25.99

How to
BECOME A
MAGE

About the Authors

K. K. Albert is a translator based in Phoenix, Arizona. Her master of fine arts degree and her years of practice in a variety of creative pursuits have led her to appreciate Péladan's teachings about aestheticism. She has intensively studied astrology, tarot, Zen, the I Ching, meditation, Qabalah, Theosophy, and dreamwork. Additionally, she is an expert in French language and culture.

Joséphin Péladan (1858–1918) was a flamboyant personality and controversial media celebrity as well as the author of combative art criticism and a series of novels with occult themes. Péladan also wrote influential nonfiction works on occult topics committed to the belief that the best way for modern Europeans to enter into communion with the guiding intelligences of humanity was through magic and the arts. He played a key role in reviving Rosicrucianism and provided a spiritual and intellectual backdrop to fin-de-siècle French symbolism. His ideas influenced the leading artists of the day, including composers Claude Debussy and Erik Satie and writer Antonin Artaud.

To Write to the Author

If you wish to contact K. K. Albert or would like more information about this book, please write to her in care of Llewellyn Worldwide Ltd. and we will forward your request. Both the author and the publisher appreciate hearing from you and learning of your enjoyment of this book and how it has helped you. Llewellyn Worldwide Ltd. cannot guarantee that every letter written to the author can be answered, but all will be forwarded. Please write to:

K. K. Albert
℅ Llewellyn Worldwide
2143 Wooddale Drive
Woodbury, MN 55125-2989
Please enclose a self-addressed stamped envelope for reply,
or $1.00 to cover costs. If outside the U.S.A., enclose
an international postal reply coupon.

Many of Llewellyn's authors have websites with additional information and resources. For more information, please visit our website at http://www.llewellyn.com.

Llewellyn Publications
Woodbury, Minnesota

How to Become a Mage: A Fin-de-Siècle French Occult Manifesto © 2019 by K. K. Albert and Joséphin Péladan. All rights reserved. No part of this book may be used or reproduced in any manner whatsoever, including internet usage, without written permission from Llewellyn Publications, except in the case of brief quotations embodied in critical articles and reviews.

FIRST EDITION
First Printing, 2019

Cover design by Kevin R. Brown
Cover illustration by Eugene Smith
Portrait of Joséphin Péladan on dust jacket is by Alexandre Séon, courtesy of the Museum of Fine Arts of Lyon © Lyon MBA—Photo Alain Basset

Llewellyn Publications is a registered trademark of Llewellyn Worldwide Ltd.

Library of Congress Cataloging-in-Publication Data

Names: Peladan, Josephin, 1859–1918, author. | Albert, K. K., translator.
Title: How to become a mage : a fin-de-siecle French occult manifesto / Josephin Peladan ; translated & annotated by K. K. Albert with Jean-Louis de Biasi; foreword by John Michael Greer.
Other titles: Comment on devient mage. English
Description: First edition. | Woodbury, Minnesota : Llewellyn Worldwide, 2019. | Translation of: Comment on devient mage / Josephin Peladan. | Based on the 1892 edition published by Chamuel, Paris, as v. 1 of the series Amphitheatre des sciences mortes. | Includes bibliographical references.
Identifiers: LCCN 2019006247 | ISBN 9780738759487 (alk. paper)
Subjects: LCSH: Rosicrucians. | Mysticism. | Hermetic Order of the Golden Dawn.
Classification: LCC BF1623.R7 P35413 2019 | DDC 135/.43—dc23 LC record available at https://lccn.loc.gov/2019006247

Llewellyn Worldwide Ltd. does not participate in, endorse, or have any authority or responsibility concerning private business transactions between our authors and the public.

All mail addressed to the author is forwarded but the publisher cannot, unless specifically instructed by the author, give out an address or phone number.

Any internet references contained in this work are current at publication time, but the publisher cannot guarantee that a specific location will continue to be maintained. Please refer to the publisher's website for links to authors' websites and other sources.

Llewellyn Publications
A Division of Llewellyn Worldwide Ltd.
2143 Wooddale Drive
Woodbury, MN 55125-2989
www.llewellyn.com

Printed in the United States of America

*This work is dedicated to all those who have borne the
Divine Image down into the life of the world, and have inspired others
to pursue the work of becoming fully human beings.*

Contents

Foreword: The Magus of Decadence *by John Michael Greer*   xi

Translator's Preface *by K. K. Albert*   xix

Author's Dedication: To the Count   xxix

Prayer of Saint Thomas Aquinas   xxxv

Creed   xxxvii

To the Ancestors   xxxix

To the Young Man of the Present   xli

BOOK ONE
THE SEVEN STEPS TO EXIT THE CENTURY 1
I. THE NEOPHYTE   3

II. SOCIETY   15

III. RULES OF SOCIAL LIFE   29

IV. ORIENTATION   43

V. MAGIC POWER   55

VI. ON LOVE   69

VII. THE AUTODIDACT   83

BOOK TWO
THE TWELVE STEPS OF MAGICAL ASCETICISM 95
I. THE QUIDDITY or THE TRUE PATH   97

II. THE ORIGIN or THE METHOD   107

III. RAPPORT or DESTINY   117

IV. MATERIALITY or EFFORT   127

V. RITUAL or SACRIFICE   135

VI. DEATH or REBIRTH   145

VII. QUANTITY or VARIETY   153

VIII. QUALITY or PERVERSITY   163

IX. TIME or IMPOTENCE   173

X. LIFE or GLORY   181

XI. THE METHOD or ENEMIES   191

XII. ACCOMPANIMENT or PROVIDENCE   201

BOOK THREE
THE TRINITY OF THE HOLY SPIRIT..209
I. THE WORK OF THE FATHER   211
II. THE WORK OF THE SON   217
III. THE WORK OF THE HOLY SPIRIT   221

Afterword *by Jean-Louis de Biasi, Illustrious Grand Patriarch–Grand Master of the Kabbalistic Order of the Rose-Cross*   227
Appendix: *The Golden Verses of Pythagoras*   237
Translator's Note *by K. K. Albert*   243

FOREWORD:
THE MAGUS OF DECADENCE

John Michael Greer

Paris in the *fin de siècle* was hardly a stranger to magnificent spectacles, but the opening day of the first Salon de la Rose+Croix, March 9, 1892, was memorable even by the standards of that time and place. The press of carriages outside the Galeries Durand-Ruel, 11 rue Le Peletier, was so great that the gendarmes were forced to close the street. Those who made it through the door found themselves in an atmosphere full of incense smoke and the scent of hundreds of blood-red roses, while musicians played the shimmering chords of the prelude to Wagner's opera *Parsifal*. On the walls were works by sixty-three artists, most of whom had been blacklisted by the French artistic establishment for years or decades for their rejection of academic standards.

In the midst of it all was a colorfully dressed man with an improbable black beard, cut long and square in the style of Assyrian kings. His name was Joséphin Péladan, and his card sported the title *Sâr*, "prince" in Hebrew. He was a bestselling novelist and art critic, claimed descent from the sages of ancient Chaldea, and headed a Rosicrucian society, l'Ordre de la Rose+Croix du Temple et du Graal, which had no less a composer than Erik Satie as its official musician. The mover and shaker behind the Salon de la Rose+Croix, Péladan had made his name challenging the officially approved painters of the day for their stunning mediocrity, and the Salon was his triumphant demonstration that the art being created outside the walls of the Académie Française was superior in every way to what was being made within it.

By the time the Salon closed on April 11, the hold of the academic establishment on the French art scene had been broken once and for all. Ironically, though, that considerable triumph did little to further the cause of the idealist and Symbolist art Péladan loved. The Impressionists and other avant-garde movements, which he loathed, took advantage most successfully of the opening he had created. That was typical of the man. He saw himself as one of the last defenders of a tradition and a world already sunk in their final decadence, and he carried out his self-imposed mission with the frantic intensity of a man who knew he was going to lose.

To comment that Joséphin Péladan was a French conservative of the nineteenth century is to guarantee that nearly every person who reads that phrase will misunderstand it. The English-speaking world has never had anything like continental European conservatism, and even in Europe the conservatism of Péladan's time is all but extinct. To go on to write that he was one of the leading lights of the Decadent Movement in French literature, the author of lushly erotic and wildly popular novels, as well as a dandy and an esthete who out-Gothed today's Goths a hundred and twenty years in advance, will doubtless leave many readers attempting to square these statements with the comment just made. And if I go on to explain that he was at one and the same time a devout if eccentric Roman Catholic and one of the most significant figures in the Paris occult scene of his time, I trust I will be forgiven for listening for the distant popping sounds of readers' heads exploding.

Péladan was all of that, and quite a bit more. He was also the man Oscar Wilde was imitating when Wilde went strolling through London in velvet clothes with a drooping lily in his hand. "Do you know what they mean when they say 'That man is a character'? Well, a mage is primarily that," Péladan wrote, and he certainly was.

All the colorful details, though, were in the service of an utterly serious purpose. Péladan belonged to that substantial minority of late-nineteenth-century thinkers who recognized that the European societies of their day were headed for disaster. More clearly than any of his contemporaries, he understood that what was facing collapse was not simply political or economic but the entire cultural heritage—aristocratic, Christian, Latin—that linked the Europe of his time with its historic roots in the ancient world. What set him apart from the sentimental conservatives of his time and ours, though, is that he recognized that this heritage was already past saving. "We believe neither in progress nor in salvation," his *Manifeste de la Rose+Croix* thundered to a mostly bemused Paris in 1891. "For the Latin race, which goes to its death, we prepare a final splendor, to dazzle and gentle the barbarians who are to come."

In that spirit, he set out to teach individuals how to stand apart from a failing society, and the means he chose for this purpose were drawn from the traditions of magic. By the word *magic*, however, he meant something rather more profound than the usual meanings the word gets assigned today. *How to Become a Mage*, Péladan's core work of magical theory and practice, contains not a single magic ritual. Its theme, to borrow a typically ornate term from his writing, was *ethopoeia*: the making (*poesis*) of an ethos—one that would enable individuals to stand apart from the collective consciousness of their time in order to think their own thoughts and make their own choices. "Society," Péladan wrote, "is an anonymous corporation providing a life of diminished emotions."

Such a life was not of interest to Péladan, and he was also intensely aware that the emotions being marketed by the anonymous enterprise of society were not chosen at random. The historian of magic Ioan Culianu, in his 1984 book *Eros and Magic in the Renaissance*, pointed out that the nations of the modern industrial world are "magician states" that rule by manufacturing a managed consensus through the manipulation of irrational images, with advertising and propaganda as vehicles for a corrupt sorcery of social control. All this would have been music to Péladan's ears, and closely echoes his own insights, but he was less interested in anatomizing the magician states of his time; his goal was to enable the individual to break free of their influence.

His unwavering focus made *How to Become a Mage* the most detailed text of its time on the fine art of freeing the individual will, sensibility, and understanding from bondage to unthinking social reactions. It was very much a book of its era, full of references to current events, and it also uses the utterly Péladanesque strategy of infuriating the reader by poking as many of those social reactions as possible. Liberal, conservative, radical, or reactionary, every reader of Péladan's treatise could count on finding a good reason to throw it at the nearest wall, and the effect is even stronger today, since the cultural differences between Péladan's time and ours step on a whole new layer of sore toes. Neither the political correctness of the modern Left nor the patriotic correctness of the modern Right has any room for Péladan's deliberately confrontational stance—nor would he have tolerated either one for a moment.

The theme of Péladan's work that tends to get the most negative response these days, however, is his insistence that Western civilization was sinking into its final decadence, from which there would be no recovery. Unpopular as it is just now, the same theme appears throughout the literature of the nineteenth-century occult revival. Partly that was because everybody in the occult scene at that time read Péladan, but it was also because the nineteenth century saw the emergence of the first generation of effective mass media, the foreshadowings of the mass movements and political thaumaturgy of the century to come, and the first drafts of today's weapons of mass destruction. Few people in the occult community missed foreseeing at least some of the ghastly potentials these things had to offer. As a result, an extraordinary range of magical literature from Péladan's time through the Second World War assumed as a matter of course that contemporary European civilization was, as we now like to say, circling the drain.

Whether "the barbarians who are to come" would be domestic or imported was a matter of some discussion—Péladan himself thought that Europe would eventually be conquered by the Chinese, a theory that seems rather less farfetched today than it did in his time—but very few people in the occult scene at that time doubted that they were working their magic in the twilight years of a dying civilization. Of course they were quite correct; the old cultures of Europe, in every sense Péladan would have recognized, died in the trenches of the First World War, and that was only the first wave of an era of traumatic change. The forty years from Sarajevo in 1914 to Dien Bien Phu in 1954 saw Europe's nations flattened to the ground by two catastrophic wars, overwhelmed by cultural shifts, and reduced from the status of masters of the planet to pawns in a game of bare-knuckle politics played with gusto by the United States and the Soviet Union.

All this made Péladan's lessons more than usually relevant, because the catastrophe he foresaw had a clear magical dimension. Read contemporary accounts of the way Europe stumbled into war in 1914 and it's hard to miss the weirdly trancelike state of mind in the warring nations, as vast crowds cheered the coming of hostilities that would cost millions of them their lives, and leftwing parties that had pledged themselves to nonviolent resistance in the event of war forgot all about their pledges and swung into step behind the patriotic drumbeats. The collective consciousness of the age was primed for an explosion, partly by the sorcery of any number of competing political and economic interests, and partly by the rising pressures of intolerable inner conflicts that, in magician states ruled by a managed consensus, were prevented from finding a less catastrophic form of expression.

It took an extraordinary degree of mental independence to stay clear of the trance state and its appalling consequences, but that was one of the things the magical training available in those days was intended to do. Péladan was inevitably the most outspoken of the period's occult writers on this subject, as on so many others, and filled a good many of the twenty-two chapters of *How to Become a Mage* with sound advice on how to open up an insulating space between the individual mind and the pressures that surround it. All this advice is aimed at the social habits of another time and has not necessarily aged well, but the basic principles still stand.

The first of those principles is to limit and control the channels by which the mainstream media and their wholly owned subsidiary, public opinion, get access to your nervous system. Now, of course, that raises the hackles of quite a few people nowadays. It so happens that, like Péladan—and largely because of his influence—I've suggested in print on several occasions that those who want to reclaim some sense of meaning from today's manufactured pseudo-culture might consider pulling the plug on popular culture as a good first step. Whenever I've done this, I've fielded a flurry of responses insisting that popular culture is creative, interesting, etc., so why do I have such a grudge against it?

It's a neat evasion of the point at issue, which is that mass-produced popular culture exists solely for the purpose of emptying your wallet and your brain, not necessarily in that order. As Péladan pointed out so trenchantly, popular culture is a vehicle for sorcery; it works, as sorcery always works, by inducing you to think less and react more. Thus, in the strictest sense of the word, it makes you more stupid. I don't think anyone can afford that right now.

One point Péladan made that remains valid today is that spending time among a crowd of people whose minds and conversation are utterly conditioned by popular culture is not noticeably different from getting your popular culture firsthand. If anything, this is even more of an issue these days than it was in his time. I suspect most of us have had the experience of hearing a conversation between two people in which every single word spoken was a sound bite from some media source or other. There's no need to become a hermit, but it's a good idea to choose your crowds with some care.

Steps such as these will cut down on the influence that the sorcery of our time has over your thoughts, feelings, and decisions. Still, the empty space has to be filled with something better, or there won't be much of an improvement; this is the second of Péladan's basic principles. The perennial mistake of Romanticism is the notion that all you have to do is fling aside the fetters of social expectations and do what comes naturally. The problem here is of course that "what comes naturally" to every one of us is the product of a lifetime spent absorbing social cues from the people around us and the media directed at us, all of which trigger a set of unthinking and unconscious reactions we share with our nonhuman relatives: social primate see, social primate do.

Thus it's necessary to replace the sorcery of the mass media and public opinion with some more wholesome and more liberating magic. Being who he was, and living when he did, Péladan phrased that dimension of the work in terms of art, music, and literature, and those are certainly among the available options. If you happen to be a dandy and an esthete, and live in a city with good art galleries, concert venues, and the like, you could do worse than to follow his recommendations—he was particularly partial to Renaissance paintings, German classical and romantic music from Bach through to Wagner, and Shakespeare's plays—though I don't recommend copying him and Oscar Wilde and strolling down the streets with a lily in your hand.

Still, the esthetic approach is only one option, and the last thing you should do in this sort of practice is rely on someone else's notions of what ought to feed your mind. "'Beware the example of others, think for yourself,'" wrote Péladan; "this precept of Pythagoras contains all of magic, which is nothing other than the power of ipseity." The important thing, as Péladan repeatedly points out, is to choose things to read, watch, hear, and do that you consider worthwhile, instead of passively taking in whatever the sorcerers-for-hire of the media and marketing industries push at you. What falls in the former category will vary from person to person, as it should.

All this seems relatively straightforward, and indeed it's quite possible to get to the same decision by plain reasoning: starting, say, from the shoddy vulgarity of mass-produced entertainments and going from there to the realization that there's much more interesting mind food to feast on. That making such choices also makes it easier to think clearly would in that case be merely a pleasant side effect of good taste. The mage in training does the same thing deliberately, not just to think clearly but to feel and will clearly as well. As the training proceeds, however, those effects begin to reveal another side, which is their effect on other people.

Péladan hinted at this effect in How to Become a Mage, though custom in the occult scene back in his time didn't favor spelling out the details. "Do not seek any other measure of magical power but that of the power within you, or any other way to judge a being but by the light that he emanates. To perfect yourself so as to become luminous, and like the sun, to excite the ideal life latent around you—that is the entire mystery of the highest initiation." What he did not quite say is that "the ideal life latent around you" is in other human beings, and that—especially in times of cultural crisis—stepping outside the lowest common denominator of the mass mind has an effect rather like induction in electrical circuits; put another way, it can be as catchy as a lively new tune.

You can catch that tune, so to speak, from a person; you can catch it from a book, which is why Péladan wrote his twenty-two novels, each of them exploring some aspect of the relation between the initiate and a corrupt society, using the major arcana of the tarot as a template; you can catch it from other sources, the way Rainer Maria Rilke did from a statue of Apollo; you can also catch it all by yourself, by climbing out of the collective consciousness for some other reason and discovering that you like the view. Now, of course, far more often than not, those who step out of the collective consciousness of their society promptly jump back into the collective consciousness of a congenial subculture, which from a magical perspective is not much better—thinking the same thoughts as all your radical friends is just as much secondhand living as thinking the same thoughts as the vacuous faces on the evening news. What Péladan showed convincingly is that there are other options.

For that reason among many others, I'm delighted to welcome this translation of Péladan's masterpiece into print. K. K. Albert has done a fine job of rendering Péladan's elaborate prose into readable English. Anyone who reads this book attentively will find it, as I did when I first read the French original many years ago, a brilliant, cantankerous, challenging, and profoundly insightful guide to the hard work and astonishing possibilities of becoming a unique individual.

TRANSLATOR'S PREFACE
K. K. Albert

How to Become a Mage was a work of Joséphin Péladan's flaming youth, a miracle with a few blunders on the side.

So, what is a mage, and why would anybody want to become one?

A mage would seem to be a master of magic—and there are probably as many ways to make magic as there are ways to make soup.

In classical antiquity, a mage was understood to be someone who practiced astrology, alchemy, divination, and other forms of esoteric knowledge; the Persian mages were a priestly caste that the Greeks took to be the conservators of this knowledge and the educators of the rulers. Theurgy, the sacred magic of the Neoplatonists, is the part of the occult tradition Péladan wanted to transmit, rather than spells and conjuring spirits: "You will never be anything but the spiritual king of a body and a soul; but if you achieve this, if your spirit makes of your body a servant, and a minister of your soul, then you will act upon others in the same proportion that you have acted upon yourself."

Péladan entered Paris in 1882 as a talented, good-looking young man of twenty-four who had, through sheer stubborn self-will, exempted himself from the punishing routine of French education. Rather than submit to the petty tyrannies of schoolmasters and peer pressure, he had dug in his heels, made trouble, refused to cooperate, and won the freedom to educate himself in the libraries. By following his own predilections, by honing his talents, and by hard application, he had made a name for himself in the literary world. In Paris he found mentors in occult and literary circles, and became acquainted with the entertainments, intoxicants, human bodies, vices, influence, and success that were all on offer—for their price. He was revolted, like a man who swats at a swarm of insects, who jumps and swats all the more vigorously when they have touched him and gotten into his clothes.

Péladan could renounce worldly pleasures and honors at that time because he was drunk on the fumes of the mysteries. The gates of heaven had opened to him in brief moments: when he had yielded himself up to the musical dramas of Wagner, to the incantations of inspired poetry; when he had imagined himself into the profound, complex expressions of figures painted by Leonardo da Vinci. And something made him very keen to pursue the Rosicrucian path. He had tasted the Mystery, and he would be satisfied with nothing less.

In 1884 he had the heady experience of his first novel becoming a bestseller. People started asking him for advice, and it seemed he had done pretty well for himself. Confrontation and persistent refusal to cooperate had paid off handsomely. For the moment, anyway.

By 1892 he had, along with friends and patrons, reorganized the old Toulouse Order of the Rose+Cross, an order founded upon notions he understood as a form of esoteric Christianity, for which he hoped to get a blessing from the Pope. Anyone who attends to all of what Péladan has to say about the Catholic Church in *How to Become a Mage* will notice quite a few criticisms and reservations, and will notice that loyalty to the Church did not deter him from spreading ideas and practices that are flagrantly heretical. He actually imagined the Church could be persuaded to accommodate them! Those who disagreed with him on this point had good reason.

Nevertheless, his belief that esoteric training must be founded in exoteric religion—or its equivalent—deserves some serious consideration. When exoteric religion functions in a constructive way, it introduces people to dimensions and possibilities of human life that are given no attention in schooling, the mass media, or the workplace. Religion provides an ethical/cosmological orientation to its members at formative stages of their lives. The few who go further to seek direct experience of the theosphere need to understand the universe as something greater than the setting for their own little ego-dramas. If this is not learned from religion, it will have to be learned the hard way.

Péladan's insistence that a French occultist should be first, last, and always a loyal Catholic put him at odds with other leaders of his Order, and at odds with developments in the occult world generally. He counseled against some practices that other occultists promulgated as the very quintessence of magic. This, along with his staunch loyalty to the Catholic Church, led some to conclude he wasn't a magician at all. Some fail to see any magic in *How to Become a Mage*.

Where is the magic?

Hidden in plain view: The book opens with an invocation of benefactors and spiritual ancestors, and moves to a prayer for divine protection. Then there are twenty-two chapters about contending with the powers that operate in the various dimensions of human life, from eating, work, and human relations (interpersonal, sexual, collective) to culture, mortality, and relation to divinity. That ascending movement—from the concrete and mundane to the abstract and celestial—parallels the course outlined by Pythagoras, as well as the ascent of the Cabalistic Tree of Life. The reader who engages fully with the book will be walked through a significant magical working and will be shown the possibility of living life itself as a magical working.

The mage is the one who acts effectively in all levels of reality, who has the faith, courage, and strength to remember the presence of God in all of them; the mage is the one who incorporates into himself the knowledge of all the realities, and thereby becomes a fractal image of God.

Péladan's preferred approach combines the receptive capacity of the mystic and the willful activity of a sorcerer: he favors the arts as a means of connecting to divine inspiration and lifting oneself up to the level of the higher powers. This path is a magical working on a different scale from what is usually understood by a "spell": this path can lead to earthly accomplishment and a magical life. He was careful to note that becoming a mage depended upon more than human effort: "The process described in this book prepares you for the light, but the light comes from above. One receives it; it is not a matter of creating it. One receives it, warmth and joy, and one radiates it, color and power." Still, if one pursues certain directions persistently—as the alchemists did, for example—or if one "gravitates toward God increasingly and without ceasing," magic can happen.

One cannot become a mage while spending 1 percent of one's time reading books on magic and the other 99 percent in the service of corrupt agendas and empty pastimes. To imagine that the portion of life spent on daily routine, work, recreation, interpersonal relations, sexual life, and family have nothing to do with gaining magical power—this is self-deception. The path to greatness demands everything we are.

One may well ask, "How can anybody stay on such a path for more than a week?"

The answer to that very important question is the reason that Péladan insists that each magician must find his very own way and create his very own magic: The only way to walk this path is to love it.

That is why Péladan's first chapter, "The Neophyte," begins by asking, "What is the aim of life?," proceeds to describe many things in the course of a conventional worldly career that are repugnant and demeaning, and goes on to ask, "Do you crave dignity, truth, honor—tell me—do you want them?" Everything hinges on what one truly wants.

What gives a person the will and persistence to do what it takes to become a mage is some combination of desire and revulsion. The neophyte must find it within himself, connect to it, and honor it. That desire, whether felt negatively or positively, is the wellspring of magic. It is the One Needful Thing, and it cannot be taught.

What can and must be taught are strategies for making the most of one's resources, and how to bring all the circumstances and activities of life into accord with one's highest aim. Much of what Péladan recommends is taken from Pythagoras, who passed on sayings that were very old when he spoke them to his disciples in the sixth century BCE. Through Plato, to St. Ignatius Loyola, the sayings had filtered out from academic and fraternal organizations into the common mind; they were repeated by people who clearly did not know—or care—that they came from a wise-guy who lived 2,600 years ago. Faced with dilemmas and important life decisions, people repeated these sayings because they had proved time and time again to be potent good counsel.

The wisdom became as common as dust, and in the past half-century, it has been largely swept out of mind. The literature of classical antiquity is no longer part of a general education, even at the university level, and the fraternal organizations that once presented the *Verses* to a vast and varied membership no longer do so. Because Péladan makes so many references to the *Golden Verses*, and since they provide the inspiration and underlying structure of *How to Become a Mage*, a version is provided in the appendix to this book.

Incorporating Pythagoras's *Golden Verses* into daily life can set one firmly on a trajectory toward realizing one's heart's desires, and it can also prevent one from falling into the same lethal traps that have been set with fresh bait every day for the past three millennia.

How to Become a Mage doesn't just spout the wisdom of the ages, however—it requires the reader to use magical powers. Péladan's method of discourse requires the reader's active engagement, and one must be ready for a challenge—in the tradition, the initiation is given only after the ordeals. His language is often peculiar: occasionally he uses words that are not in the dictionary, and ordinary words are sometimes used in unexpected ways—all in the venerable tradition of occult dialect. His intention in writing this way was not primarily to show how mystical he was but to make an adept of you. Being *automatically* or *immediately* understood was not always his first priority. Magical reality, after all, does not necessarily conform to the comfortable familiarity of the mother tongue and everything you think you already know.

Péladan chose his words with great care, for the purpose of activating the faculties required of a mage. By paying attention to the points where he perplexes you—stopping a bit to examine the problem, allowing yourself to be uncertain, and continuing to read—you may find bafflement yielding to insight. In the process you will find yourself exercising some mental/spiritual muscles that the rest of your education may have neglected. You might think of it as an ordeal of magical initiation.

Péladan also employs outrage as a teaching strategy, throwing out incendiary bombs on almost every page about politics, religion, career, family life, personal grooming, sex—you name it, he's got something irritating to say about it. He believes that a magician must be a Catholic and nothing else, that political democracy and a national military are abominations, that theocracy is the ideal form of government. But what does all this hot air have to do with learning how to be a mage?

It has to do with getting a handle on our own assumptions. Our basic assumptions are often invisible to us until they are challenged, and Péladan is a born challenger. Yes, he actually believed some of his ludicrous assertions, but he also fully intended to arouse indignation. Throwing the book to the floor can be an occasion for the indefatigable reader to pause for an examination of what is going on in your heart and mind: What is it that rises up so forcefully within you against his ideas? Just what is offended, what cries out to be defended? Is it really yours? Is it more important to defend old assumptions or to get a maximally clear view of reality? Must you give up the one to have the other?

Coming to terms with Péladan's outrageous ideas may be a process that takes some time and reflection, but it is invaluable preparation for confrontations with entities more daunting than an offensive book. If the reader engages fully with the text, it can generate a great advancement in self-knowledge, not to speak of *savoir-faire*.

Although most of Péladan's outrageous statements are deliberate strategy, one of them disturbs early-twenty-first-century readers to a degree he may not have foreseen: Péladan was convinced that women were inferior to men because they lacked the faculty of intellect. Today we are apt to find that claim patently false, sexist, absolutely unacceptable, and grounds for total discredit.

But before going any further, I must point out that he was no hate-filled misogynist. Evidence from Péladan's words and his life testifies that he had ample respect for women and was quite fond of some of them, as some of them were very fond of him.

How, then, could a man of goodwill write such egregious slander?

His ideas about women's lack of intellectual capacity were partly shaped by social conventions that denied women access to higher education, while the universities were the sole arbiter of what nineteenth-century Frenchmen understood as "intellect." In nineteenth-century France, young men and women of the genteel classes were almost completely isolated from one another. From the time a boy started school at about seven years old until he finished his education at about twenty, if he did not have sisters, the only young women he saw were old or "disreputable." And even when he entered adult society, his contact with women of his own social class was limited to highly artificial situations. Péladan did not have sisters and had not yet married, ensuring that his ideas about female intellectual capacity were based on incomplete and insufficient information.

Of course, he was not untouched by that male arrogance that is the gender equivalent of nationalist pride, both remarkably virulent in his lifetime.

Péladan's ideas about women were also to a large degree dictated by occult theory. As a student of Cabala, Péladan was reading and listening to authorities propounding elaborate and venerable doctrine to explain how women, by nature and by divine dispensation, lacked the faculty of soul that corresponded to intellect. Those doctrines did, however, allow room for female greatness, albeit in forms different from those of men.

Since *How to Become a Mage* was written with young men in mind, it does not elaborate on those ideas. Speaking to young men on the subject of women, Péladan was most concerned about alerting them to the dangers of walking blindly into sexual entanglements and marriage, for much the same reasons that the Church required its priesthood to be celibate: family obligations and other consequences can make it impossible to pursue one's chosen course.

To address women, he wrote a counterpart, *How to Become Fey* (*Comment on devient fée*, 1893), in which he gave parallel advice to young women, urging them not to accept being treated or portrayed as sex objects, even suggesting strategies for repelling sexual assault. In that book he also maintained that women, like men, have to divest themselves of pernicious social conditioning in order to cultivate individuality of soul. The domain of women's activities is, like that of men, corrupted by collective insanities; Péladan challenged the sentimental notions of women as "domestic angels" and embodiments of love, and blasphemed those stereotypes in terms just as infuriating as those he applied to journalism and political cant. In this, he anticipated the feminists of the mid-twentieth century who maintained that women were diminished and trapped into a false position by being "put up on a pedestal." Péladan's attitude toward women was by no means enlightened, but it was not misogynist. In his perception of women's capacities and potentials, he was in alignment with that branch of feminism that emphasizes the need to respect some women's preference for the traditional female roles and the need for a reappraisal of "women's work" that acknowledges that its immense value is beyond quantitative calculation.

We are not obliged to share Péladan's ideas about female intellectual incapacity, but we can turn them to good account by taking them as a glaring illustration of the perils of conventional thinking: "What everybody knows" may seem self-evident in a particular setting, but it may well be regarded as ridiculous, or worse, in the future. The fact that a contrarian like Péladan perpetuated a notion that we now understand to be pernicious nonsense just goes to show how very difficult it is to avoid partaking in the insanities peculiar to one's own time and milieu. If we can learn to recognize this pitfall from a book rather than from hard experience, we are fortunate.

All that being said, Péladan's ideas about women elicit no greater horror in twenty-first-century readers than the fury aroused in French readers in 1893 by his views on religion, democracy, patriotism, and the military. My guess is that he would be delighted to be raising another ruckus a full century after his death.

In 1892 Péladan envisioned the Order of the Rose+Cross of the Temple and Grail as a cadre of disciplined and idealistic young men who would, at the turn of the twentieth century, achieve something comparable to what the Knights Templar had won in the eleventh century: a recovery of the Holy Land from the Infidels. Time, age, and sad experience would eventually temper his illusions, hopes, and boldness. But the handbook he wrote in 1892 to pitch the ideals of his new order was written in the passionate hope that great things could be brought to fruition. The genuine enthusiasm for beauty and wisdom and the incandescent energy of a brave, resolute, and daring young man are palpable in *How to Become a Mage,* giving it an infectious power that more mature works often lack.

I need to thank John Michael Greer for showing me what a mage is, and for introducing me to the work of Joséphin Péladan. Great credit is due to Elysia Gallo and Jean-Louis de Biasi, who each deserve many thanks and my deep gratitude for their important contributions toward making this work available and comprehensible to the English-speaking world. The knowledge and expertise they brought to the project have supplied much that I lacked, and their patience and good cheer made it possible to produce an English edition of *How to Become a Mage* that does justice to Péladan's own erudition and the high hopes had for the book.

The thirty-five-year-old individual who wrote *How to Become a Mage* had not yet withstood every test of time, but the wisdom he gathered together in it has been road-tested for three millennia. There are some truths that are easier to say and to hear now than when Péladan was writing, but there are other truths, some very important truths, that could be said in 1893 and are almost unspeakable in the early twenty-first century. Péladan tells them—oh, does he tell them!—and that's one thing that makes *How to Become a Mage* invaluable. From the wisdom of Pythagoras to brotherly advice about choosing careers, friends, and spouses, it has been practiced, remembered, and repeated because it has given real people the freedom required to make magic.

May it do so for you!

TO THE COUNT
ANTOINE DE LA ROCHEFOUCAULD
GRAND PRIOR OF THE TEMPLE
ARCHON OF THE ROSE+CROSS

BROTHER IN THE WORK,

Your ancient and brilliant name,[1] let it shine upon the face of the favored work; Surely, I pledge both my warmest friendship and my formal admiration.

In our restoration of the Rose+Cross of the Temple, your credit is extreme: it surpasses my own.

I brought to you a dream of a militant ideal, and you have realized it.

During the recent journalistic clamor, my fortune, always extreme on the right as on the left, would have it that you read what I had written about art; You rediscovered there your own aesthetic in print and in action.

From our first meeting it seemed that each of us revealed to the other his own thoughts. A few hours sufficed for us to conjugate our Verbs into a pact that already embraced the whole of Western culture.

Your enthusiasm plunged itself into a courage rarely seen in this country. With what unmoved serenity you have received a baptism of injury, the infernal sacrament that Paris imposes upon any chivalry of light!

---

1. [Translator's Note, hereafter appearing as "[TN]"] **Count Antoine de La Rochefoucauld** was heir to one of the most illustrious families of old French nobility. He served as Grand Prior of the Rose+Cross of the Temple and the Grail from 1892 to early 1897. His connections in high society and in the art world, along with significant financial support, were indispensable to the success of the annual art exhibitions sponsored by the order.

Descended from the most completely annihilated race of mankind, without country, without prestige, I was forced to become great, at risk of not being anything at all.

But you, showered with advantages from the cradle, might have spent your life as a simple d'Orléans[2] going between stable and drawing room, occupied only with sport or adultery, after the manner of your peers.

No! Works of art revealed to your seer's eyes the one and only aristocracy, and taking up your tools, you have shown the talent of a master; you, to whom an illustrious name would have authorized decorative sloth.

Here begins the merit that you expanded into Glory.

At this point on the intellectual horizon it appeared to you that men, times and places have worth or lack it, in proportion to their adoration for Beauty.

A singular zeal overtook you, beating in your soul, and raised it to the realms of abstraction.

Our hands joined not in mutual emulation, but in a vow of light, to take up the Rose+Cross.

To Deliver the Holy Sepulcher where, since the Renaissance, the Beauty of Salvation has been entombed, to defend the pilgrims that still wear the blazon of the idealist, and to uphold the banner of heaven in the face of the century: this is the work for which our two beings joined in a single effort.

Between the noble enterprise of Bayreuth and the movement of the Rose+Cross, as between you and Louis of Bavaria,[3] there is a resemblance.

There and here, the idea of celebrating intellectual culture manifests according to the same formula.

"Religion is made into art to speak to the masses: Art is made into religion to speak to the few."

Bayreuth is the temple of a single genius, and Louis of Bavaria did not love art except in one art and one unique body of work.

---

2. [TN] **d'Orléans** is the surname used by several branches of the royal family of France who descend from Hugh Capet, the founder of the dynasty deposed by the French Revolution. It had been the custom to grant the revenues of the duchy of Orléans to support the second surviving son of the king. As a member of the Orléans family, Antoine de La Rochefoucauld was heir to enough wealth that he had no material need to concern himself with anything but his own pleasure.

3. [TN] **Louis of Bavaria** (1845–1886), known as Mad King Ludwig, was a hereditary monarch of Bavaria whose patronage enabled the composer-librettist Richard Wagner to build the Festival Theater at Bayreuth, where his operas could be presented as Wagner envisioned them.

Accomplishing in theatrical form that which I conceive, I will not achieve the magic of the daimon of Wahnfried[4]; even you will not be able for a very long time to accomplish this unprecedented realization of Bayreuth.

But, just as I have attained a level where my own work represents for me only the authority to devote myself to the aesthetic of others, to serve it in guiding it; similarly you love Beauty mystically and in God.

The Rose+Cross of the Temple celebrates not the rites of an art or an artist, but the entire cult of all the arts and all the Masters.

Therein lies its beauty; from that comes its power.

Scrupulousness as to its means, and wisdom in the face of the temptations of the always-imperfect moment may impede the great aesthetic venture of 1892.[5]

No matter! For the first time in thirty years, the fine arts, all in service to a strict metaphysic, will be exhibited; traditional in their essence, while being modern, current, avant-garde, by the preference given to any completely new technique that does not contradict the norms of magic.

---

4. [TN] **The daimon** (genius) **of Wahnfried** was Richard Wagner (1813–1883), whose residence at Bayreuth was named Wahnfried. Wagner was a German composer, librettist, conductor, and theorist best known for his operas, notably the four-opera cycle (tetralogy) *Der Ring des Nibelungen* (*The Ring of the Nibelungs*). Wagner transformed the art form from light entertainment to a quasi-religious experience in which visual and musical elements were subordinated to a drama with profound ethical-mystical content. In order to be staged as Wagner envisioned them, his works required the construction of a special opera house, the Festival Theater at Bayreuth. Such ambitious undertakings involved a well-coordinated army of musicians and stage personnel, staggering amounts of debt, and the recruitment of music lovers of various European cities into "Wagner societies" to generate a constant stream of publicity. In fact, Wagner was the organizing head of artistic forces that were fully comparable to a military operation. In his day, Wagner was a media celebrity; his accomplishments as an artist, along with gossip about his personal life, were heavily covered in the popular press.

5. [TN] **The aesthetic venture of 1892:** The first exhibition (salon) of arts by the Order of the Rose+Cross of the Temple and Grail opened on March 10, 1892, funded by La Rochefoucauld. Sixty-three artists showed 250 works, and the two-week event included musical and theatrical performances, all selected as examples of a Rose+Cross aesthetic that Péladan called "idéaliste." The aim was not to represent banal reality, but to "paint the invisible"—religion, mysticism, myths, legend, dream, and allegory—in line with Péladan's motto that "There is no other Reality but God. There is no other Truth but God. There is no other Beauty but God." (Péladan, *L'Art idéaliste et mystique*, Paris: Chamuel, 1894, 33.) The composer Erik Satie supplied music for the exhibition, and his composition *Le Fils des étoiles* functioned as incidental music for Péladan's play of that name, performed as part of the event. The salon attracted huge crowds; yearly Rose+Cross salons followed through 1897.

I promise you honor in centuries to come for this undertaking, which will doubtlessly be ridiculed by the man in the street.

In this way, Grand Prior, the nobility of your role surpasses that of Louis II who raised a temple, to a demigod, certainly, while you dedicate a Pantheon to all the glories, and you open a refuge to all the devotees.

The Rose+Cross of the Temple actualizes divine charity for the likes of the Signorellis[6] *and the Palestrinas,*[7] *for the Marsiles*[8] *and the d'Olivets,*[9] *restoring their altars that have been deserted or extinguished; and also relighting for the young navigators of the eternal Argo, the lighthouse of salvation that is called Magic in the Orient, Eleusis in Greece, and Rome for the Christians before 1600.*

---

6. [TN] **Luca Signorelli** (c. 1445–1523) was a painter of the Florentine school who was noted in particular for the scientific naturalism of his portrayals of the nude human figure from all angles of view and in many poses of energetic movement. He was one of a group of artists commissioned by Pope Sixtus IV to decorate the Sistine Chapel, and Signorelli's work influenced that of Michelangelo.

7. [TN] **Giovanni Pierluigi da Palestrina** (c. 1525–1594) was an Italian Renaissance composer of mostly sacred, mostly vocal music, including 104 masses. He composed according to a strict set of rules that made his music elegant, balanced, and serene, and set the standards for sacred music well into the nineteenth century. The music of Palestrina has been kept active in the sacred repertoire during all of the past 450 years.

8. [TN] **Marsilio Ficino** (1433–1499) was a Florentine Italian philosopher, Catholic priest, linguist, and astrologer. Cosimo de' Medici commissioned him to translate many ancient Greek texts into Latin, with priority to the Corpus Hermeticum. Based on those studies, Ficino investigated therapeutic measures based on astrology and sympathetic magic. He went on to write translations and commentaries on the entire corpus of classical philosophers, including Iamblichus, Proclus, Plotinus, and early Christians, providing the basis for the Florentine Platonist Renaissance.

9. [TN] **Antoine Fabre d'Olivet** (1767–1825) was a French author, occultist, poet, and composer. He received a Pythagorean initiation in Germany in 1790; he later translated *The Golden Verses of Pythagoras* into French verse, in a style he called "eumolpid": subject to measure and harmonious cadence but free from rhyme. Fabre d'Olivet also wrote music and a book on music as a sacred art, and his example sparked a revival of public interest in Pythagoras. His biblical and philosophical interpretations of history influenced many occultists of the Rosicrucian tradition, including Éliphas Lévi, Papus, and Péladan, although archaeological discoveries made since Fabre d'Olivet's time have shown most of his linguistic theories to be unfounded. In *Hermeneutic Interpretation of the Origin of the Social State of Man*, Fabre d'Olivet asserted that republican government is, by nature, hostile to religion. This offended Napoleon I, who declared Fabre d'Olivet a non-person; and after hearing that Fabre d'Olivet had healed a boy of deafness, Napoleon sent him an official notice that he was never again to heal another person of deafness.

Every Word has a brain and a heart when it becomes flesh, when it is manifest; if my intellectual atavism and my sufferings for the sake of the Ideal are worthy of the unequaled honor of serving as the brain of the Order, You, by the sublime enthusiasm that moves you, you are the heart, the dear heart of the Rose+Cross.

You are the aesthetic Siegfried[10] *that will slay the dragon of realism; or more likely, since Catholicism dominates our efforts as symbolism dominates those of Wagner, you are, not the hero that Vigny*[11] *despises among his ancestors, so prominent in the history of your noble house; you are the chevalier of Montsalvat,*[12] *the envoy of the Grail.*

Ah! A toast to Gurnemanz,[13] *I owe you one. In vain do the Falsots and the Fafners, the Abériches and the Mimes, the Telramunds and the Ortrudes*[14] *join their dirty hands to halt your step, raising their strident voices to drown out your prayer.*

Look, look the Beauséant[15] *unfurls its black and white, the Holy Grail blushes, and the cruciform Rose palpitates with the beating wings of the Holy Spirit that inspires it.*

On the white mantle, the drivel of journalists becomes fringes of silver; in every battle the miracle of the Grail glows redder and the Rose enchants the consoled cross with its perfume.

---

10. [TN] **Siegfried**, who "knew no fear," was the hero of Wagner's opera of that name.
11. [TN] **Alfred Victor, Comte de Vigny** (1797–1863), was a French poet and early leader of French Romanticism. He also produced translations of Shakespeare and wrote the first novel based on French history, *Cinq-Mars*, in 1826. Its protagonist is based on Henri Coiffier de Ruzé, marquis de Cinq-Mars (1620–1642), a favorite of King Louis XIII, who was eventually executed for leading a political conspiracy against Richelieu.
12. [TN] **Montsalvat**, the Grail-castle as portrayed in Wagner's opera *Parsifal,* can be found only by one who is called by the Holy Grail. Inhabited and guarded by a chaste brotherhood of knights with the vocation to serve the Grail, Montsalvat was built for the safekeeping of this holy relic, along with the Holy Spear used to pierce Christ in his side during the Crucifixion.
13. [TN] **Gurnemanz** was a "wise old man" character in Wagner's *Parsifal.*
14. [TN] A list of villains from Wagner operas: Fasolt is a giant in *Das Rheingold*; Fafner is the last of the giants, disguised as a dragon in *Siegfried*; Alberich and Mime are malevolent dwarves in *Das Rheingold*; Telramund and Ortrud are the murderous Count and his witch-wife who plot against the hero Lohengrin in the opera of that name.
15. [TN] **Beauséant** (also spelled Baucent, or Baussant): The black-and-white banner of the Knights Templar. The upper half of the banner was black and the lower half white: black for danger to foes or for the sin of the secular world, and white for fairness to friends and the purity of the Templar Order. Beauséant was the war cry of the Knights Templar, and as they went into battle, they yelled "Beauséant!" as an exhortation to "Be noble!" or "Be glorious!"

O my noble partner, journalism in its cave huffs and puffs at us—a dreadful monster? No, just blather; just ridicule.

O you muttering naysayers, whatever the earthly result of our human labor may be, it is manifest in heaven, for the infinite century.

In the afterlife the Archangel Arthur will receive us at the round table of the Paraclete.[16]

Your glory, my friend, is in the hands of the angels, and not of the wiseacres.

With a serenity that only a ray of the Holy Spirit can shine onto a mortal work;

In the name of Joseph of Arimathea, our father in piety, in the name of Dante, our father in thought, in the name of Hugh de Payens,[17] our father in action:

You who come at the moment when idealism succumbs to the slander of the age, I commend you to eternal glory—Lohengrin[18] of the Ideal!

SÂR MÉRODACK PÉLADAN

Paris, October 1891

---

16. [TN] The **Paraclete**, from the Greek word *parakletos*, meaning "a person called alongside another" to comfort and give assistance. In the Gospels, the Paraclete refers to the Holy Spirit, the third person of God.

17. [TN] **Hugh de Payens** (c. 1070–1136) was the first Grand Master of the Knights Templar. With Saint Bernard of Clairvaux, he founded the order and created the *Latin Rule*, its code of conduct.

18. [TN] **Lohengrin** was the heroic Swan Knight in Wagner's opera of that name.

PRAYER
OF
SAINT THOMAS AQUINAS
BEFORE STUDY
VERY APROPOS FOR GUARDING THE READER
AGAINST POSSIBLE ERRORS OF THIS BOOK

O ineffable Creator, Who, out of the treasure of Thy wisdom, hast ordained three hierarchies of Angels, and placed them in wonderful order above the heavens, and hast most wisely distributed the parts of the world; Thou, Who are called the true fountain of light and wisdom, and the highest beginning, pour out upon the darkness of my understanding, in which I was born, the double beam of Thy brightness, removing from me all darkness of sin and ignorance. Thou, Who makest eloquent the tongue of the dumb, instruct my tongue, and pour on my lips the grace of Thy blessing. Give me quickness of understanding, capacity of retaining, subtlety of interpreting, facility in learning, and copious grace of speaking. Guide my going in, direct my going forward, accomplish my going forth; through Christ our Lord. Amen.

CREED

I believe and declare that the Catholic, apostolic and Roman Church is the Truth. I profess to be its son and I pledge to it my intelligence and my blood.

I recognize the infallibility of the Pope in pronouncements upon dogma *"ex cathedra"* and *"urbi et orbi."*

Although neither my conscience nor my thought reproaches me for any heterodoxy, I am ready to burn my work with my own hands, if the infallible Peter should judge it to be wrong or excessive.

TO THE ANCESTORS

Your glory, O Babylon, I have displayed.

By the virtue of my art, human lips pronounce anew the names of your divinities.[19]

O Chaldea, I have dreamed night and day of restoring you, and here I erect the first chamber and the first level of the great tower: THE AMPHITHEATER OF DEAD SCIENCES.

As a poet, I have sung of your beautiful nights of pious science,[20] of the home of the patriarchs, the land of Abraham and Moses.

I have made lamentation over you, Merodack Beladan, last Sâr of history.[21]

May your wisdom—august race, my race, rivals of the Egyptians, who educated the Celts and from whence came Orpheus[22]—may your wisdom that has

---

19. The heroes of the ethopoem *LA DÉCADENCE LATINE* are named for the Chaldean gods:
    I. *Vice Supreme* (MÉRODACK)
    II, III & IV. *Curious, Initiation,* and *To Lost Heart* (NEBO)
    V. *Ishtar* (ISTAR, NERGAL).
    VI. *Triumph of the Husband* (ADAR).
    VII. *Heart in Pain* (BELIT, TAMMUZ, ISOUBAR).
    VIII. *The Androgyne* (SAMAS, AGUR).
    IX. *The Gynander* (TAMMUZ).
    X. *The Panther* (BRIN and SELA).
    XI. *Typhonia* (SIN and URUK).
    XII. *The Last Bourbon* (ANOV and NAMTAR).
20. *Le Fils des étoiles (Son of the Stars)*, Chaldean pastorale in three acts, with music by Erik Satie (will be refused by the Odéon).
21. *The Sâr Merodack Beladan*, eumolpid tragedy in four acts (will be refused by the Comédie Française).
22. In *The Origin of the Orphakasd*: Orpheus kasdean = Chaldean.

given priests to every people, O you who through the Tuscans made Babylon reborn in Florence—may your wisdom, Race of Thought, Race of Leonardo and of Dante—may your wisdom illuminate me.

The prophet of Israel has pronounced against you words of negation, words that kill, words that enslave, land of the Chaldeans!

Yet behold, the last Sâr has confessed Jesus and his Church: and by the All-Powerful Crucified, by His name and by his sign that saves the world: in the name of God, the only God, who descends upon the hosts:

Lazar of the Chaldeans, the first revelation, Lazar of the ancient mystery, arise—and march to convert or confound the Aryan Barbarians.

And you, winged bull with your human face, who has watched so long over the threshold of my palaces, stand at the threshold of this work.

Spirit of the Earth, remember!

Spirit of the Heavens, remember!

TO THE YOUNG MAN OF THE PRESENT

Here is the book I did not have when I was twenty. Brother, take this precious gift I make to you, not from my own thirty years' experience, but from human genius.

Don't try to figure out if some precept comes from me or if I borrow it from Pythagoras. Is he the better man? Follow him![23]

All the sons of the Prostitution they call Journalism will warn you away from what I have to say: even those I've initiated will argue with my ideas, and if you are disappointed not to find here the ideological light and shadow that are sterile but seductive, you, too, will pass them by.

Never has a book been published with more indifference to its fate: It is done to keep a tacit promise, to repair the wrong I may have done in spite of my good intentions.

Before 1881, Magic was missing from French culture. I have given it illumination and glory, not by bold and dangerous treatises, but through a specific art that did not involve the Sacred Knowledge in my own possible departures from it.

---

23. [TN] See the appendix, *The Golden Verses of Pythagoras*.

I have unveiled magic, which is to say I have accommodated it to the present time. For those who were bewildered by Mérodack of Vice Suprême,²⁴ for those who have come to me asking them to resolve the confusion born within them from reading my work, I offer this practical method of self-magnification.

To obey my Lord Jesus, I have charitably established my program of self-correction in terms sufficiently general and moderate that they may be practiced by poor and rich alike, by artist and socialite: only the priest and the soldier are excluded, the one because he belongs to the Church of which I am myself a devoted son; the other because he belongs to the Absurd, and because he would come away from this book as a deserter or a renegade.

Again, I warn those who take part in collective infamies that I teach contempt for the rights and duties of citizenship.

From my father, the knight Adrien Peladan, affiliated since 1840 with the neo-templars of Genoude, of Lourdoueix, who for fifty years wielded the pen of light for the Church against the parpaillots,²⁵ for the King against the mob—I belong among the followers of Hugh de Payens.

---

24. [TN] *Le Vice Suprême* (Vice Supreme) was Péladan's debut novel, published in 1884, with its protagonist named Mérodack. The name is taken from the Chaldean name for the planet Jupiter and is the equivalent of the Mesopotamian deity Marduk. The character is also Péladan's alter ego: in his public persona, Péladan claimed to be a spiritual descendent of the Chaldean theocratic rulers, or Sârs, and he was frequently referred to as Sâr Mérodack. The character Mérodack reappears in later installments of his 22-volume "ethopoem" *La Décadence latine (The Latin Decadence)*, a series of novels depicting the spiritual dilemmas of life in a dying culture. (See author's note 19, p. XXXIX.) Péladan wrote, "Every novel has a Mérodack: that is to say, an abstract Orphic principle facing an ideal enigma." (Péladan, *L'Art idéaliste et mystique*, Paris: Chamuel, 1894, 275.)

25. [TN] **Parpaillots** were opponents of Catholicism.

Following my brother, the doctor Peladan, who was with Simon Brugal, of the last branch of the Rose+Cross, from Toulouse, like Aroux,[26] D'Orient,[27] the viscount of Lapasse[28]—and who practices occult medicine, without remuneration—I follow Rosencreuz.

In my work I am the steward of contemporary Magic; by my name and by my Word, I belong to the sacred race of the Chaldeans, but I belong above all to Peter, my sovereign, and to the Holy Order that has entrusted its destiny to me.

May my luminous will be blessed by you, my God, and may my work be valiant for my salvation—and for yours, my reader.

Let it be so!

---

26. [TN] **Eugène Aroux** (1793–1859) was a lawyer who held a number of posts in provincial government, and researched and recorded Rosicrucian traditions. The title of his major work, published in 1854, summarizes his ideas: *Key to the Anti-Catholic Comedy of Dante Alighieri, Pastor of the Albigensian Church in the City of Florence, Affiliated with the Order of the Temple: Explaining the Symbolic Language of the Fedeli d'Amore in the Troubadours' Poetic Compositions, Romances, and Epics of Chivalry*. Joséphin Péladan perpetuated these ideas in his own books: *Le Secret des troubadours: De Parsifal à Don Quichotte*, 1906, and *La Doctrine de Dante*, 1908.

27. [TN] **Arcade d'Orient Vial** (1790–1877) was a jeweler and goldsmith in Paris who educated himself in languages, physical sciences, theology, esoteric philosophy, and history. D'Orient's two-volume *Natural Philosophy*, published in 1820, discussed magnetism, the possibility of many inhabited worlds, the transmutation of metals, the philosopher's stone, and the philosophical triangle, all in light of scientific knowledge. His best-known work is *Des Destinées de l'ame*, 1846, in which he discusses metempsychosis (reincarnation). D'Orient, as a devout Roman Catholic, supported his un-Christian thesis with texts drawn from scripture, church fathers, saints, and theologians.

28. [TN] **Louis Charles Edouard, Viscount of Lapasse**, was a doctor and occultist from a family of the old Spanish nobility and the first head of the Toulouse Rose+Cross, circa 1850, who published practical alchemical texts. In his book *Les Péladan* (Lausanne: L'Age d'Homme, 1990, 48), Jean-Pierre Laurant suggests a possible succession of the heads of the Toulouse Rose+Cross Order as the Viscount of Lapasse, Arcade d'Orient Vial, Dr. Adrien Péladan, Joséphin Péladan.

BOOK ONE

The Seven Steps to EXIT the CENTURY

FINIS LATINORUM
(Epigraph of the ethopoem
The Latin Decadence, 1881)

We believe neither in progress, nor in salvation. For the Latin race, which goes to its death, we prepare a final splendor, to dazzle and gentle the barbarians who are to come...

Let us be the All-Past in the face of All-Paris. Let us be enthusiasm in the face of ridicule. Let us be patricians facing the mob. *Let us be ourselves*, and may our personalities, refractory to those among whom we move, triumph over sin and the public.

(*Figaro*, September 2, 1891, *Manifesto of the Rose+Cross.*)

I
THE NEOPHYTE

The first concern of the superior man, from the time he becomes conscious of himself, is to chisel and sculpt his moral being: the theory of Christian perfection is but the sublimation of initiation.

Yes, man has the duty and the ability to create himself a second time, according to the Good. One asks, What is the aim of life?: it can only be, for the thinking man, the occasion and the means of making a masterpiece from this block of soul that God has given him to work upon; and since most do not dream of accomplishing this one work commanded of them, Hell, having become necessary, will be populated with obsessed perverts who have no wish to recreate themselves. Heaven may be defined as the Company of the Good; one does not enter without having made a masterpiece, that is to say, having themselves separated "the earth from the fire, the subtle from the gross," as the Emerald Tablet says, having finally disengaged his soul from the yoke of instincts, and having extracted by religious or magical efforts, a statue from the block one was. (*Supreme Vice,* first book of *La Décadence latine,* Dentu, 1882.)

I
THE NEOPHYTE

Divine Name: ׳ (Yod) [29]
Sacrament: Baptism
Virtue: Faith
Gift: Fear of God
Beatitude: Poverty of spirit
Work: Instruction
Angel: Michael
Arcanum: The One
Planet: Samas [30]

The first sacrament of the Church signifies washing, and purifies from Original Sin. At his first effort, Magic releases the individual from the encrustations of plaque with which education has encased the personality, so that in gaining consciousness of himself, his efforts may enable the proliferation of grace: effort taking here the widest sense of the word "merit."

The Church gives us baptism without our being in a condition to desire it; magic does not yield the mystery unless we are aware of baptism: it enjoins the baptized to works as children of the Church and children of the mystery, simultaneously.

---

29. [TN] The Hebrew letter Yod.
30. [TN] **Samas** is the Chaldean name for the astrological deity of the Sun, which the author preferred to use over the traditional planetary name.

Please imagine for a moment that in taking up this book you have hit your elbow against a fragile keepsake, the souvenir of a dearly departed being. Now, sadly you have remembered, and to the degree that the memory has unfolded, you have noted the vulnerability of your heart, now full of forgetfulness, now full of pain, and, with rising melancholy, this idea came upon you that man is a poor thing undone by the first gust of passion or even the whiff of a memory. Analyze: the breakage, sensation; regret, emotion; a general idea, spirituality.

As many things as you have locked up inside, just so many keys has life has written into you. You are body, soul, and spirit: so Saint Thomas tells you, along with Paracelsus.

I am giving you to understand that this book will teach you to govern your soul.

You might object that you have heard the same thing from your family and in church, and you are disgusted with it.

The Church has prescribed the great work of emotional passivity; she has told you to obey your father and your priest; but if you are destined for an exceptional destiny, your father and your priest cannot guide you; their very dignity prevents it: because it requires giving the advice of an accomplice, to incite you to dangerous deeds.

I have promised to teach you *How to Become a Mage*.

Do you know what they mean when they say, "That man is a character"? Very well, a mage is primarily that. Up to this point, Hermetic teaching has spoken to you of omnipotence, of making gold, talismans and charms: all fraud and humbug. You will never be anything but *the spiritual king of a body and a soul*; but if you achieve this, if your *spirit makes* of your body a servant, and a minister of your soul, then *you will act upon others in the same proportion that you have acted upon yourself.*

Do not seek any other measure of magical power but that of the power within you, or any other way to judge a being but the light he emanates. To perfect yourself so as to become luminous, and like the Sun, to excite the ideal life latent around you—that is the entire mystery of the highest initiation.

Catholicism, this perfect religion, like her imperfect older sisters, is based upon the plane of the emotions, for the compelling reason that spirituality is a fairly rare phenomenon; so that the essence of religion focuses on the point at which the greatest number can converge. Every life and every hour of life contains divine charity; how few the existences and the moments where intellectuality takes place! Even for a genius, even for a mage, manifest inspiration and undisturbed meditation are never customary, so long as their souls, like those of the simple, are in action, and up for grabs. Here then, is a course of ideal influence I undertake:

"What," you will ask, "I will be a mage the day I know how to feel a certain way?" Yes, brother, and the day you have put a bridle on your instincts and have groomed your heart according to the ritual of clarity, you will have only a few more books to read; I would reduce them to one, if the French barbarians didn't prevent it. You may believe for the moment that the spiritual exercises that you will read here represent unimagined difficulties; and that even as stupefying as that idea may be, there is within you a will unfailingly defiant and a soul equal to the task.

You are twenty years old, you live in a city that pretends to be civilized; yesterday your morality was poisoned by the national locust, the University; tomorrow you will be delivered up to torture, also national. College boy one day, soldier the next; between the grind from which you emerge and the one you will enter tomorrow, do you feel within yourself the urge of a proud being? Are you someone, or are you a social unit?

Hardly out of high school, sent to the barracks upon graduation, browbeaten by your professors, soon-to-be victim of your officer, do you crave dignity, truth, honor—tell me—do you want them? You make trouble for yourself, my friend: I play the devil's advocate, my subversive words alarm you, and you believe I want mostly to teach you hate.

O my friend, you may rest assured: I will tell you to whom you owe respect, to whom to pledge your love. But it requires that you renounce the collective in order to be born into your personality.

Society is an anonymous corporation providing a life of diminished emotions. Born in France, you may consider France as a travel agency. Once you are off the academic treadmill, the corporal will succeed the monitor, and then you will be a lawyer, that is to say a conman, accomplice to every crime, the fence for ill-gotten goods, in on all the rackets. Between wrong and justice, you will throw yourself into the role of an actor, the lies of a woman, the bad faith of a Protestant. Your glory will be to have the guilty declared innocent; and such is human injustice, that as an obstructer of justice, you are useful.

Will you limit yourself to being an accomplice of thugs? Oh, no! Son of a respectable family, your actor's role, your effeminate lies, your bad faith, your journalistic cynicism, you owe all of that to your country. Rotten and lazy, ignorant and cross, what are you good for? Total incompetence—where will it get you?

Into politics! No hesitation, the affairs of your country, patriot, the fate of the city, O citizen, that's the issue that will allow you to batten on the mob. You do not have to corrupt the judgment of three bored loiterers nor the torpor of a jury, you have only to spew a mixed hash of Robespierre and Prudhomme, to become deputy of the people; then leadership of the state is nothing but a question of nullity, and the thickness of your wallet a question of how low you can go. If you know how to behave yourself as a young cabinet officer, you may become an ambassador, or a Commissioner of Fine Arts.

A lawyer without cases or a candidate without a party, which will you be? Society has granted you two credentials of superior ability: a bachelor's degree, and a license, you don't bat an eye—you will be a journalist! In that trade you can smoke, drink, and see a lot of the world, and it would be a lot like prostitution, if there were no other considerations.

Once upon a time there was journalism that was political; progress has marched forward, now journalism is pollutional! You may choose between false news and false literature, between reporting and blackmail. The honest, the brave, and those whom you do not esteem, you may insult them; you are the priest of opinion. Meanwhile, if you want to outdo your fellow pimps, learn fencing; a duel provides the last social role for a civilized scoundrel, and the man on the street knows a gentleman who fights is always proper.[31] The

---

31. [TN] When this book was being written, two of Péladan's associates in the Rosicrucian Order had been challenged to duels in the public press. At the center of the controversy was "Abbé" Joseph-Antoine Boullan, who had served as an informant and a model for a major character in Joris-Karl Huysmans's bestselling novel of 1891, Là-Bas. In 1886, the order had denounced Boullan for fraudulent and immoral practices (see pp. 168–169). At Boullan's death in 1893, the journalist Jules Bois openly accused Stanislas de Guaita, then the head of the order, of having murdered Boullan by means of black magic, and issued him a public challenge to a pistol duel. Not long after, Bois also challenged Papus to a duel with sabers. All this was covered with breathless excitement in the daily press—much more thoroughly than it covered the wars in which the French military was engaged at the time. Neither of the two duels resulted in anything more than minor injuries.

Press inherits from feudalism this fail-safe means to get people to pay tithes for the latest gossip. You will have your reserved seat at all theaters and railway cars, and even the handshakes of honest folks, because their jobs and their pay depend upon your good humor.

If I have harped on the criminalities of the lawyer and the journalist, it is because they render one unlikely to become a mage, since, in the former case, you deliberately falsify the truth, and in the latter case you are the entrepreneur of darkness, the universal pimp: these are the two blemishes of the age.

Soldier, you cannot be a mage; passive obedience spoils those who impose it and those who offer it. In the military you are always a potential criminal, and furthermore you are always liable to rob and kill for the collective interest, to profane the idols and even the temple of the true God, as in 1880.[32]

You see already two conditions of this catechism:

Never lie, never serve yourself by means of The Word, but serve it; and on the other hand, subject yourself to nothing but The Word of Divine principle.

"But," you will protest, "what should I do?"

Whatever survival, in accord with your values, dictates to you.

If you wear a uniform like one of the defeated, you will suffer, and your suffering will protect you from contamination; if you wear it with ease, you are not worthy of going without it.

To its youth the social order opens up brothels without voluptuousness and schools without God; it proposes degrading careers for your active manhood and ridiculous honors for your ripe age. I step forth and tell you: Young man, isolate yourself to grow tall.

By your triple nature, you have the life of sensations, emotions and ideas; to realize your ideals, you must first transform instinct into emotion; in other words, you must become incapable of a pleasure that does not include imagination.

This poses the most difficult operation for you; it is a matter of analyzing yourself, so as to discover your vocation, and then learn what you must stimulate and what you must restrain.

---

32. [TN] In 1880, as part of the French government's policy of secularization, the French military seized the Abbey of Frigolet, a monastery in southern France, and forcefully evicted the monks. Joséphin Péladan was foremost among a group of Catholics from Nimes who demonstrated against this seizure.

The human personality, for my ancestors, was refracted into seven planetary types, each corresponding to a type of personal vocation.

Samas: The Sun, the eternal expansive self
Sin: The Moon, the intermittent, receptive self
Adar: Saturn, the eternal, self-contained self
Merodack: Jupiter, the radiant self
Nergal: Mars, the tyrannical self
Istar: Venus, the seductive self
Nebo: Mercury, the egoist self, penetrating others

Are you blonde, with yellowish skin, eyes sensitive to light, small hands, a narrow, noble but not large nose, self-confident and without any need of praises?
Are you pale, round-headed, with prominent eyes, whimsical, dreamy, gentle or perverse, lazy, changeable?
Are you big, slow, irritable, somber, suspicious, a zealot, a thinker?
Are you plump, rosy, vain and good-natured, a hearty eater, already balding, generous and ambitious?
Are you effeminate, open only to nervous impressions, without ideas or will?
Are you small, agile, with tapered fingers, a jack-of-all trades, without sympathies except for yourself?

For more clarification, Leonardo was a solar type; Beethoven was lunar; Michelangelo, Dante and Wagner were Saturnians, Rubens and Titian were Jupiterians, Ribera was Martian, Raphael was Venusian, etc. But these great men each had two secondary planets.

The Solarian is destined for glory and misfortune in love.
The Lunarian poet or musician must live a wandering and adventuresome life.
The Saturnian, the type who founds orders, is designated for great works of science and faith.
The Jupiterian is born for social functions and pontificating on everything.
The Martian represents the active life, and violence.
The Venusian is passive and passionate.
The Mercurian is the smooth operator, the abnormal and the practical egoist.

For fuller delineations there is insufficient space here. For more details, I would steer you to my *Chaldean Astrology*. Below is a brief indication of the seven methods of individualism:

Solar method: To appear in life presenting a work, say a word and disappear. To wait for fame before wanting to be loved; to live alone without intimates, and demand glory.
Lunar method: travel, observe, give oneself to the wind and to chance; ideas come to this type as impressions, and emotions as ideas.
Saturnian method: physical and moral self-containment, chastity, contemplation, life of isolation until circumstances ripen for a single slowly-prepared flash of life.
Jupiterian method: taking part in contemporary movements, if only to combat them. The personality here has force only with the consent of society.
Venusian method: Operating by charm of character, manners, seduction; flirting with life, and playing Don Juan with others.
Martian method: belligerence and violence, aggression, unreflective effrontery: incapable of thought.
Mercurial method: persuasion and flexibility, sorting things out without making judgments, careful and patient diplomacy.

Gift of the Sun, glory; pitfall, moral solitude
Gift of the Moon, poetry; pitfall, perversion
Gift of Saturn, thought; pitfall, fanaticism
Gift of Jupiter, honors; pitfall, egoism
Gift of Venus, passion; pitfall, foolishness
Gift of Mars, energy; pitfall, brutality
Gift of Mercury, skill; pitfall, deceit

Samas (Sun) is tempered by Nebo (Mercury)
Sin (Moon)   —   by Samas (Sun)
Adar (Saturn)   —   by Sin (Moon)
Mérodack (Jupiter) —   by Adar (Saturn)
Istar (Venus)   —   by Nergal (Mars)
Nergal (Mars)   —   by Mérodack (Jupiter)
Nebo (Mercury)   —   by Istar (Venus)

Are you an artist, poet, thinker, pompous, impassioned, impatient, competent—or unknown, perverse, fanatical, egotistical, dull, brutal or deceitful?

For the rest, whatever astrality you may be, this book gives general commandments that fit most natures. Nevertheless, if you are lunarian, venusian or martian, you may not find your equilibrium within yourself, you will succeed only in collaboration. On the contrary, if you are Sun, Jupiter of above all Saturn, you should not accept any but the leadership role in any undertaking. If you are Mercury, you may shift between active and passive without advancing in any sense.

What is called Fate is the malefic influence of a star that determines an individual's chief propensity: In order to mitigate such an influence, the Saturnian who vows himself to solitude must, in order to draw the influences of sociable Venus, take up effeminate forms and manners. A Venusian who would counteract the softness of his nature must, on the other hand, dress soberly and surround himself with objects of a somber character.

I have told you enough that you will be able to sense the degree to which my teaching may apply to you. As to the six collective sins and the seven harmful habits [33] of modern life, you must absolutely give them up; any single one is enough to sterilize all your efforts toward the light, since any one of them is enough to bind you to your companions, and from there you will be torn between the social routine and the demands of individuation that contend for your will.

---

33. See chapter III of this book, "Rules of Social Life."

CATHOLIC CONCORDANCE

ARCANUM OF THE SAMAS [34] or of BIRTH

Baptism makes us children of God, but Society pledges us to Evil by its laws and its education.

Faith gives us light, but it is in perpetual conflict with Society.

In order to render baptismal grace full and vibrant, the initiate must renew his renunciation of Society, renouncing its limits and its crimes in order that the *Fear of God* shall cause him to prefer inner grandeur to the dishonorable favors of the state.

He will be truly poor in spirit when he has renounced everything given by the present time, and in order to arrive at this poverty of spirit that is nothing less than the disdain for his country, he practices upon himself the work of mercy: he teaches himself (the ignorant) about a subject he is most ignorant of, the triplicity of elements that constitute his essential unity.

---

34. [TN] The Sun.

II
SOCIETY

As to the general disintegration of ideas and concepts, for the individual lacking high will and the knowledge of how to resist the current of the times, it results in a dreadful phenomenon of bewitchment. (*Supreme Vice,* first book of *La Décadence latine,* p. 48.)

The West, the West denies God, and to deny God is to invoke Death and to proclaim the void.
There is a moral and metaphysical equilibrium necessary to social existence. The day when the human Word no longer contains a sum of truth at least equal to its errors, when egoisms impose upon the charities, and when there are more people in the brothels than in the church, on that day the metaphysical law of equilibrium that is poetically called Providence will wreak justice upon a people. (*Ibid.,* p. 331.)

Caliban reigns over the island (France);[35] his sons begat their atrocious and godless sons; they deserve each other. You, my Ariel, hide your trembling wings, as I hide my wisdom—they are treasonous among the swine. Prospero disdained to defend a molehill from the moles, or to pick a flower that so many slugs had beslimed. (*Curieuse,* second book of the ethopoem *La Décadence latine,* Dentu.)

---

35. [TN] France is being compared here to the island upon which the main characters of Shakespeare's play *The Tempest* are all shipwrecked. In the play, the wise magician Prospero prevails over the vicious plots of Caliban, a subhuman creature indigenous to the island.

II
SOCIETY

Divine Name: אל הי (El-Yah)
Sacrament: Confirmation
Virtue: Hope
Gift: Piety
Beatitude: Gentleness
Work: To counsel
Angel: Gabriel
Arcanum: The Binary
Planet: Sin [36]

Before you think or choose, society grooms your being and fashions it according to its standards. As soon as you think and choose, erase the creases it has put into you, that is to say, free yourself from modern habits according to your duty.

---

36. [TN] Chaldean name for the moon.

To make your choice, know that you have three destinies: you may be an animal like the degenerate that the superficial call savages; an astral[37] being, ruled by your temperament, like most people; or spiritual, like Saint Thomas or Dante. Animal, be beautiful; astral, be good; spiritual, seek the Grail.

To become beautiful, astralize[38] your instincts; to become gentle, spiritualize your emotions; to grow toward the Absolute, develop abstraction in yourself.

Democracy is the ultimate ugliness; militarism is the supreme malevolence; the supreme inanity is Progress.

The free man is the one who submits only to sickness, misery and the police. Brother, as I cannot give you either the elixir of life or the philosopher's stone, even less can I give any assurances that you will not be unjustly imprisoned or executed; I can only emancipate you from instinct and from society; I can only isolate you morally from the brutes said to be your peers, make you aware of the continence that will allow you to avoid two thirds of the foolishness that an honest man commits, and of the social indifference that will save you from losing time and committing sins.

Regard the sexual act as a very inferior thing, and political acts at that same level.

Restrain your physical life, annul your civic life.

---

37. [TN] Péladan's term is *animique*, a word with no precise English equivalent, derived from the Latin word *anima*, meaning something like "life force," sometimes translated as *soul*. The word *astral* seems to be the closest one-word English equivalent, since the English language has loaded up the words *anima* and *soul* with meanings that Péladan did not intend. In his way of thinking, the *anima* is the middle part, in the three-part structure of a fully developed human being: the flesh, the anima, and the spirit. The flesh is involved with sensations and instincts. The astral-animic faculties are involved with emotions, desires, imagination, and ordinary discursive reasoning. Spirit involves abstract thought and consciousness itself, and permits intuition and direct experience of the divine. Astral awareness draws from and communicates to both flesh and spirit. Humans relate to one another mostly through astrality, while they relate to God through spirit.

38. [TN] Péladan's term is *animise*—to suggest a process in which the astral-animic faculties are brought to bear upon the instincts, to channel their operation into conformity with human values.

Neither fornicate nor vote; consider that those men who are the favorites with the ladies are the biggest fools, and that booksellers are awarded the Legion of Honor,[39] as well as those who laid heroic siege to Frigolet.[40]

Don't settle for being someone in a phantom country, who survives but no longer lives; and be aware above all that only you can ennoble yourself, decorate yourself, and elevate yourself. There has only been a single dignity in the world: to be fully yourself on the spiritual plane; and only one true glory: to teach someone to become an entity.

Then you will quit the seven habits of this decadence by virtue of hyperphysical laws.

If you wish to evaluate modern society, and evaluate France with its divine language, take the Ten Commandments and interrogate the French people:

I. *I am the Lord your God: You shall have no other gods before me.*—The City Council of the City of Light [Paris] has willed the omission of the divine name from Fontaine's *Fables*; the Committee of Public Instruction distributed to schools of the country a catechism that denies God. Every morning five hundred blasphemers, whose voices are multiplied by the enormous diffusion of their papers, insult both Jehovah and his son Jesus. In sum, the era of State atheism is upon us.[41]

Is this to say that the French have another God? No, they have fallen lower than the savage who, at least, has his fetish.

---

39. [TN] **The Affair of the Decorations** erupted in late 1887, when a prostitute with a grudge against her madams told the police that more than one kind of corruption was going on in the house. Political allies of Jules Grévy, the serving President of the Third Republic, were selling awards (decorations), including memberships in the Legion of Honor, to businessmen and provincial opinion-makers in exchange for their support. This scandal forced Grévy to step down, and opened the way to the presidency to Sadi Carnot.

40. [TN] **Frigolet,** see note 32, p. 9.

41. [TN] The policy of *laïcité*, or secularization, was encoded by the Ferry Laws passed in 1881–1882. They made primary education in France free, secular, and compulsory. Further legal measures from 1901–1903 provided for the separation of church and state: secularization of hospitals; subjection of seminary students to military conscription; provision for divorce and civil marriage; legalization of work on Sundays; abolition of public prayers before parliamentary sessions and legal proceedings; removal of religious language from judicial oaths; and the prohibition of military personnel from frequenting Catholic clubs or participating in religious processions.

O, the irony! I cite the Second Commandment:

II. *Thou shalt not take the name of God in vain.*—The name of God is forgotten; only the drunk speaks it as he rolls in the gutter; but the crocodile that sprawls on the throne of Saint Louis,[42] Carnot,[43] chief of the savage Latins—the last avatar of the reptile[44] that the degenerate Egyptian priests showed to Saint Clement[45] as the very dignity of the Misraim[46]—does not pronounce that name.

III. *Remember the Sabbath Day and keep it holy.*—They have only one Sabbath: Bastille Day, the national holiday; it commemorates only a drunken public that took over a tower defended by some invalids.

IV. *Honor your father and mother.*—The fathers and mothers of a society are the enlightened spirits who formed it; France, like all the West, was raised in the lap of the Church, and France, that parricide, at the instigation of a wise-guy that Louis XIV wouldn't have accepted as a personal servant—France now denatured, persecutes the cloisters. Oh, the barbarians of 1880 did not look like Huns. They are not greedy ignorant nomads; they spread across their country as many schools as brothels and barracks, they speak of liberty at every op-

---

42. [TN] **Louis IX** (1214–1270) was canonized as a saint in the Roman Catholic and Anglican Churches. As a French king who personally led Christian forces in the Seventh and Eighth Crusades, he was one of Péladan's heroes.
43. [TN] **Marie François Sadi Carnot** (1837–1894) served as the President of France from 1887 until his assassination in 1894.
44. [TN] The **crocodile**-god Sobek was worshipped in Egypt from the earliest times through the late antiquity, as a protector from the dangers of the Nile River and as a representative of the Sun, fertility, pharaonic power, and military prowess. In the Ptolemaic period, in the oasis city now known as Fayum, a sacred crocodile named Petsuchos was kept as an avatar of the god in a special temple pond where he was adorned with gold and gems and fed by priests with offerings brought in by his worshippers.
45. [TN] **Clement of Alexandria** (c. 150–c. 215) was an early Christian theologian who taught at the Catechetical School of Alexandria in Egypt. He had extensive knowledge of pagan mythology and mystery religions, and sympathies with pre-Christian Jewish esotericism and Gnosticism.
46. [TN] **Misraim** is the Hebrew and Aramaic term for the land of Egypt.

portunity, and keep a zoological garden where the public can come to gawk at some Fuegians[47] who, it seems, believe in Manitou.

We have seen an army corps besiege forty monks, we have seen the closure of churches, and finally we have seen priests required to become assassins. The Fifth Commandment is clear and requires no interpretation:

V. *Thou shalt not kill.*—Is it really true that the human collective is exempt from the duties laid upon the human individual? All the public wealth is dedicated to maintaining the national assassins; all scientific activity serves to invent new means of destruction. Do the foreign enemies force us to defend ourselves? That goes to show that the foreigners are barbaric killers like the French, and I do not see any moral progress we have made over the Goths, I see only various modes of homicide. ...

A Corsican bandit stretching his bloody hand in the nineteenth century—how does he differ from the bandit whose brutal march of triumph opened the thirteenth century? Between Genghis Khan and Bonaparte, in what degree of infamy do they differ?

At Alise-Sainte-Reine the French were taught to bow before the four thousand human hands cut off by Julius Caesar; at Quiberon[48] they gave academic awards to the grandsons of the martyrs in the form of a portrait of General Hoche.

France has even succeeded in sullying the propagation of the Faith: behind the missionary comes the national assassin.

By what right, if not that of might, do the French assassins crush the Arab race? They send them the Cross at the point of a bayonet; what they call bringing civilization, as if an army was anything else but systematized barbarism.

---

47. [TN] The **Fuegians** were indigenous people from Tierra del Fuego, eight adults and three children, who were brought to Paris and studied by the Anthropology Society of Paris in the "Garden of Acclimation" in 1881. Fifty thousand visitors came in one day to gawk at them, and they were also put on display at the Berlin Zoological Garden, as though they were animals. Manitou is a deity worshipped by the Algonquins of North America, not a deity of the Fuegians.

48. [TN] The **Quiberon Peninsula**, on the southwest coast of Brittany, became, in 1795, during the French Revolution, a base of operations for French Royalist exiles, in their attempt to recapture Brittany with British assistance. General Lazare Hoche commanded Revolutionary forces that defeated their invasion.

A thug, the same one who chased the monks from their monastery, the greatest wrong-doer of his period,[49] thought one night that it would be convenient to massacre the yellow man, the Germans being nearer, but too dangerous: then the national assassins sailed the oceans to eviscerate women, topple idols, steal, pillage and kill like Goths: and that was called the glory of France.

The Chinese, however, are civilized, in accord with the sentiments of Pythagoras, to consider the professional soldier as an inferior being: they refused to negotiate with the generals; while the French, for their part, chose soldiers as their diplomats: this demonstrates the great inferiority of the French Empire to the Celestial Empire.

VI. *Thou shalt not commit adultery.*—Adultery, pffff! How medieval! We have invented divorce. You are no longer pleased with your wife, leave her: Ah, the family. Family is a Chinese thing for the French! The children grow up while their father lives with another mother, and their own mother with another father? We think about children only when we make them, according to the witty French saying.

VII. *Thou shalt not steal.*—Robbery is almost the sole motive of the assassin, all war turns upon plunder. The last woman who sat on the throne of France accepted in front of her people a necklace stolen by Montauban, the arsonist of the Summer Palace of Peking. The French assassin prefers destruction to theft: for the rest of it, the State undertakes highway robbery. Isn't it wonderful the

---

49. [TN] **Jules François Camille Ferry** (1832–1893) was a French republican statesman and a promoter of secularism and colonial expansion who was twice president (1880–1881 and 1883–1885).

   In order to prevent the restoration of a monarch to power in the early years of the Third Republic, Ferry ordered a wide-scale purge of many known monarchists from top positions in the government, army, and civil and diplomatic service. As a minister of education, he passed laws in 1881 and 1882 that made primary education in France free, secular, and mandatory. His policies toward Germany were based on his perception that France was not strong enough to win a military confrontation, but his popularity suffered for this.

   As minister of foreign affairs and as president, Ferry worked for the expansion of the French colonial empire, principally for the sake of economic exploitation. He promoted ventures into Tunisia, Madagascar, and Indochina—which brought France into conflict with Qing dynasty China. Public outrage over military spending in Indochina forced him out of the presidency in 1885.

way people submit to monopolies, in other words, the cheapest merchandise at the highest price!

VIII. *Thou shalt not give false witness.*—Now, lies constitute the whole of the discourse of the two Chambers of government, and of the press. Monuments carry the word liberty, in a country where *habeas corpus* laws exist in no form whatsoever.

IX and X. *Thou shalt not covet thy neighbor's wife, nor thy neighbor's goods.*—Now, envy is the principal sentiment of all democracy, and it is no slander to claim that the bourgeois rise to power only by inciting vanity and the burning thirst for the Good Life. The France of the past twenty years is a population of traveling salesmen and drunken laborers.

Compare, my disciple, the worst of men to the French collective, put the blackest blackguards up against Society, and you will see that the adulterer has at least some family feeling, and that the thief takes very little, while France robs a whole people, that the assassin kills at most a family, while Bonaparte exterminated fifteen million lives.

If you are on the street at the moment when someone engages in wrongdoing, you will change course for fear of being mistaken and arrested as a perpetrator, or an accomplice. And if you are in the country at the moment of the greatest wrongdoing in history, you had better take a wide detour, for fear that the law violated, which will crack down soon, does not fall upon you.

Shake the dust from your sandals, wash your hands and renounce this society that forgets God, when it does not blaspheme Him. Flee the foul embraces of the bourgeois mob; do not pass the salt among such reprobates. Set yourself apart from this nation of thieves and assassins, where deceit attacks every reputation, where people live like ravening dogs.

Renounce here below what God has renounced in his Heaven; only at this price will you become a Mage, only at this price will you be saved.

Isolate yourself, meditate, listen to silence, and if the abstract speaks to you, then you will have returned to the foundations of moral retreat. As an apostle or genius, try to save the Latinity that was once sublime, and this France, which will at least always live through its incomparable language.

POST-SCRIPT ON FRENCH BARBARISM

On Friday, September 11, the *Figaro* covered three separate events that allow the reader to make some judgments about this sweet country.

Firstly, the mayor of la Mure, railway station of Grenoble, 3,600 inhabitants, forbade women to wear white frocks with ribbons, for fear that they would defect to the procession organized in a neighboring town; the tribunal passed their judgment on the 8th.

That is the liberty that reigns in France.

A very literate Shiite pilgrim monk had, in obedience to the spirit of his order, which encourages the search for truth by means of travel, wandered for years through Persia, the Caucasus, Armenia, Mesopotamia and Asia Minor, on foot, without hindrance. Having arrived in Paris, he was imprisoned, and left to rot for three days among thieves. Without the intervention of a Persian student of Advanced Studies full of wisdom and virtue, Goulam, Riza Seystani, he would still be sitting in prison.

That is French hospitality.

And the arts of Paris! Lamoureux had his life threatened by the musicians of the Grand Opera, for having required them to respect the score. He was forced to set his revolver on the podium: America would have been truly ashamed. The opera houses do not dare to advertise *Lohengrin*; they will advertise *Robert le Diable* and play *Lohengrin*; as neither the patriots nor the syndicate of music publishers want the performance of masterworks; and the mob of patriots prefer the bellowing of Massenet as the music of the nation.

To sum up, what I say about society should be understood only of the present. If the corpse of egalitarianism was not already in a ripe state of decomposition: if, instead of living in this period of degenerate insanity, we were in the time of Saint Louis or Louis XIV, my language would be completely different. Anywhere that the principle of theocracy presides, there is still sanity, but for a century God and tradition have been blasphemed; France will die in its impenitence; it is even useless to pray for her. Reserve your zeal for the Church and beware of the collective.

Get it into your head that the seven thousand years of documented history contain no period so debased, nor a place so foolish that equality has been proclaimed. That this term contradicts science, reason and faith; and faced with 36 million equals, you have only the duty of the tiger—that is, to show yourself dangerous enough that they will leave you in peace in the wilderness, where you want to grow, progress and become a Mage.

CATHOLIC CONCORDANCE

ARCANUM OF THE SIN[50] OR OF BELIEF

The sacrament of Confirmation is a counterpart of Baptism: one can receive it only once, it obliges us infinitely because we receive it with a certain awareness, it engages us to fight for the Faith.

Hope of eternal life is worth the renunciation of the more immediate advantages offered by society.

The initiate obtains the fervent aspiration towards the better, to become holy; and piety engenders sweetness, but also impatience for the reign of God.

It is not enough for one to be gentle. After having been established in this virtue one must perpetuate it around oneself with great energy.

Confronted with society, the initiate must be a Knight Templar confronting the Infidel, never to bow before the French Mohammed, petty officer or judge: so that his battle-tested personality can disengage from the ignoble collective to rally around the Church, the only homeland of the Christian and the Mage.

---

50. [TN] Chaldean name for the moon.

III
RULES OF SOCIAL LIFE

Metals are precious by reason of their density, and the soul rises higher to the extent that it offers less porosity to the mundane current.

The initiate's relation to the State should be limited to self-defense. (*L'Initiation sentimentale*, third book of the ethopoem *La Décadence latine*, Dentu.)

But there have been those like Orpheus, who refuse base joys, fleeing the maenads, knowing how to live for a name and to die for a dream: Eurydice.

Here's a toast to the incorrigibles who get intoxicated only from cups bearing the seal of their rank. (*Istar*, fifth book of the ethopoem *La Décadence latine*, p. 266.)

III
RULES OF SOCIAL LIFE

Divine Name: שׁוּי ישׁו (Yeshu, Shaddai)
Sacrament: The Eucharist
Virtue: Charity
Gift: Science
Beatitude: To weep
Task: To console
Angel: Samael
Arcanum: The Trinity
Planet: Venus

There are seven customary abominations that you must first detest and repudiate: the bars, the group of buddies, the news, gambling, sports, the brothel and vulgar entertainments.

These are the seven heads of the imbecility of the West and of the French country; the plague of any single one will debar you forever from the Temple of Magic. Now, these are unspeakable uglinesses that the Orient does not know, and they are spawn of the dragon of error that the prostitutes of the pen call progress.

Beer, dirty language, media filth, thievery, nonsense, cynicism, and the profanation of music all offend the Holy Spirit itself, the rector of the magical domain.

Write your letter of resignation from your gang of buddies, cancel your newspaper subscription, try to avoid smoking, drink nothing but water or wine, and listen to me.

We are going to reform your outer life, because it is the easiest way, and because I do not wish to discourage you.

LAW: Every meeting between individuals exudes a fluidity with the same name as the state of their soul; this effluent creates a moral atmosphere strong enough to act upon the soul, in a degree of intensity similar to that of gas fumes acting upon the body.

Consider the state of the soul of the man who sits in the bars; multiply it by the number of individuals to be met there, and tell me: if this influence leads to idleness, laziness, showing-off and vulgarity, how should it not be forbidden to anyone who desired to perfect himself?

LAW: What is called a game, in other words, a mechanical means of preempting thought, constitutes a voluntary act of imbecility.

A game of cards or billiards corresponds to the lowest stage of humanity, to the rube, the officer, the confirmed bachelor and the traveling salesman. Read, dream, sleep; but never allow your spirit to slip into drawing numbers from a sack or knocking balls against each other. If you have no respect for time, if you speak of killing it, pass on by—you will never be anything better than a senator or a notary.

LAW: Gaming as a way of making money is a formula for thievery practiced by the lazy or the mindless.

As a matter of morals, the act of taking someone else's money constitutes thievery; to rob the player leaving the game table after having won—that is to say, having succeeded in stealing—is a crime. But these are less culpable than the practice of the gentleman who uses the social convention of a game as a pretext to steal.

LAW: Whoever relies on the accord between secondary causes that is called chance, without making any mental efforts, will never rule his own destiny, nor other men.

What I have said about the bars you may apply to your group of buddies, in capital letters.

LAW: As soon as men gather without a lofty goal (councils), or without the motivation of need or action (corporations): the electrified atmosphere of the same name engulfs even the intelligent in an enormous volume of nonsense; and this because—in the spiritual sense only—men beget men; opposing aspirations cancel each other out, and their bad instincts are reinforced.

The law above applies to debaucheries as well as to the national assemblies, today. The corollary is this:

LAW: When the people assembled are not acquainted with one another, they are hypocrites (at the theater); when they are known to one another, and have no fear of one another, they are cynical (as in a club).

In a social club or other circle, you find all the same dangers as in the bars; and more, a kind of intimacy with the vicious. Their cynical and brutish manner of treating matters of love, their bragging, the battalion of broads that hovers just outside such a circle, is dirt that will rub off on you.

A club consists of drunks, jokers, good-for-nothings who think of little beyond themselves, which is to say that they live only to drink, fornicate and out-do their competitors. As individual as you are, you will be overwhelmed by these waves of vulgarity, inundated and crushed.

Moreover, you read the news, which is idiocy itself. No perceptiveness is possible among journalists; they lie all the time about everything.

If you have any generosity of soul, you will not be able to look at a newspaper without indignation; and as the news is only ephemera, don't waste your attention upon it until you are established on the path to self-realization, when it may become useful to know what idiot winds are blowing through Paris.

LAW: The man attempting to perfect himself should not interest himself in ephemera, as it would diminish his breadth of vision.

As for sports, like all social life, it is a compendium of adultery, vanity and brutality. Nevertheless, it has a venerable prestige. Falconry has its decorative aspects if it is practiced in archaic costume; stag-hunting, seen through the eyes of Rubens and Snyders, has the power to seduce the nobility, but not the initiate.

LAW: Whoever kills an inoffensive animal without excuse of poverty, charges his aura with the reflection of murder. The woman cruel enough to accept the gift of game will weep for it; the tears of the stag do not fall with impunity.

Note well, real hunters are all brutes; Homer, Dante or Shakespeare never mixes a butcher into his plot. Beware of the enthusiasts of the hunt. Nimrod, the great brute who stands at the dawn of history, Nimrod and his sons were never civilized despite the efforts of my Chaldean ancestors: the father of the Sennacheribs and the Sargons, father of genocides like Bonaparte, is called a great hunter in the books of Moses.

LAW: Whoever attends the bullfights, cockfights, quail-fights, is a being accursed. These are barbarities.

As for the horses, it is a great idiocy; if you are competent, well-read, to give your attention to a derby—don't sully my pages any longer with your deluded eyes.

Physical culture has its place, because of the enormous importance of a body capable of serving the will, and of sustaining the necessary cerebral excesses. Physical force is never good for anything more than that. It once conferred royalty among the Germans and Scandinavians; it attracts the favors of only very dull women, which are negligible. I do not believe that a modern man can weigh his nerves against his musculature and have any hesitation in choosing between the two. It is to be noted that the muscular, sportsmen or officers, *do not think*, particularly horsemen.

The brothel always seems to come along with an army: it proliferates in cities in proportion to the garrisons. Must I say more?

LAW: The sexual act always takes place doubly, in the hyper-physical as in the physical; the prostitute receives through her contacts the lowest astral emanations, and no one takes her without being tainted astrally. The sex act leaves traces of the indignity of the contact and also of the sum total of the indignity of all its precedents.

If the vulgar sexual contact infects the soul, the gross spectacle of the Palais-Royal[51] and scandalous entertainments corrupt the sensibility.

Anyone who can easily endure shows of patriotism and filth yowled by bimbos with no talent, or the bombastic bellowing of someone like Horloge, anyone who can dine in peace on the Ambassador Terrace,[52] that one will never be a mage.

To take pleasure in inferior literature and art is to lose the comprehension of the masterworks and to become resistant to their purifying action.

The Parisian who is seen as often at Bayreuth as at the Alcazar (a café-concert)[53] will never feel the art of Bayreuth; the reader of Zola will never understand Dante: in a curio cabinet that contains Japanese prints, one does not see the works of Leonardo. The muses are imperious mistresses, and if one is unfaithful to them, they abandon the boor to the music of Auber, the bellower

---

51. [TN] The **Palais-Royal** was built in 1639 as a noble residence and was converted in the 1780s into a venue that included cafés, gambling houses, theaters presenting works of doubtful taste, and women displaying themselves in the street arcades to those who came to buy their company.

52. [TN] The **Ambassador Terrace** was an open-air café-concert along the Champs-Elysées that was very fashionable among members of high society. The musical entertainment was popular but very artful, including singers such as Aristide Bruant and Yvette Guilbert. The venue was bustling and noisy.

53. [TN] A **café-concert** was a type of venue that was very popular in France during the Belle Époque; *music hall* and *vaudeville* were the British and American equivalents. A French café-concert typically served light refreshments, including wine and beer as well as coffee, and featured popular musical and theatrical entertainment that might range from extremely artful to uncouth and pornographic, depending on the particular venue.

to the blare. If you are one of those who take the *Marseillaise*[54] as your Grail theme and an obscenity for the rites of spring, put this book down. The mage closes his ears to the songs of the vulgar, in order that the Beethovens, Bachs and Wagners may prepare him for the divine music of the spheres.

> LAW: *Two men who look upon one another act upon one another; each of the two men who spend much time together has the other's morals in his keeping.*

Antiquity attributed an extreme importance to the choice of friends: in our time, chance encounters are the sole determinant. Choose for your friend the friend of virtue, said Pythagoras, a handsome term, vague, of no practical use.

Choose for your friend the one who shares your interests, who walks the same path of destiny: since the tying and untying of the knots of love and friendship are the bifurcations of existence.

In theory, one should not choose companions of one's own age: and above all, not young writers, with their brains addled by cerebral effort, unquiet souls, embittered by the desire for success. You will profit only from your elders; only they will take pains to form you, because without knowing it, you prolong their lives.

> LAW: *In the visits between an old man and a young man, the enfeebled organism of the one inhales and incorporates a bit of the vitality of the other. In return, the understanding of the elder polishes and refines the intelligence of the youth.*

You would be a fool to spend your time around an old man who has no wits or whose life has not mixed him into other great lives and great works. The old officer, for example, the man who gave blind obedience, flee him; look for priests and those who were respected, whose memories are the pages of civilization.

As you cannot completely avoid contact with those of your own age, take this rule, to never let them *make fun of you*: where they mock you, leave. Never stay in a group in which you are considered small.

You should be difficult to approach: Don't give your hand until you have judged the person in front of you.

---

54. *La Marseillaise* is the national anthem of France, first sung to rally support for the French Revolution.

Be more careful for your ideas than for your person, for what you admire than for your own reputation.

But as soon as you have given your hand, be unfailing in your courtesy; observe the good manners of the world you are in; exaggerate, even. If someday you accomplish something, you are not relieved of being civil, but you may be civil in your own fashion.

Do not be familiar: men usually have scant respect for those closest to them.

Give no deference to those who represent the State; reserve your respect for the artist.

As mother and sister, women appear to you at first in their admirable aspects.

The mother belongs to the Divine.

The woman seen in your house, the woman related by blood, is nothing like the wife or mistress, she of whom you will demand pleasure or love.

Do not chase girls; flee them, not because they are the occasions for sin, but because they are infected with vulgarity. By girls, I refer to any woman who makes money from sex.

See only honest women, that is to say women you can be seen with in public. When it comes to defending yourself against their manipulations, there is no such thing as public opinion.

LAW: A woman never separates her interests from her emotions, her destiny from her loves: and the superior man, in yielding to his emotions, must defend his interest; in love, safeguard your destiny. Where a man seeks pleasure, the woman does business. Her nature forces her to employ her only means of influence, sexual attraction; she wants to keep the man.

Never forget this fatal opposition of interests: let it turn you away, first of all, from those beneath you, and then from all young girls.

You may think I am recommending adultery—certainly not—because I put you on guard against anything that would disturb your life. Do not imagine I forbid fornication to push you into marriage. No! Marriage, the best form of love, should come down to a matter of destiny, not entrapment. Do I vow you to continence? I wish I could do so; but you will not listen to me, any more than you listen to your priest. Speaking only in the name of wisdom, I can give you counsel in relative virtue although it does no good to teach anything but absolute virtue:

> LAW: *The companionship of women is profitable by this analogy: that the nervosities, like the electric charges called positive and negative, strengthen one another. Only the companionship of honest women is beneficial, because their goodwill emits upon us the thing that corrupt women substantially dissipate. Befriend honest women.*

I mean by honesty not only that precise virtue, but also that good judgment that minimizes and hides faults. You will observe that a woman's charm depends upon your unsatisfied desire. Consequently, even in high society, avoid the too-easily pleased, who do not require you to earn their esteem.

Finally, ask nothing of women but refreshment for your eyes, the spectacle of grace, and obtain their friendship if you can. It is only then that this formidable adversary disarms and becomes favorable. This apparently chaste commerce contains a certain voluptuousness that you can almost smell, which is enough for fine natures: it prevents feelings of emptiness; plus it renders one singularly refined and psychologically perceptive. Finally, my disciple, the most precious gift a woman can give is not herself, but her illusion.

> LAW: *A woman is the prism through which male desire is refracted, she is not the light of life, but only Eros' means of analysis. Consider her as the material point, the concretion of the ideal and, in parting, love with only half a body, if you can, with only half a heart, as you must.*

Do not play Don Juan: it is a bad role, and the commanderesse[55] always comes. Acquire the double reputation for never demanding favors, and of being a collective heart.

---

55. [TN] In the traditional story, we are told that Don Juan had murdered the father of a girl he had duped, a high-ranking military man known as the Commander. Toward the end of the drama, a statue of this commander, with the portentous and powerfully menacing air of divine retribution, comes onstage to give Don Juan his due punishment. Péladan notes: "A great departed spirit, Armand Hayem, in his dramatic version of *Don Juan*, had the bright idea of replacing the commander with the commanderesse."

LAW: *The female instinct being that of possessiveness, half of the human race has been fettered by this very thing, so imperious it is. Feminine jealousy has ruined two astonishing political fortunes, those of Gambetta[56] and Boulanger.[57] So that you may love one alone, appear to love many: only that will give you peace: let the word mistress have no more meaning for you than the word master.*

56. [TN] **Léon Gambetta** (1838–1882) was a French statesman who was prominent during and after the Franco-Prussian War. In 1871 Léonie Léon became his mistress and a trusted political advisor. He continually pressed her to marry him, but she did not wish to compromise his public career. Finally, in late 1882, when she had finally consented to marry him, Gambetta was wounded by the accidental discharge of a pistol in his home, in her presence. The injury was not life-threatening, and the consensus seems to be that it was unquestionably accidental. A month after the accident, he died of natural causes.

57. [TN] **Georges Ernest Jean-Marie Boulanger** (1837–1891) was a French general, a politician, and an enormously popular public figure when scandal over political corruption in 1887 brought the government of the Third Republic into disrepute. General Boulanger won a series of elections and had enough popular support, along with political backing in Bonapartist and monarchist circles, that he was expected to mount a *coup d'état* in 1889. At the decisive moment he did not make his move, and this was widely believed to be due to the influence of his mistress, Marguerite Bonnemains (née Marguerite Crouzet), a wealthy and beautiful divorcée he had met in 1887. After passing up the opportunity to become a dictator, General Boulanger fled Paris and went into exile along with his mistress. Marguerite died in his arms of tuberculosis in July of 1891, and Boulanger committed suicide two months later by shooting himself on her grave. He was buried in the same grave.

CATHOLIC CONDORDANCE

THE ARCANUM OF ISTAR or NUTRITION

The Eucharist is such an ineffable mystery that we would voluntarily sacrifice symmetry, if the beneficial sense of our work would not suffer from it. By this sacrament, the creator gives himself for the love of his creatures: in order that a supreme love might be born in us.

The initiate must isolate himself from his surroundings until the day when he is able to give himself as a sacrifice: as the gift of wisdom ends in the work of consolation, and the poets like the artists are great consolers through the beautiful reflections of the ideal by which our senses can taste Heaven. To console the suffering requires them to weep, not the vain tears of the body, but the tears of the mind such as man's iniquities drew from Jesus.

Love and friendship are the refuges for our failing hearts; but it is in God that we must look for our vision and our complement, and, having seen by illumination, retell it to men in a word of art, science or goodness.

IV
ORIENTATION

Between knowledge and love, like Alcide long ago, Athena, Aphrodite surround me as I travel the thirty-two holy paths. (*La Victoire du mari*, sixth book of the ethopoem *La Décadence latine*, p. 231.)

Oh! Yes! I envy you, my catholic heroes; your role, aristocrats of holiness, is the good one: to have your steps marked out by the spitting of the crowd, and then at last to fall into the light, and risen to heaven and become a star, to vindicate yourself in the sun. (*A Coeur perdu*, fourth book of the ethopoem *La Décadence latine*.)

IV
ORIENTATION

Divine Name: יהוה (Jehovah)
Sacrament: Penance
Virtue: Prudence
Gift: Strength
Beatitude: Thirst for justice
Task: Correction
Angel: Anael
Arcanum: The Quaternary
Planet: Nergal [58]

Aware of the dangers you ran as a member of the social collective, be on your guard against the hazards of sociability: Orient your being. I assume you have found your astrality and chosen one of the seven methods. Whatever the result of your *nosce te ipsum,* the time has come to formulate a theory of will.

The magnet, in whom strength increases by the increase of the weight he pulls, provides the image of will.

The Church tells you: weep for your sins, because the Church thinks of the many and, for that reason, counsels passivity. Magic tells you: erase your sins by exercise of the corresponding virtue.

Take a catechumen who committed the sin of base fornication; as religious hygiene he weighs his sin, the better to detest it; the magical exercise is to wash

---

58. [TN] Chaldean name for Mars.

himself of his moment of instinct by several hours of metaphysic. Where the devout repent, the initiate reforms himself.

Thomas à Kempis's *Imitation of Christ* is written about the monastic life; obedience is always prescribed. Look where this commandment takes you in real life: to brutality and wrongdoing.

Your superior is called teacher, priest, or sergeant in turn; the one falsifies the heart in vaunting the savages of Rome, Caesar and Bonaparte, the other requires you to listen to the orders of a Lavigerie [59] or the *Marseillaise* from his pulpit; as for the sergeant, he makes you into an assassin and a sacrilege.

Brother, disobey your time and your country, in order to obey the Eternal and the light from which you have come.

Understand that all the ways of the present are the ways to perdition; tear up the social contract, if you are ever to attain full being in eternity. I cannot promise you will become like Pythagoras or Plato, unless you cease to be a Frenchman in 1891, a Westerner.

I have told you to repudiate the laughable rights and fraudulent duties of citizenship, I have warned you against your university professors, I relieve you of the hierarchy of Bottoms who weigh down your individuality: I assume you are now isolated from outside influences—isolate yourself still more from ambient ideas.

> LAW: *Ephemeral human groups (the bars, friends, theaters) release an astral influence; permanent human agglomerations release an abstract oppression. It is a phenomenon of bewitchment through the unconscious mind.*

At a nightclub, for example, one perverts his taste in accustoming his eyes to vulgarity, his ears to *filth*. A military uniform, for another example, corrodes one's notions and leads to mental incapacity.

---

59. [TN] **Charles Martial Allemand Lavigerie** (1825–1892) was a French cardinal who was active in missions and establishing Catholic institutions in the French colony of Algeria. In his famous "Algerian Toast" of 1890, he proclaimed, in front of a large assembly of French officials, that in keeping with Pope Leo XIII's encyclicals of 1884 and 1890, French Catholics had a Christian duty to adhere to their republican government. This policy was in direct opposition to the Church's previous alignment with monarchist opposition to the republican governments of France. French monarchists, including Péladan, considered themselves betrayed.

It is certain that if the modern army could take down forty monks by means of starvation, it will stop at no imaginable infamy. It is no less certain that even if the army had not been dishonored by the siege of Frigolet,[60] one would judge it to be as totally mindless as a thrown rock, and just as irresponsible.

The permanent, mindless and irresponsible institutionalization of all infamies should strike any thoughtful person as the most horrible thing in the universe, and the most potent, in the fatal sense of the word. So, every intelligent being in France risks his life or his intelligence at the age of twenty-one.

A man of Alsace-Lorraine admitted to a journalist that, in civilian life, he conspired against Germany, while as soon as he put on the [German] uniform he became a military thing, and proceeded mindlessly to march in step with his mates. This imbecile is a prime example of the modification of the individual by the collective: his heart beat for France, and his rifle shoots for Germany. Be on guard, then, lest the currents of opinion rob you of your reason.

Beware *the example of others, think for yourself.* This precept of Pythagoras contains all of magic, which is nothing other than the power of ipseity. However, on this point you may not be able to achieve clarity by your own lights, and even if you follow my lessons, they do not exactly unfold for every case into an independent existence.

Be a Catholic, that is to say, pray morning and night, go to mass, and let your sign be the sign of the cross. An improvised prayer, spoken or murmured, is a big part of magic. Let your prayer be an exorcism of this age, whose influence is not at all that of a would-be mage.

After the prayer that raises you toward the divine, admiration is the second power; read nothing but masterworks, books sacred to all peoples, but since the epics treat antiquity, while the modern litany blasphemes Jehovah Sabaoth Lord of Hosts, keep to the following:

> LAW: *An act is beautiful not because it is powerful, but it is powerful only because it is beautiful. To admire strength for its own sake is to return deliberately to the animal state; the hero is not the one who kills his adversaries, but the one who, whether he kills or is killed, has upon his sword the ray of divine justice.*

---

60. [TN] **Frigolet**, see note 32, p. 9.

Anyone who admires ugliness victorious and injustice triumphant will never enter into the glory of eternity.

To put my finger on the nub of this matter, I declare that the Vendome Column[61] shames the people servile and savage enough to have made themselves the instrument of the fearful monster that Hell vomits up onto France to punish it with an orgy of anarchy.

England in the Indies, and France in Tonkin[62] and Algeria may be called by their true name, that of systematized piracy; and my head explodes when I must add that it is a stain upon the propagation of the faith when the missionary serves as a tool for French banditry.

A naïve reader of the daily papers will reply that if France had not done it, someone else would have.

I doubt there's a single low blow that the national army has ever neglected to strike; but I have no doubt, either, that justice is the most effective policy for states as well as for individuals, and that God's blessing upon a people is worth more for its prosperity than any number of East India Companies.

I bring together here a certain number of laws that will help you to resist the pressure of false ideas, and they follow from this axiom:

LAW: *There is only one cause, and that is God; only one end that is Eternity; only one reality that is Beauty.*

It follows then, that any act must adhere to the divine plan, aim at the immutable, and manifest beautifully.

The divine plan is divided between perfection and expansion; the immutable into a gradation of ascendancy; beauty into subtlety and charity.

---

61. [TN] The **Vendome Column** is a monument to the French Revolution.

62. [TN] The French military was involved in Southeast Asia (French Indochina) from the late eighteenth century to 1954, and these ongoing wars were characterized by much the same atrocities on the field and fraudulent propaganda at home that have characterized the wars undertaken by the US in the late twentieth and early twenty-first centuries. The French often justified their military operations as efforts to protect Catholic missionaries and their activities.

The conscious being perfects itself in order to shine, and by this imitation of the Sun, and by this merit, to achieve the highest ascendance, of which the terrestrial gages are understanding and goodness.

Now, my disciple, submit your questions to this criterion: What signifies *the name of the French people?* What is this people one names with a single name? A human collective is nothing but a sum total of equalized units, and consequently, lower than the individual.

Now, you do not obey an individual; are you going to obey something worse, the nation? If so, any commandment according to this formula is vain.

But this human collective called France has prisons and police; you can outsmart rather than fight them. Outsmart the law, in an original way if you can. You can't do better than that as the head of a rebellion, or as a thinker. If you write, tell the truth: truth is worth more than your safety.

If you enter adult life with five hundred francs per month, on the condition you do not marry, you must consider any work in society as servile and unworthy of yourself.

It is not permissible to debase yourself in order to make your fortune. At least pursue a beautiful goal, like Schliemann [63] who wanted to be rich in order to excavate the remains of the Homeric world.

This proscription against pursuing wealth will astound you, above all when you imagine that if my ideas caught fire in the heart and veins of a rich man, it would be a victory for the ideal. I tell you, brother, it is the nature of gold to destroy every noble quality of soul. Look around: not a single intelligent rich man. I have known only one, an extraordinary spirit, Armand Hayem, who dreamed of reconstructing the Temple of Jerusalem. As for the Rothschilds, that clique of climbers—what do they do with their gold? They give out a few ten-franc tickets to the literati, so as not to be excoriated in print, and a few hundred thousand francs to the princes of Orleans in order to be received as guests. To pay the gambling debts of the nobles whose houses they visit, that is the light shined by these clowns, who do not partake of the brilliance or the insolence of their gold.

---

63. [TN] **Heinrich Schliemann** (1822–1890) was a German businessman who became a pioneer archaeologist. In order to substantiate his conviction that the works of Homer and Virgil reflect actual historical events, he excavated sites now presumed to be the Bronze Age sites of Troy, Tiryns, and Mycenae.

If fortune comes to you of herself, accept her and lead her, but don't chase her. A dethroned king may accept any crown, but may not stoop to get one.

Know! Above all, cultivate your intelligence. Dare! Stand firm upon the evidence, and constant in your Will! That which the mind has conceived, the soul will execute. Be silent! Silence is the source of the Word and of the work. Such are the four magic words as the Chaldeans established them six thousand years ago in the form of the sacred bull.[64]

Study this symbol: The human head carries a royal crown of three tiers of horns, the privilege of the gods, signifying: initiated, no longer obedient, you are a king if you think. The king does not seek to reign; the triple horns destine you only to the conquest of eternity. The wings indicate that you must be inspired by a higher world, without failing to manifest light in this world below by the strength of your bull's hooves.

Another teaching comes from the relationship of the wing to the hoof, analogous to the precept of Pythagoras on the excellence of the golden mean. By its hooves, the colossus stands upon the earth; by its wings it may rise above; this indicates that the Mage need not seek the heights of ecstasy, nor persist in bringing light to his earthly milieu. Abstractly, the Chaldean orientation of this symbol yields thought, supported by enthusiasm (wings)—by means of vigorous flanks (work)—will be everlasting, ever-present, and victorious. May your unending efforts be in obedience to abstraction, without your enthusiasm carrying you away from reality, without reality diminishing your enthusiasm.

Meanwhile, at the beginning of your initiation, do not fear to abandon your soul to the excess of zeal; mistakes being the truest teachers, make your mistakes on this path where nothing fails to yield fruit. Make your mistakes, but I forbid you four offenses: any notion of using magic in your emotional life, any "magnetic" or "spiritualist" phenomena, any affiliation with an occult society. Would-be sorcerers are simply robbers and assassins, magnetizers of mindless malevolent forces and spirits, an assortment of mental cases. As for the legitimate desire to instruct yourself in hermeticism, from anyone who professes it, I forbid it because magic cannot be taught, because memory plays no role, be-

---

64. [TN] The **winged bull** represented a celestial being, a protective deity known as a *lamassu*. It was often represented by colossal sculptures placed in pairs flanking the entrances to palaces and cities of the ancient Near East. The cover of the current edition of this book features a pair of winged bulls, as did the cover of the original French edition.

cause reading books by Fabre d'Olivet amounts to a simple effort of erudition and, finally, because magic is man creating himself a second time; consciously doing for himself what his family and society tried to do while he was unconscious. But here there is no director; as in mysticism, one must, after the example of Siegfried, forge one's own sword and suit of magical armor.

> LAW: *There is no magic that realizes badly conceived intentions, since to realize signifies as much to conserve as to obtain, to conquer as to keep.*
>
> *Magic consists of formulating only such intentions as harmonize with one's own nature and with the circumstances. Success is a series of accords struck by the will, according to the rhythm of life.*

It is thus an illusion to think that the occult serves all ends, that the voluptuary can turn magic into a pimp, or the wastrel into a source of money. If they could, black magic would exist.

The force of a word resides in its prudence, as there is no power against reason. In modeling the soul upon eternal justice, the will takes on the *force of law* and manifests itself. Do not worry then, my disciple, about the manner and the quantity of will, but about its purity. Your thought, if it be as a ray of light, will extend at the speed of light; if it be like a stone, it will fall suddenly and heavily.

Directed, this common word resumes its power, as the whole dynamic here depends upon mental focus.

A navigator has nothing but his compass, and the initiate depends on his orientation. The currents and the winds, that is to say circumstances and coincidences, favorable and unfavorable by turns, must not change your eternal course, but only the set of your sails; and the better you know yourself, the more surely you will grasp the tiller. Your life or voyage will be happy according to your management of your being, your vessel, first according to its tonnage and rigging, or your temperament and faculties, and then by the currents, rocks and winds.

CATHOLIC CONCORDANCE

ARCANUM OF NERGAL or SECURITY

Extreme unction, which is the sacrament of the sick and not for those in agony, tends to cure as much as purify, despite the catholic ritual, and it corresponds to the pentagram of occultism.

The word extreme comes from the existence of three unctions [65] that one may receive before it.

The just receive the gift of counsel that leads them to holiness of the merciful. The initiate always forgives what is done to himself, but never forgives an offense given to God, be it what he considers his dignity in relation to other men, or whether he sees his nothingness in the presence of God, pride or humility of the mage does not permit him to have any outrage except about matters of abstract justice.

His perpetual effort to produce equity in himself renders him steadfast in the face of death that is near or violent. God will judge him as he has judged, and he will have judged according to God.

---

65. [TN] **Unction, or anointing,** is the ritual of applying aromatic oil so as to introduce a divine influence or presence, to ward off dangerous spirits and demons and as a form of blessing. In Christian ritual, the oil is usually dabbed onto the recipient's forehead. The three occasions on which a Catholic layperson is likely to be anointed (receive unction) are Baptism (in which oil is applied before and after water), Confirmation, and in one's final illness. The Roman Catholic Church no longer uses the term *extreme unction*, preferring instead *anointing of the sick* or *last rites*. Anointing is also part of the coronation of European monarchs, the ordination of priests and bishops, and the consecration of altars, chalices, and patens used in the Eucharist.

V
MAGIC POWER

Lightning is like heat; Sound is like Color; and Life is nothing but the power to work miracles in Matter.

Perception and emotion are each a modality, the microcosm can rule the macrocosm by the conscious play of secondary causes. (*Istar*, fifth book of the ethopoem *La Décadence latine*, p. 128.)

V
MAGIC POWER

Divine Name: יהצוה אלהים עליון (Elyon, Elohim, Yehoshua)
Sacrament: Extreme Unction
Virtue: Justice
Gift: Counsel
Beatitude: Spirit of mercy
Work: Forgiveness
Angel: Raphael
Arcanum: The Five
Planet: Nebo [66]

Never fight except in the name of a principle; forget yourself for your cause, take no pride in anything except the blows they strike, and let disdain be the whole of your vengeance. The news media, the moron media, have told you of sorcery: this is a literary device that does not exist in magic.

> LAW: *If your adversary is unjust, redouble your justice; it will bewitch even him, because the will to injustice does not prevail over the will to justice. But know well that to be in the right is not enough for you to be safe; this righteousness must be coupled with will; the will manifests in signs still only appreciated by the catholic faith. "I've been bewitched," you think; open Genesis and say, "Great Moses, may your Word cover me," and it will cover you.*

---

66. [TN] Chaldean name for Mercury.

Neither metaphysicians nor mages can be bewitched: they live in a domain to which the nerve-fluid, vehicle of malevolence, does not ascend.

Be truly absorbed in Plato, or Paracelsus, and during this time, even if they stick pins into a waxen head in your image, you will not suffer as much as a headache.

One overriding reason that sorcery has never been done, according to the word of Eleonore Galigaï:[67]

> LAW: *Malevolent fluidic transmissions are so depleting that in order to produce a headache in his enemy, the operator uses up vital force that would normally last him for a year; even if the spell works, he will not regain the force emitted: if it is a failure, he will lose three times more.*

You must clear yourself of all anger against a being who offends no one but yourself: never give any more importance to your enemy than if he were a thing: drop it; don't confront anyone, unless you want to raise the enemy to your own level and then let him go free.

In treating the hostility as a thing, do not set yourself against it like the sailor who curses the bad seas; calm yourself in order to reflect, and reflect in order to pardon. But understand this of forgiveness: it consists of desisting, before God, from your just complaint—not of ceding any other point.

---

67. [TN] **Leonora Dori Galigaï** (c. 1571–1617) was a favorite and confidante of Italian-born Marie de' Medici, who reigned in France as regent between the assassination of her husband, Henri VI, and the coronation of her son, Louis XIII. Leonora was in charge of the queen's hair and wardrobe and was also paid to repel black magic by working exorcisms and white magic. She and her husband, Concino Concini, both Italians, became very powerful and wealthy due to their influence over the queen; the French courtiers and the French people detested the lot of them, viewing them as foreigners looting the country. After Louis XIII overthrew his mother's regency in a coup, Leonora's husband was murdered and dragged through the streets, and she was arrested and charged with bewitching the regent and practicing magic. When questioned, Leonora insisted that her only power over the queen was that of a strong mind over a weak one. Nevertheless, she was decapitated and her body was burned at the stake.

A Ramollot[68] will brutalize you; forgive, consciously, those who know not what they do; but exercise your severity upon whatever represents Ramollot, Nimrodism.

Let all your most passionate emotions arise, and abstract them.

This way you will present a very small target to ill will: as the great work of magic, this is deceptive to the superficial.

> LAW: *Magic is the art of quickly wearing away ordinary human lust and greed; and the mage finds himself in possession of much he no longer desires; in the sense that the death of a desire makes it an absolute negative.*

It makes me angry to see people taking seriously the amusing affirmation about transmutation attributed to the Rose+Croix: The philosopher's stone consists of simplifying, reducing things to quintessences, in order that contingencies no longer affect us.

Magical asceticism reduces gross sensibility in order to sublimate it into spirituality; and the sore spots of the ordinary man, the triggers for lust and anger, are almost dead in the Mage.

> LAW: *Magic is an asceticism that, wearing away human lust and greed, replaces them with the extraordinary aspiration to be angelic, even; and the Mage finds himself wanting things made all the more precious because he will find them on the other side of death, in absolute positivity.*

I would compare the Mage to a navigator whose compass is set toward a point invisible to the many, and who, after having been buffeted by the winds and waves, sails with supernatural speed and serenity.

> LAW: *Magic consists of seeing and desiring beyond the horizon.*

The vision of the beyond is developed in solitude, the will by exercise.

---

68. [TN] **Colonel Ramollot** was a fictional character invented by Charles Leroy (1844–1895) as the protagonist for a series of illustrated novels and stories for penny brochures, published over a period of more than ten years. The colonel, a blustering imbecile and a foul-mouthed bully, caricatured a type of military officer very well known to the French public.

Solitude does not consist of shutting yourself up and smoking; it is fertile only if great thoughts preside.

The exercise must be unceasing.

TYPICAL DAY FOR AN INITIATE

He goes to sleep the previous night perhaps mulling over an idea, or absorbing himself in a question that might be resolved for him in the astral life of sleep.

Waking up in the morning should never be abrupt, but a review, even if vague, of that idea.

The second awakening, more complete, should be appreciated like *Gloria in excelsis Deo*: and the sign of the cross upon you and around you should precede a brisk exit from bed.

One should never linger in bed, nor read in bed. The horizontal position, essentially passive, is too much like death and does not suit the morning, the daybreak of activity.

The initiate grooms himself meticulously; washing with water at body temperature is recommended in default of a quick one-minute bath in the tub.

After washing, a prayer performed while kneeling should include the *Lord's Prayer*, the *Ave Maria*, the gospel according to St John; with the first lines of the *Lord's Prayer* spoken, and an improvised closing prayer of one's very own, requesting more specific blessings upon the work of the coming day.

Next, if one has not written out a plan for the day, quickly detail what needs to be done; knowing that accomplishment depends upon the cooperation of circumstances and other people.

Supposing that someone fails to do their part, do not become upset, but move on to other parts of the plan.

Theoretically, the morning is the time for efforts requiring clarity; but this is not practical except in the provinces or in the country. In Paris the nightlife rules, and makes midday a time for rest, physical care and interior concerns.

Gluttony, the lowest of all sins, is also the most inimical to initiation.

As to vegetarianism, I do not recommend it; it diminishes combativeness; and since a Mage is destined to fight, he must as far as possible eat the meat of wild and/or aggressive animals. I would recommend, for their phosphate, fish, dairy foods and caviar.

Other points of nutrition I would prescribe here: fruit is especially good for the intellectual, fowl should be avoided. As for drink, no beer nor cider, nor hard liquor; you may have wine, and if possible, nothing but water, except for occasions when one wants to stimulate the organism. These are matters of moral hygiene.

> LAW: *The ordinary man cares for his body in order to have health and fullness of life. The initiate cares for his soul, persuaded that the physical body will receive the influence of the astral body.*

Eating too heavily and drinking to drunkenness are faults.

One who consults a menu and saves his appetite for a specific dish, or who does not stop eating at the first sensation of a full stomach sins against initiation. One must, like Leo X, remain temperate at the table of Lucullus; follow one's needs and not the attractions of a dish. One who allows himself to be seduced by food is a fool.

One should not read at the table, nor after a meal unless aloud; declamation may improve digestion at the same time it prepares one for mental work. The afternoon is good for reading, research and gathering material for the work of the evening.

The hour preceding the sunset, infinitely well suited to enriching the emotions, must be for the initiate what it is for Nature, a moment of recollection in which one listens to life and ponders.

Nightlife was born in Chaldea to accommodate climate, whereas in Paris it accommodates a false conception that pleasure depends on being released from work. This is a matter that each must work out for himself. The theatre, when dominated by Racine, Corneille, and above all Shakespeare, and beyond him Wagner, is the sole beauty of civilization.

Mornings in church, afternoons in the museums and libraries, evenings at the theater—that is the outer life of the initiate.

If the evening is given to labor, no purification is required, but if one has gone into society, one should burn some incense as an astral disinfectant.

Never close your eyes to sleep without asking yourself: What did I forget? What did I do today?
If it was bad, abstain from it; if it was good, persevere.

This advice from the *Golden Verses*,[69] which also imparts piety, is always of colossal importance, if, having examined your failings of the day, you form a plan for the next day accordingly.

This done, make the same prayers as those of the morning, except that the improvisation should always express the needs of the moment.

As for using sleep for the notary art[70] or for work, I discuss it in a later volume: It will suffice, remember, that your last thought be abstract; your last sight before turning out the light should not be a portrait, but a masterwork such as the *Last Supper* by Leonardo. He who closes his eye upon a ray of the ideal will have no nightmares; phantoms never come near the worshippers of great art.

Ideally, one prepares for sleep, as for meditations, by listening to some approximation to divine harmony, some measures of Beethoven, Wagner or Bach.

Lie down to sleep in a noble posture and always on the side.

Practical magic, under rigorous precepts, has no laws when it comes to matters of personal detail. What suits a country person may not serve a Parisian. Someone attached to a piece of land will not be able to follow the training indicated for an unattached individual at all hours.

But I suggest to everyone three magic reminders during the day: upon rising, prayer and resolutions; at sundown, remembering to listen for the unknown superior; when going to bed, prayer and self-examination.

Anyone who, every morning, prays and wills; at every sunset, dreams; upon going to bed every night, prays and wills again—that one will become a mage.

---

69. [TN] See the appendix, *The Golden Verses of Pythagoras*.

70. [TN] The **Notary Art**, or *Ars Notoria*, were a series of prayers and invocations that could be used to secure divine aid in enhancing one's memory, eloquence, and general academic capability.

Three times a day he affirms his will, both according to the communion of saints and according to the communion of sages.

Saint Teresa of Avila said: "Give me a quarter hour of reflection every day and I promise you salvation." Give me three quarters of an hour of reflection a day and I promise you magic.

Nothing should be allowed to preempt the threefold exercise, not fatigue, nor sickness, nor even laziness. Better to do it imperfectly than omit it. This ternary suffices to make you into an adept, if you add to it two rules, one of which applies to the moral course, and the other for which you will be detested, if you admit it.

The first demands that you be a gentleman, that is to say a man who does not lie, intrigue, or indulge in finance of any sort. The second demands that you renounce society, country, and your times.

If you are a soldier or, even worse, an officer; if you're a customs officer or, worse still, a minister in the government; if you are a player in the infamy of this land and this century, you pray in vain. You are of the collective, a servant of evil; patriot, go back to your absurdity, you will come to nothing when the luminous pentagram [71] unleashes its dreadful justice upon mankind.

You must defend yourself, but you do not have to fight; so consider each hostility as if it were a thing, and push it out of your way, or avoid it, as you would a crumbling rock or a violent wind; never designate any being as an enemy, as that would be to put it on a level with yourself and to recognize its destiny as equal to your own. Since persistence is exceedingly rare in this world, it is rare that hostility endures very long. Besides, gratuitous hostility, that is, hostility in the face of a blank wall, wears itself out, peters out and expires.

Forgiveness does not seem the magic word of the concept it contains. Does one forgive the wind that blows off a roof, or the rain that drowns a crop? Just so, the one who offends you is no more than a wind or a rain: protect yourself, step aside from that which threatens you, and let it pass. Whoever slanders you, or usurps your place somewhere, acts under the influence of corrupt instincts much more miserable than the harshness of the elements.

---

71. [TN] This pentagram consists of the five Hebrew letters of the name of Jesus, *Yeshua*, according to Christian Kabbalah: YHShVH, *Yod, He, Shin, Vav, He*. This pentagram is displayed on the symbol of the Kabbalistic Order of the Rose+Cross, which is taken from an engraving by Heinrich Khunrath.

When you have arrived at the point where you disdain the wicked, you are very close to overcoming them, since to ignore one who is unjust is almost to defeat him. Ignore your enemies. Wipe off defamation as a sailor does when a squall has passed.

There is nothing redoubtable but what you believe to be so, and when a human thing is ignored, it retreats, impotent as an octopus that cannot find a foothold.

CATHOLIC CONCORDANCE

ARCANUM OF NEBO [72] or RECOVERY

The sacrament of penance consists of contrition, confession and restitution.

Here I am forced to contradict the catechisms: restitution does not consist of reciting a few prayers—that is unworthy of the name of penance. Restitution consists of making amends for your misdeeds. Whoever has slandered must recant his lies in the same assembly in which he spread them; this penitent who has sullied a reputation must seek out everyone connected with the matter, in order to redress it.

If the same benighted priests who forbid artists the study of the nude were to force their flocks to make reparations, there would be fewer frequent communions, and even fewer unworthy communions.

The catechists reduce the works of restitution to three: prayer, charity and fasting. This last method of penance is truly so simple as to be completely childish.

Magic demands that the initiate repent through an act of light opposed to his sin: such are the personal corrections and scientific measures that strengthen and develop a hunger and thirst for justice.

---

72. [TN] The Chaldean name for Mercury.

VI
ON LOVE

This faculty of being exalted by nervous vibration, and of reproducing, prismatically transposed, the influence given by a man, makes a woman a fey creature whom only the superficial or the feeble denigrate: the one because he is incapable; the other because he is afraid. (*Coeur en peine*, seventh book of the ethopoem *La Décadence latine*.)

The universal Library does not contain a single female philosopher; nevertheless, the eloquence of Saints Teresa, Brigit, Maria d'Agreda, is admirable, because God touched them. A woman, always lunar, can only refract the light radiated in her by Love. (*A Coeur Perdu*, p. 38.)

VI
ON LOVE

Divine Name: אלגבור (El Gibbor)
Sacrament: The Order
Virtue: Strength
Gift: Intelligence
Beatitude: A pure heart
Task: Support
Angel: Zachariel
Arcanum: The Six
Planet: Mérodack[73]

Love is the permanent desire for the good; to understand this word in the sexual sense is to fail to understand it. To confine the voluptuous between a table and a bed, and to give to women the sovereign empire of love, is inconceivable. The Greek Eros signifies the Desirer, and his myth has no connection with conjugal passion.

Unlike the woman, who in the economy of providence must subordinate herself to her husband, the man must give a woman second place in his mind and his life, and the figure of Don Juan seems to me as idiotic as can be; this dull man who endlessly repeats the same exercise, this negligible man who thinks that changing his instrument makes for better music, this frivolous man who doesn't recognize the emptiness of the woman and who has a soul too

---

73. [TN] Chaldean name for Jupiter.

feeble to create that which he desires,[74] Don Juan represents the diabolical privilege of art, the prodigious exercise of cerebral free will, by which man attempts to justify himself by a rationale that defies Reason.

The contemplation of the mystery of faith or of poetry, study of a Bach prelude, of a drawing by Leonardo, of a metope, is not work appropriate for the many; and a woman fills the whole ideal horizon for the one who does not raise himself into the abstract.

Mark the distinction in my thinking by which, like the apostles, I esteem celibacy above marriage, as more fitting to the perfection of the individual.

Marriage will always remain the only form of love compatible with magic; a wife is always worthier than a mistress, by virtue of the law that I have already cited, according to which the woman pursues her interests and her destiny as soon as she loves; sanctified union disarms her by uniting her destiny with yours.

As an initiate, marry only if you are materially independent, or where the marriage brings material independence: From the day you are married, your first duty is to defend the woman from want, as well as your children; and without money, you will be forced to march to the tune of the times, to serve the social abomination. You may still be a saint, but you are no longer fit for magic.

As for the celibate without virtue, I have given you in the rules of sociability advice that would profit all. Wagner has represented women more fully

---

74. [TN] The author expands on this thought from the woman's point of view in another of his works:

> A. XVIII. *As a woman does not possess a fixed personality; she models herself after the desires that surround her, and reflects them: An idealist, if the men around her are idealists; soon a cynic if they are gross and brutish.*
>
> Your beauty depends upon those who look upon you; your emotions upon those who love you, in all the acts of those who surround you. You will then be beautiful, lovable, and noble in the same proportion to which the men who approach you are handsome, loving, and noble. It is said that the auditorium makes the orator, the public the mime, the occasion the thief, the robe the monk, and the situation the joke. In just this way men make women, that is to say, producing the reflections of their own tendencies.
>
> —Joséphin Péladan, *Comment on devient fée (How to Become Fey)* (Paris: Chamuel, 1893), 93.

than Balzac: Elsa[75] would press endlessly for the revelation that killed her, and Kundry, femininity personified, wavered between the Grail and Klingsor,[76] equally excessive in her rights and wrongs.

Neither wife nor mistress should dominate you: remember that the woman, all-powerful in intimacy, is powerless over one who is away. Never argue; should the woman forget her duty of obedience, leave her. Go to the next room, the house next door, or to the neighboring country. Leave her for an hour, or a day, or a month. It is up to you to judge your own case, I can only tell you the secret: "Get out." For, on the one hand, this strikes at the essence of the woman's sense of possession, and what's more, only brutes can prevail in intimate battles.

In submission to the man, resonating, the woman becomes his equal, in that she is his double, his zealous and enthusiastic alter ego; ideally husband and wife will become the platonic androgyne, a single being in two forms. In dominating the man, she disdains him; a woman loves only one who is her master.

Am I saying that one must tyrannize the being so little responsible and so mindless? Certainly not, one must only subordinate her to the ideal, without humiliating her. Never say to her, "You are incapable of such a sentiment"; she is capable of anything, high or low, and give her credit: the eternal coquette will metamorphose her sentiments in order to seduce you. Show her a chimera and tell her: "This is what I love and what you can become." If she loves you, she will manage it; if she does not love you, there is little harm in it. Nothing resembles such a love as much as all other love.

The tendency of this gender, like that of the people, is always to test the temper of one she loves: oppose all rebellion with silence and absence. You risk only being fooled in revenge, which is no big deal, or being dropped, which is even less.

---

75. [TN] In Wagner's opera *Lohengrin*, that hero's power to lift an evil spell depends upon his keeping his name and origin a secret, but his newlywed wife, **Elsa**, persuades him to divulge his identity.

76. [TN] In Wagner's opera *Parsifal*, **Klingsor** was the implacable foe of the hero and the other Grail knights, while **Kundry** was Klingsor's female accomplice.

Balzac, the greatest literary genius of the century, has written a naïve book on the subject of the fear of cuckoldry,[77] and the writers of popular romance novels have not known the torments of being loved.

Never be jealous, and try to defend yourself from the jealous: they can ruin your life without remorse.

"I am suffering," the woman says, and soon that will be her justification for anything. Do your best, my disciple, never to inspire extreme emotions; they are ephemeral and leave a trail of ruin behind them.

We become responsible for an act of madness when we are its object; the initiate is mindful not to throw any soul into disorder. We are also responsible for the suffering we may cause; and our name must never be spoken with tears, not by a single soul.

Always when destinies collide, when the woman mixes her love with business and pursues the fight for life along with the fight for love, one must brush the woman aside without hesitation.

Art has largely spoiled the human spirit by its outrageous sentimentality. What intoxication there is in the poem *Tristan and Iseult*! But they can only die, as real life does not permit such vertigo to endure; and the mad passion that kills in works of art, becomes brutal in reality.

Think of true love as tender generosity, more attentive than poignant, more enduring than extravagant. Think of sensual pleasure in the serene and gracious style, and not as ferocious, but meditative and smiling. Beautiful hearts reflect deeply, but serenely; beautiful bodies vibrate under a calm caress.

Let the ideal be the third party in your love.

I certainly do not intend that you should intellectualize your wife. A woman never knows anything; whatever efforts she makes, she ends up in the role of the parrot, and the bore. But a few rare ones burn with precious enthusiasm: the chosen can only admire.

---

77. [TN] **Honoré de Balzac** (1799–1850) was the author of the novel sequence *La Comédie humaine*, which presents a panorama of post-Napoleonic French life. His novella *Ferragus*, which first appeared in 1833 in the *Revue de Paris*, focuses on a good and honest stockbroker who suspects his wife of cheating on him. Miscommunication and fear of losing social status aggravate the trouble.

If you should encounter one of these, stimulate in her this beautiful faculty of enthusiasm; so that she may serve the ideal mass in the cult of human genius: what her vibration will add to your own is indescribable.

Night falls upon the arcades of the cloisters, the angelus is rung; if your wife then adds her impression to yours, you will know the admirable second violin that is a woman in the sexual duet.

The musical domain, so substantial, so ethereal in its mode of impression, appears to me as the only one in which a woman can celebrate the mystery: the soul of the modern woman, the best of her soul manifests at the piano.

Love must be serene in order to be truly love; otherwise it should be known as passion, which one suffers as an overwhelming instinct.

You will probably not avoid the phase of emotional development in which popular culture and the example of your peers presses you to subordinate everything else to sexual obsessions. I cannot suppose, without making myself ridiculous, that you are wise and prematurely great enough to overcome the sphinx of passion from the first, nor fortunate enough to resolve by a good marriage the problem of being twenty years old—take this advice which is not a command from the ideal, but an accommodation to your frailty.

Love does not germinate, that is to say, does not awaken in us, by multiple impressions, but through imagination and desire; thus it is wrong to do the work of the flesh—the less the better.

Pleasure is not in the spasm, but in the progression of energies that leads up to it.

Never sleep with a woman as a lover; I do not forbid the bed, I forbid sleeping together that belongs to man and wife.

Be apprised that marriage is a resolution to join your destiny to another destiny, and that love is an artistic attempt to restore the primordial being, the artificial androgyne of Platonism.

The man who marries must first be a statesman; the one who loves must be a lyric poet. Am I saying that the two cannot be found together? Certainly not, but since love does not bring along with it endurance or clairvoyance, to marry for love is an impulse of instinct and foolishness; to marry without love, an act of darkness and equally foolish.

Be warned that where you may see moonlight and kisses, the woman always sees a better living situation. That is no sin, but it does not require you to play the fool, to fall into dreamland and awaken in the arms of necessity.

Also, a young man's life is enclosed by two barriers: the one forbids you fallen women and the daughters of the poor, because any woman whose life offends social conventions can too easily threaten your own destiny; the other forbids you married women and virgins, because you would disorder their destinies.

So, what's left to you? You don't see, and it is not my place to point it out to you; but widows and divorcées would seem to be exempt and free, and the least sinful; and I insist upon this point, that the emotional exercise is enough, that temptation does not require you to yield to it, and that an affectionate flirtation satisfies refined natures, in the form of amorous friendship.

The poets, those quasi-divine beings, have wrongly falsified the Western imagination by propagating the exaggerated gallantry of the Spanish moors and the caliphate.

A woman is not love incarnate, nor the ideal, and in a frank assessment of this terrain, she falls short of the imagination. The sister of charity and the mother of a family are incomparably higher than lovers, even if one assigns equal value to the level of charity and the level of the passions.

Ask of a woman whatever her sense of charity permits her to offer, and not the materialization of your dreams.

Imagine Cleopatra not as the queen of Egypt, but as the daughter of an insecure bourgeois of Lyon, and you will see that a woman's prestige is made from a million extraneous things, such as her name, rank, wealth, influence.

There once existed among the royal families of Atlantis and Babylon admirable princesses; but in order to produce such meteors, it takes two thousand years of monarchial splendor.

You may encounter Hatshepsut and Nitacrit, or Semiramis, in the features of an inspector's wife, and you don't recognize them, because she is only seen in a destiny related to her own; and there really is no other destiny than to be Madame Wagner,[78] Madame Récamier,[79] an abbess, or a saint.

Furthermore, a modern man does not know how to give a woman the joys of the past, for the usual reason that the wife of a general is always prettier than the general.

Only art can make your dreams come true; live among masterworks and ask a woman only to give her heart and to temper your sensibility.[80]

The woman who passes by should leave a mirage; the woman who abides, a calm; and marriage is only so beautiful because it reduces passion to a minimum of importance.

These notions are not fashionable but neither should they be taken lightly; they do not flatter the senses. To the superficial they will appear misogynist, until the wisdom of Love has been explicated with qualifications not possible to develop here.

What I want to indicate is the ideal of love, at the same time as that of marriage; peace in both desire and destiny finds realization only in the case where the wife understands her role as the satellite to the man, understood to be a superior man.

---

78. [TN] When Wagner met his first wife, Christine Wilhelmine "Minna" Planer, she was a leading lady in one of his opera productions. The marriage lasted thirty years until Minna's death in 1866, but it was tempestuous, full of mutual infidelities, and plagued by financial difficulties. Minna became emotionally imbalanced, which wore down Wagner's health and ability to work, leading to their estrangement after 1850 and a separation in 1862. Wagner's second marriage was to Cosima (born Francesca Gaetana Cosima Liszt), daughter of the Hungarian composer and piano virtuoso Franz Liszt. When Wagner met Cosima in 1863, she was married; she bore three children by Wagner before her husband agreed to divorce her. Despite Wagner's infidelities, his second marriage endured from 1870 until his death in 1883. Cosima continued to direct the Bayreuth Festival for over twenty years after Wagner's death, promoting his music and philosophy and establishing the festival as a European cultural institution.

79. [TN] **Jeanne Françoise Julie Adélaïde Récamier** (1777–1849) was celebrated as the most beautiful and graceful French woman of her day. The brilliancy of her conversation, manners, and taste set the tone of a social circle that exerted great influence on French letters. Because her husband, a banker, was ruined by Napoleon's policies, her salon was characterized by opposition to the government.

80. [TN] **Sensibility** is a word from the vocabulary of Romanticism that combines the notions of sensitivity, emotional capacity, and artistic taste. Péladan's work as an art critic, impresario, novelist, and head of a Rosicrucian order was largely aimed at cultivating sensibility.

In our day, the word superior has been usurped by blue-stockings and their ilk, I cannot deny that some beings have existed, still exist perhaps, equally superior to both sexes; these are androgynes such as Saint John, Mozart and Raphael: but this third sex is never a woman writing articles, nor a man weaving tapestries.

One should not forget that the Celts who once submitted themselves to sacred priestesses, were driven by these beings who claimed to be civilized into human sacrifice; remember that wherever women rule, madness reigns, and that you have no duty to obey them.

Never should the word mistress ring proud in your ear. Have women as friends or take a wife, and no one else.

There is no point in mentioning binges and debauches: the pleasure-seeker is always an imbecile.

There is room, between the priest and the layman, for a third type who renounces the base sins of the layman without pretending to sacerdotal purity. To pillars of the Church who breathe calumny after each *Our Father*, to hateful people I may appear to give license to immorality, while by advocating that lapses be kept as small as possible, I might obtain more improvement than by exacting a rigor that would be laughed off.

Without revealing the esoteric secrets of love, I can let it be known that voluptuousness plays a great role in the ferment of the soul, as the yeast in the making of the bread of perfectibility. A single word will make this teaching clear.

Suffering is recognized by all thinking people as the condition of moral elevation; now, is it not true that sexual love presents the most astounding temptations to cause suffering, and is it not true that passion is a suffering that one accepts and finds pleasing?

Not speaking to one who would be Ariste,[81] not to one who wishes to become a Mage, but speaking to an ordinary man, I would nevertheless urge him to love, as the only salvation that can keep one of the collective from rot and childishness.

---

81. [TN] **Aristé** is a major theme in *Comment on devient Ariste [How to Become Ariste]*, which Péladan published soon after the present work. *Aristé* is a neologism that plays on the similarity of the Greek word for personal excellence, *aristos*, to *artiste*, the French word for artist. He explained it this way: "Between devotion and magic there is an intermediate perception; more subtle than sensation, less ethereal than an idea—the sentiment and the taste of the divine, that I will call Ariste… Aesthetics is the art of sensing God in things: and whoever experiences this sentiment I call Ariste, signifying "excellent, the best." Joséphin Péladan, *Comment on devient Ariste* (Paris: Chamuel, 1895), 6, 9.

CATHOLIC CONCORDANCE

ARCANUM OF MERODACK [82] or COMMAND

In times like ours, when there is a separation between Art and Faith, between Science and the Clergy, it is the duty of exceptional Christians to employ themselves where the anointed are incapable.

When the Catholic curia is remiss, the French Bishopric under oath, catholic councils senile enough to forbid the study of the nude and to renounce Baudelaire [83] and d'Aurevilly, [84] there is room to restore, as I have done, the Order of the Rose+Cross of the Temple. The clergy of today want only docile followers, because it suits their own ignorance and laziness.

The paragons of the Rose+Cross assume the burden of holding the holy cross high and steadfast in the most elevated sphere, that of subtlety and beauty.

---

82. [TN] Chaldean name for Jupiter.
83. [TN] **Charles Pierre Baudelaire** (1821–1867) is best known for his book of lyric poetry, *Les Fleurs du mal* (*The Flowers of Evil*), which explores his own love-hate relationship with reality in a rapidly industrializing Paris. He was one of the very first of the French "decadents," who used that word proudly to indicate his rejection of banal "progress."
84. [TN] **Jules-Amédée Barbey d'Aurevilly** (1808–1889) was a French novelist and writer of short stories whose work influenced Péladan, to whom he was a friend and mentor. Aurevilly's preface to Péladan's first novel helped it to become a bestseller in 1884. Barbey d'Aurevilly was also known as a dandy and a creator of his own persona. Péladan emulated Aurevilly by creating a persona for himself that was even more flamboyant.

VII
THE AUTODIDACT
(The Self-Taught)

A true Christian has two neighbors: others and the otherworld.

Deeds, masterworks, honors, ideas, ideas above all, the heights of heroism, resplendent art, thaumaturgy of faith, ascensions of gnosis: these are paths, these are vows, these are orisons and merits. (*L'Androgyne* and *La Gynandre*, eighth and ninth books of the ethopoem *La Décadence latine*.)

VII
THE AUTODIDACT
(The Self-Taught)

Divine Name: אראריתא (Araritha)
Sacrament: Marriage
Task: Temperance
Gift: Wisdom
Beatitude: Peace
Work: Necrolatry
Angel: Orifiel
Arcanum: The Seven
Planet: Adar[85]

> *Fear the example of others. Above all, think for yourself.*

The most profound of the *Golden Verses* tells us that in order to wed the mystery, one dies to the world. All greatness is the child of solitude, not the material solitude so easily realized on an island, but the mental solitude practiced in Paris, in every place, and that demands a rare and tenacious force of personality.

For it is not a matter, as in mysticism, of losing oneself in God; but of searching for God by every way of understanding; these paths are the testaments of human thought. The commerce with the departed great ones, meditation on

---

85. [TN] Chaldean name for Saturn.

the texts of Moses, of Pythagoras, of Plato and the Church Fathers, this is the only necromancy, and the great secret of the power of magic.

For the initiate, the present is nothing but the way into the future; only the past presents a mental foothold.

There is a communion of genius as there is a communion of saints, and only solitude admits you into it.

> *LAW: The mage is in subtlety what the mystic is in exaltation; the mage proceeds by understanding, the mystic by ecstasy; the one is an enthusiastic mind, the other a heart becoming cerebral, and there is a point at which the heart engenders the abstract, where the abstract leads to ecstasy; Saint Thomas and Saint Francis personify the double ideal, and it would be impious to prefer one over the other of the two sublime mages.*

The Italian school loves a motif often depicted by its incomparable masters, the mystic marriage: the Virgin holding her child appears to Saint Catherine, the Divine Jesus holds a ring of gold that he put on the finger of the saint, and this is the symbol of the seventh arcanum.

The initiate, aware of himself, freed from everything social, prepared by experiences of will, becomes the fiancé of the tradition; he does not become a mage unless the past accepts him as a new link in the uninterrupted chain of thought.

From then on, the soul being prepared, the culture of magic may begin. But woe to anyone who takes the occult as his profession. One is not a mage as one is a painter or a journalist.

The initiate does not become adept until the day he adheres to an abstract, and this is not to be understood as some teaching or other, but as an actual effort of impersonal light.

The misfortune for magic is this swarm of men of letters who swoop down to batten on it as an untapped source of copy, along with the idlers who amuse themselves with magnetism, and the hysterics that delude themselves with mediums.

The true initiate knows that magic cannot be taught, for it is science itself, not a branch of science; it is a universally applicable method, not a subject matter.

Besides, pedagogues of the occult carefully avoid demanding any moral worth from their audience; they address the intellect, but one may learn metaphysics and still be a scoundrel. In order to become a mage, one must become noble and good; there is no black magic, any more than there is true error, or shady light: there are men with cultivated minds whose souls remain a wasteland, that's all.

So-called sorcery is nothing but bad-will tainting a certain culture.

The crimes of sorcery are ordinary crimes; when perpetrated in an age of faith, they take on the character of superstition. What is the medieval Klingsor, if not a simple criminal who also plays at occultism? The calumnies of Don Bazile [a journalist] work evil much more powerful than sticking pins in a wax doll, and Gilles de Rais[86] who sought gold by smothering and raping children seems no more satanic to me than Jules Ferry who, by his foul invasion of Tonkin[87] is provoking the Mongol invasion that in a half-century will be camping in La Place de la Concorde. One should not be duped by forms and styles of permanent acts. Orpheus charming the savage beasts is called, in times closer to us, Lamartine quelling a revolution by a lyric phrase.[88]

---

86. [TN] **Gilles de Montmorency-Laval, Baron de Rais** (1405–1440) was a lord, a knight, and a leader in the French army. He fought alongside Joan of Arc against the English and their Burgundian allies during the Hundred Years' War, for which he was appointed Marshal of France. After 1432, Gilles was accused of occult practices and of committing a series of child murders, with victims possibly numbering in the hundreds. In 1440, he was condemned to death and hanged at Nantes.

87. [TN] The **Tonkin Affair** that erupted on March 30, 1885, brought an ignominious end to the career of French Prime Minister Jules Ferry. News came that a position in Lang Son, gained by French troops the previous month at great cost of life, had been abandoned so as not to risk defeat by a Chinese army equipped and prepared to fight a European-style battle. The announcement triggered a tumult in the National Assembly, when Ferry used the occasion to ask for more funding. Mobs gathered in the streets to express hatred for Ferry and the Sino-French War.

88. [TN] **Alphonse de Lamartine** (1790-1869) was a French poet and politician who, as Minister of Foreign Affairs, played a part in establishing the Second Republic. He was put in charge of the government for two months during the revolutionary turmoil of 1848, and on February 25 he stood on a balcony of the Hotel de Ville in Paris to announce the establishment of the Second Republic in the traditional ceremony. In that declaration he spoke eloquently for the retention of the Tricolor as the national flag, rather than taking up the red flag of the revolutionists.

Is it not stupefying that a panel of certified experts will study the phenomenon of momentary suggestion upon the individual, before looking into this colossal suggestion that made military service acceptable to a purportedly civilized population? Instead of stirring up images of the Middle Ages, ask yourself which sorcerer cast a spell of passive obedience over the West. The State finds enough victims that it wants to ship them over to die in Tonkin, and that merits a bit more explication than the displacement of a chimney brush onto the kitchen table.

Since I cannot prevent you from undergoing experiences of phenomenal determinism, I will only indicate that the Second Reality is not hidden in the abnormal, but among permanent phenomena.

Explain to yourself the succession of ideas that visit you in a single day, this is worth more than analyzing the phases of hypnosis.

As I have taught you to keep to yourself and to isolate yourself from the age and your surroundings, I would encourage you to limit your studies to your own personality, until the day you will have perfected it. Then you will pay attention to the present in order to sow seed for the future. Until then keep your eye and your mind on the past.

Without restricting your readings, be always defiant before the Hindu Word; because you should, as a Catholic, accept only the philosophers, and Buddhism is a religion.

The Semitic tradition, the purest and strongest, is entirely conformed to the Church: but since the Semite, the supreme theologian, is no artist, seek what is missing from the Kabbalah in the Greek genius of Pythagoras, of Plato and even the Alexandrians.

Taking the Catholic Creed as the standard of truth, choose from the Chaldo-Greek Word whatever suits your nature best. God is not only extremely various, but infinite, and to a great extent indefinable. To define God, use the word that seems most noble to you, call him Artist if you like; or use no name at all, since even the language of the angels does not suffice.

Let the major portion of your meditations be outside of time: imagine the meditations of an angel who has seen the unfolding of the whole creation and the reign of mankind, and that is the point of view you must take.

Try to find in yourself an intense interest in your own perfection, cultivate yourself like the pious seek salvation, in a kind of obsession, as if hypnotized by the Abstract.

Hide your initiation—it is the first golden circle of your crown. In our day the assassins of Louis XVI and Marie Antoinette are the masters, and their detestation of royalty is exceeded by their detestation of Catholic intelligence.

The affairs of the West are forever ruined; there is nothing left to save in France; but tomorrow the French language will be the third classical language, and that is why you still have a duty of high culture.

I certainly do not want to push you into lecturing, nor into literature: even if your desire is a noble one, and your circumstances favorable, write late, publish even later.

Magic resides neither in books nor in rituals, but in the Word: if you think straight and you think continuously, the hour will come when your thought will be realized and take a life of its own—if it is beautiful.

Regarding your neighbors, be peaceable, not indifferent. On any occasion when they insult God or genius, protest—it is your duty.

The execution of orders given by that shameless Ferry, Fiorentino's attempt to assassinate *Lohengrin*[89]—these are examples where anger is holy: for, literally, you must live from admiration as well as from piety.

As an initiate, you owe a cult to Pythagoras as you do to Phidias, to Leonardo, to Orpheus, to Fabre d'Olivet[90] as to Delacroix.[91]

Only a state of religious admiration can bring you into the company of geniuses.

The *Golden Verses* say, in their third exhortation:

Revere the memory
Of the beneficent geniuses of the semi-divine heroes.

---

89. [TN] **Pier Angelo Fiorentino** (1811–1864) was an Italian-born playwright, journalist, poet, and translator. In France he worked for the major newspapers as a music and theater critic. His reviews of Wagner were scathing and not only targeted the music but extended to personal ridicule of the composer and the dresses of the German ladies in attendance.

90. [TN] **Fabre d'Olivet**, see note 9, p. XXXII.

91. [TN] **Eugène Delacroix** (1798–1863) was a French Romantic painter and lithographer regarded as the leader of the French Romantic school. His expressive brushwork and his study of the optical effects of color influenced the work of the Impressionists, while his exotic subject matter inspired the artists of the Symbolist movement.

LAW: The Word of genius does not die, any more than genius itself; the thought of Plato hovers always living in the ether, and the initiate, by rites of admiration, attracts to himself the radiation and the fertilization of the Spirit of which he makes himself the disciple.

Nothing is more firmly established than the cult of the apotropaic saints: by invocation of Saint Anthony of Padua, I quickly find a lost object; the image of Saint Christopher is a protective talisman against accidents; so why don't the intellectuals use the same thaumaturgy?

In magic, the sign of Solomon (or of the macrocosm) is said to be all-powerful, even though his Word has been absent a very long time from our culture; in magic as in religion, the sign of the cross appears as the supreme symbol.

Never allow intellectual intoxication turn you away from religion, yet be sure that knowledge is worth as much as virtue. Above all, initiate, remain faithful: whatever your doubts about Catholicism, it is your proper routine.

Go to mass mindfully, with the attention of a theater critic, and you will be bowled over by its splendor.

Return to what I have called the moral atmosphere. Forsake the barrooms in favor of the Church; it is the only place in which the air, figuratively, is wholesome and vivifying.

As for the clergy of today, a French bishop isn't worth a dime; but he does the work of God, and that is enough for you to defend him, even if you despise him. You may doubt the competence of Roman congregations, but don't antagonize them. Your hand may be full of truths, but if the truths are controversial, close your hand.

Render consecrated worship to the immortal gods.

That is the first word of Pythagoras, and it will be the last idea in this chapter. Anyone who does not go to mass will not enter into the temple of mystery.

I am attempting to detach you from everything. The zeal left to you, give it to the Church. She may force you to translate Nahash[92] as serpent, but she must serve the greatest number before considering you.

---

92. [TN] **Nahash** is a Hebrew word usually translated as *serpent*, as in tempter of Adam and Eve. Kabbalistic tradition associates Nahash with the survival instincts: appetites, sexuality, egotism, and aggression. Other esoteric interpretations link it to metallurgy, divination, prophecy, magic, and sorcery.

Be Catholic in order to become a mage, and do not forget that while your masters are among the dead, you have a superior among the living, His Holiness the Pope.

CATHOLIC CONCORDANCE

ARCANUM OF ADAR[93] OR PERMANENCE

In magic the rite corresponding to marriage is the union of the initiate with the tradition contained in the masterworks; and this corresponds with the concern of Roman Catholicism to combine all the dispersed parcels of truth, including some belonging to cults that have disappeared.

The virtue of an initiate is formed out of serenity: it is equivalent to the blessings accorded to the peacemakers.

The highest work of mercy consists in making a museum of sublime thoughts within one's mind; to reassemble the beautiful ideas lost in ancient books, and—I speak it aloud to Roman congregations—to raise a monument to Plato in one's understanding, to rethink the sublimities of Confucius or of Zarathustra will always be the highest of pieties, and the rarest.

St. Augustine, after having enumerated his seven degrees of perfection, offered an eighth as the sign of the realization of the preceding seven: "To suffer unjust persecution." I admit that for the mage, this blessing is infinitely more realizable than for the ordinary Christian. Persecution comes from the State or the individual, and the mage distrusts the one as much as the other.

The mage does not profess any moral system.

Universal prejudice and misunderstanding—what do they matter? I declare that what they call dishonor, military degradation, loss of citizenship, inspire in

---

93. [TN] Chaldean name for Saturn.

me only a smile of pity, and that, if not for the material penalties, it would be desirable and glorious to be thus repudiated by the State.

When Theophile Gautier[94] said that he would give all his rights of citizenship to see Julia Grisi[95] in her bath, he spoke a great and noble thing, and there isn't a superior man who would not second the thought.

I do not counsel you to call attention to yourself, even if you wait (as you must) to support yourself by a work; but if the world tries your temper, address it. Make a scene rather than be just like everybody else, and meditate upon the words of Massillon,[96] that in all times, superior men have been singular, and it is better to suffer for being too much oneself than to pay the price of being like all the others.

---

94. [TN] **Pierre Jules Théophile Gautier** (1811–1872) was a French poet, dramatist, novelist, journalist, and critic of art and literature.

95. [TN] **Giulia Grisi** (1811–1869) was an Italian opera singer who was widely considered to be one of the leading sopranos of the nineteenth century.

96. [TN] **Jean-Baptiste Massillon** (1663–1742) was a French Catholic bishop and famous preacher. Because Massillon's sermons put little stress on dogmatic questions that had divided French society in previous generations but focused on moral subjects, he was more acceptable to the rationalists of the eighteenth-century Enlightenment than most churchmen of his time.

BOOK TWO

The Twelve Steps of
MAGICAL ASCETICISM

> Something is dying in humanity that has survived everything for seven thousand years; we touch upon unforeseen times where goodness, beauty, and truth will be impossible. Twenty centuries after Christ, there is no longer a place for a messiah. Paths corrupted to the point of complete rottenness give way under the footsteps of the theurgist: the soul of the world is damned. (*La Gynandre*, ninth book of the ethopoem *La Décadence latine*, p. 319.)

I
THE QUIDDITY or THE TRUE PATH

Divine Name: Sabaoth Elohim
Sephira: Kether
Spiritual Rank: Seraphs
Sign: Aries
Arcanum: The Eight

After having conducted you to the point of asceticism, I owe you a definition of magic: It is the art of the sublimation of man. Nothing else is worthwhile.

Sublimation operates upon your ideas and your behavior: one must be sublime in order to think straight, and think straight in order to act in the light.

You will find here neither the promises made by Éliphas Lévi,[97] nor the erudition of the most recent dissertations. I can only promise you that results will be in proportion to effort. As for erudition, I would only need to cite Fabre

---

97. [TN] **Éliphas Lévi Zahed** (1810–1875), born Alphonse Louis Constant, was a practitioner of ritual magic who wrote influential books, including *Dogme et rituel de la haute magie (Doctrine and Ritual of High Magic)*, 1854, and *Histoire de la magie (The History of Magic)*, 1860. Central to his ideas, although not original with him, was the concept of the astral light: he considered it similar to ether, a fluidic life force that fills all space and living beings. Lévi's works triggered the occult revival on both sides of the English Channel.

d'Olivet,[98] along with Drach[99] to astound you. In your own best interest, I want to dispel your fantasies; to satisfy my conscience I join the catholic ideal to the magical ideal! Emotional adoration and intellectual adoration of God; piety and mystery.

Mystery—is it higher than piety? Yes, if piety is its basis.[100] Here is the most important point of my instruction, that magic is not compatible with dishonesty. A journalist mage, a lawyer mage, a bureaucrat mage: ridiculous!

As for those who read lots of books and have written books on the matter, are they mages?

A predilection for reading and study do not signify as much as that.

The doctrine of the hierophant is animated by his own essential characteristic, and Renan[101] would have expended the same devoted and perverse attention upon the occult as he expended upon Christianity, had he been no more of an adept than he was a theologian. All the same, this present mania for didactic expositions of occultism—for no ambition higher than to advertise one's library and one's curiosity—is a great misfortune. Hermeticism is becoming just another branch of literature, and it suffers contamination from the others, which are inextricably entangled with the most toxic of evil weeds.

Joseph the acting father of Jesus, although a prince of the Davidic line, was a member of the guild of carpenters; the Medici of Florence had their name listed with the medical association. No man has the right to call himself a mage without an epithet: one is a poet, metaphysician, novelist, painter,

---

98. [TN] **Fabre d'Olivet**, see note 9, p. XXXII.

99. [TN] **David Paul Drach** (1791–1868), born a Jew, was thoroughly schooled in Talmud and went to Paris in 1812 to fill a prominent position in the Central Jewish Consistory. After converting to Catholicism, he studied patristic theology and the Septuagint in order to investigate rabbinical claims that its Alexandrian translators had been unfaithful to the original Hebrew. He concluded that the Jewish scriptures supported Christian belief. In 1827, Drach was appointed librarian of the Propaganda in Rome, a post he held for the rest of his life.

100. [TN] Here, Péladan writes from his conviction that sound esoteric practice must be prepared for and grounded in exoteric religion.

101. [TN] **Ernest Renan** (1823–1892) was a French philosopher, historian, and scholar of religion, as well as a leader of the school of critical philosophy in France. In his view, the Church's teachings were incompatible with the findings of historical criticism, but he retained a kind of faith in the religion. Best known for his book *Life of Jesus* (1863), he was very influential in his lifetime; he was excoriated by the Church but considered by many intellectuals to be the "incarnation of modernity."

chemist, or scholar—and one performs magical exercises, and one works according to the magical method. Demand of one who calls himself a mage that he should excel in his art—the work certifies the doctrine. If it were otherwise, a hodgepodge of ideological archaisms or an apocalyptic pastiche would suffice to crown you the greatest fool among your followers.

Even then, you must not yield to the temptation of writing until you have sensed that a voice is using your pen; even when you will have decided to cultivate yourself in silence, choose a field of activity in the fine arts or letters, in order to avoid lycanthropy.

It is not possible, except for the elect member of a large order, to establish oneself in pure abstraction. Perpetual contemplation of the mystery does not grant increase of illumination. Fixity of the mind, like that of the eye, soon becomes a muddle of images; stabilize them by squinting, and this squint becomes error.

Besides, the specialization I command is necessary, as a prism into which the mystery enters to sort out its contents. Your specialization will be the concentrating lens of the divine light. As your choice will not be influenced by external necessity, you will at the same time find your vocation, that is to say your principal aptitude.

Then you will walk simultaneously upon three paths, which is to say that when you make an effort—whether to perfect yourself, to create, or to abstract—at the moment you act on one level, you write the bass lines for the two others.

On the first level of self-culture, set yourself a task: have you overcome a habit? A parallel acceleration is produced on the two other lines, as if a melody, which might be written on any one of the three lines, generates its accompaniment on the two others: thought profits at once from artistry and soul; or art is perfected by the echoes of soul and mind/spirit.

Historically, and also in modern custom, most Jasons [102] of the occult are ruined in body and fortune; the shore of Colchis has earned its name as the Bay of Sinners. This danger has two causes: using the sword of the angels in service to one's own passions, or the cultivation of either soul or mind to the

---

102. [TN] A reference to the Greek tale of **Jason and the Argonauts**: Colchis was their destination, the scene of their adventures and their catastrophes.

exclusion of the other. The agnostic, or anyone who concerns himself with contingencies and appearances, may strike hard blows to no effect.

The mage's will acts upon the secondary or etheric causes that crush the being who wishes to materialize them.

One of the thirty-seven teachings of Pistorius:[103] *the mind dresses up to descend and undresses to rise*, warns us that the will of the initiate must divest itself of passions in order to rise to conception, or he will suffer insanity or illness. One who thinks of demanding from hermeticism the power to seduce, to conquer his enemies, to surpass his rivals, will perish.

The initiate may attract or repulse the desire of another, but does not seek it, just as he waits for his enemies to destroy themselves, and relies only upon his own merit in the face of his competitors. The strength of any force lies in its adherence to the divine plan: victory always comes seeking those who wait for her.

According to the verses of Hebrew history, Israel identified itself with Yahweh, and equated the enemy of God with the enemy of this powerful people: we should view this as much more than an artistic ploy, and as a priceless lesson in practical magic.

If you have been wronged, examine whether in doing wrong to you, your adversary has offended God; if so, give up your hatred, you have the guarantee of sacred Providence; if not, give up your hatred. The quarrel that has not touched the divine is not worth a minute of your attention.

The other peril in the study of the occult may be seen at once in the exclusive focus upon a single branch of achievement.

Woe and delusion to the one who seeks metallic perfection without being first a saint and a genius.

Woe and delusion to the one who makes a public display of magnetism and occult phenomena, without a pure will and a perfect disinterestedness.

Woe and delusion to the one who, in the pride of his collection of strong and beautiful thoughts, lives miserably and contrary to his doctrine.

---

103. [TN] **Johann Pistorius** (1546–1608) was a German physician, theologian, Kabbalist, and political advisor to the Holy Roman Emperor Rudolph II of Bavaria. Raised and educated as a Lutheran, he turned to Calvinism, and finally to Catholicism in 1588. He studied Kabala and published a Latin translation of the *Sepher Yetzirah*.

Sanctity embraces magic within itself; all the learned doctors of the Church were mages; but how few occultists were satisfied to be virtuous!

Know this, without making an excuse of it: unbalanced intellectuality produces degrading repercussions even in the geniuses themselves, and will not, like the despicable bourgeois, absolve your debaucheries just because Dante was unchaste, or absolve your drunkenness because Musset[104] was a drinker. You don't even have the right to judge those men; you must kiss their work and admire; the high pleasures that you owe to them, you owe to their boldness. I guide you toward becoming a mage, not to becoming a torch: an extreme rigor becomes the law of any being who manifests his thought: artist and thinker alike put their eternal destinies in play every time they speak a word.

If the genius who made *Parsifal* is certain of happiness without end and without limits, if Gluck[105] played with the fullness of noble love, if Plato is seated at the foot of the divine throne, be assured that an imbecile such as Auber or Scribe,[106] a lout like Zola or a prig like Luther[107] will be damned, and in quite another fire from that which took their works!

In leaving this life, a dazzling light will make us cognizant, with the clarity of the sun, of all error. The error of a Word will be the eternal garb of the one who spoke it.

---

104. [TN] **Alfred de Musset** (1810–1857) was a French dramatist, poet, and novelist. Along with his poetry, he is known for writing the autobiographical novel *La Confession d'un enfant du siècle* (*The Confession of a Child of the Century*).

105. [TN] **Christoph Willibald Gluck** (1714–1787) was an Austrian composer of Italian and French opera in the early classical period.

106. [TN] **Daniel Auber** (1782–1871) was a leading composer of French opera from the 1820s onward, collaborating with the librettist **Augustin Eugène Scribe**. He is known mostly for his operatic comedies.

107. [TN] **Martin Luther** (1483–1546) was a German professor of theology, composer, priest, monk, and a principal figure of the Protestant Reformation.

In a century of centuries, Auber, the man of Médan[108] and Luther will be hounded by the scorn of the worlds and the angels.

Furthermore, my disciple, beware of premature acts, hasty words; restrain yourself in word and deed.

Since in our time magic has fallen so low as to come into the hands of journalists, and socialites dare to have pentagrams embroidered on their bathrobes, you might imagine that a mage is a sort of scholar, or that a woman can understand anything of the occult.

Beware of such nonsense: the true mage is neither a pedagogue nor a chronicler, he proves nothing and doesn't deign to astound anyone; in antiquity, in silence, for long ages he offered only prayer and orders.

Modern people, liberated from this sublime tutelage, tread the paths of the demented, and one can no longer even pray for egalitarian societies, those who have wed themselves to shadows.

Your duty consists of preparing the future, the present being so rotten that to touch it at all would just make it fall into dust all the quicker; while you must reveal eternal verities so as to make them perceptible to those who will come after.

The function of thinkers is to cast the eternal wisdom into forms appropriate to their time.

Egypt, that left such beautiful monuments of its power, has bequeathed us its wisdom only through its inscrutable forms.

Chaldea astounds us with its formidable priestly organization, which came out of an intellectual dynasty that reigned in Memphis and Etruria alike. But its doctrine is not manifested in the winged bull that guards it, nor will the bi-

---

108. [TN] **Émile Zola** (1840–1902) was a French novelist, playwright, journalist, and a founder of the Naturalist movement in literature. Zola presented his novels as exercises in dispassionate, quasi-scientific observation; his shocking accounts of life in the nineteenth-century working class were admired for their realism by some, but aroused much objection on aesthetic and moral grounds. He spent his summers in a house in the village of Médan, a suburb of Paris, in which he hosted artists and other writers, including Alphonse Daudet, Guy de Maupassant, and Joris-Karl Huysmans, who became known as the "Médan group." In 1880, as part of their promotion of literary realism, Zola and five other authors produced a collection entitled *Les soirées de Médan* (*Médan Evenings*), in which every story was a realistic, nonheroic depiction of the Franco-Prussian War.

lingual tablets of the Library of Nineveh teach us any more of its philosophy than its superstitions.

Nearer to us, Greek thought has become just as inaccessible. In those shameful holes they call universities, do they not tell the young that the Greeks worshipped adulterous goddesses and sodomite gods? Of all human duties, the noblest is to unveil, that is, to lift off the old indecipherable forms of truth and to replace them with new forms that make it more evident and potent.

The name of God in a single letter contains the mystery of the government of a people; the two-letter name of God contains the mystery of the government of all peoples; the three-letter name of God contains the mystery of the government of a man by himself.

In the form that is dated by a redaction from well after the Babylonian captivity, what do we see now but a singular enigma, *J, el Yeshu.*

The government of a people should be the office of a single individual: Royalty.

The government of the world should be the office of two: the Pope and the Emperor.

The government of a man is the office of three: Body, soul and mind.

That is extremely clear, and nothing remains but to lay out the panorama of historical experience to demonstrate that royalty is the rational form of limited power; the imperial authority submitted to the papacy, the form of total power; and for the individual to prove, by analyzing an hour of the life of an intellectual, that this hour has been occupied by phenomena of three ranks: sensations, sentiments and concepts.

A great occult secret that is very seldom spoken, because it is embarrassing, is that eternal truth perennially requires the creation of new forms that will reveal it.

Art is either worthless or a treasure for eternity. To say that a work has aged is nonsense; we should say it was no good. The book of Job and the Psalms have not been displaced by modern poets. Any aesthetic form is either definitive or negligible; no one argues that Wagner detracts from Palestrina, or Shakespeare from Aeschylus, nor Balzac from Homer: From the moment one is, one is eternal in art.

Why? Because art has its complete evolution within one man, while science evolves only through civilization. Likewise, religion evolves slowly and with a great shaking of peoples and territories.

Well then! Magic is admirable in that it partakes of religion by the same stability of foundations, while at the same time goes through its complete evolution in the individual, like an art.

The mage is an artist of wisdom and a savant of art; his soul takes on an extreme importance, and if it is not supremely beautiful, it incarnates a deformed truth, and the deformity of truth is called Error.

By analogy, a doctrine is not only a spiritual operation: it is also an emotional manifestation.

Only beauty of soul can allow sublimity of spirit to bloom; and I have started my instruction with cultivation of the emotions.

CATHOLIC CONCORDANCE

EIGHTH ARCANUM

Religion is the collective form of truth; magic will be the counterpoint played along with that truth by the exceptional man. In ancient times the Mages were directors of religion, then inexcusably became its adversaries.

To overcome superstition that they could not uproot, the early fathers of the Church damned the names of the cosmic forces. In order to achieve doctrinal unity, the councils renounced any sacred college of intellectuals. These things are facts; were they mistakes? I cannot decide this here; it would require a great deal of discussion.

In asking of the exceptional man an intense cultivation of mind, I command the same culture of the soul as the Church. Just because an assertion appears to contradict ecclesiastic practice does not mean I must defend myself for such a trifle!

The whole theory of hermeticism can be summed up in this way:

Balance mind and soul, but give precedence to mind.

From pride in one's origins and ends, do what the mystics do from humility.

Walk the path of pride with the same works as the path of humility.

I speak for the future cardinals of the human mind, not for the cretins that befoul the church with music of a Rossini,[109] with the words of Lavigerie,[110] with the painting of Signol.[111]

---

109. [TN] **Gioachino Rossini** (1792–1868) was an Italian composer noted for his operas (especially his comic operas), including *The Barber of Seville* (1816), *Cinderella* (1817), *Semiramide* (1823), and *William Tell* (1829).

110. [TN] On **Lavigerie**, see note 59, p. 46.

111. [TN] **Émile Signol** (1804–1892) was a French artist who painted in the neoclassic style of the previous generation. He received commissions through government institutions and was a member of the Académie des Beaux-Arts. The subject matter of Signol's paintings fit well into King Louis Philippe's cultural agenda of encouraging French enthusiasm for their history. Signol provided six imagined portraits of Merovingian kings and contributed six large canvases of historical events to the palace of Versailles. His religious paintings can be seen in many famous French churches. Péladan believed that portraiture and history painting failed to carry out the spiritual purposes of art; he may have objected to the religious paintings in the Church of Saint-Sulpice because they were commissioned by the City Council of Paris in 1868.

II
THE ORIGIN or THE METHOD

Divine Name: יהוה צבאות (Sabaoth, Jehovah)
Sephira: Chokmah
Spiritual Rank: Cherubs
Sign: Taurus
Arcanum: The Nine

God created us fit to attain eternal life: what they call salvation is affective eternity, happiness: one prepares by renunciations, one achieves it through sublimation of the whole soul into charity. For charity, the state of radiant love without distinction of object, approaches the state necessary for the experience of paradise.

Added to happiness and the emotional personality, is an elevation of the intellectual personality.

Without being able to expound the theory in this book, I teach that a blessed outcome has no fixed destination; that the gravity that draws one upward is beyond time; the seeker is not resolved in God, but gravitates towards God increasingly and without ceasing. The more one advances into the light, the more one is oneself, that is to say, individual. This departs from the claims of many theosophists that the goal of evolution is a sort of nirvana or collective divinity.

If the personality is the sovereign good, then it will be the sovereign means of all perfection.

Now, the personality elaborates itself out of itself, that is to say, the more solitary one is, the more one is oneself, *ipsissimus*.

Unsociability that comes from bad temper is worthless; on the contrary, it corrupts our impressions and deprives us of the blessings that sometimes come from another's radiance.

But easygoing Philinte is just as far from the ideal as the fuming Alceste;[112] the one accommodates himself to wrongdoing while the other gives free rein to passionate, impotent anger. An honest woman yields nothing to a flatterer; the initiate must yield nothing to his surroundings.

To go to the theater of the Palais Royale—that house into which art has never entered,[113] to suffer the company of fools, to take any part in the ambient mindlessness, is to dirty oneself. This is why the hermetist avoids any place consecrated to killing time: Time—this most precious commodity by which we are measured and by which we enter eternity!

The primary solitude is mental; it is always possible, endlessly fecund. I have pronounced imperious commands in the *Seven Exits from the Century*. I insist upon them again, such is their great importance.

Upon rising, to set one's course, upon retiring, to evaluate oneself, these are the midwife operations of solitude. You will soon see the advantages of planning each day, if the day ends for you as for a fisherman who takes in his nets and chooses his fish, rejecting the worthless and keeping the saleable.

Discrepancies between your plans and the results will force you to know yourself at a profound level and to learn how to manage yourself.

You may have been struck by the simple-mindedness of pleasure-seekers, of the mental poverty of people who have been around the world many times; the inanity of professors with five PhDs.

For the first, thousands of experiences have flowed through their eyes, through their senses; the next can describe forms and colors in admirable variety, and a library has gone into the memory of the last. What is lacking in

---

112. [TN] **Alceste** is the misanthropic protagonist of Molière's comedy of manners *The Misanthrope*, while **Philinte** is his easygoing sidekick and foil. Alceste makes a career of criticizing everything and everyone, including himself, and Philinte is too ready to go along with anything. *The Misanthrope* was first performed in June 1666 at the Théâtre du Palais-Royal in Paris by the King's Players.

113. [TN] The **Palais-Royale**, see note 51, p. 35.

those who have lived everything, seen everything, and learned everything, which keeps them from being superior? They lack the consciousness that reigns in solitude.

Had the pleasure-seekers reflected every night upon their emotions, the captains reviewed their impressions, the professors classified and synthesized their knowledge, they would all be admirable. They have only omitted to sort out their fish; they have gone around life, around the world, around knowledge; but they did not know how to feel life through their senses; or see the soul of the world through their spectacles, or to see wisdom in between their exams and publications. They have not abstracted, and this failure renders them inferior.

There is a dietary axiom, "Ingestion is nothing, only digestion nourishes," which applies the same way to the mind, and stamps as worthless any superiority based upon memory applied to a narrow field such as the typical degree program of a university.

Ingestion must be the careful work of the adept, but I will deal with the subject in a book on metaphysics.

The second solitude is emotional: one must examine one's personality of the day and harbor within oneself no exaggerated vibration either pleasant or painful: forbid yourself the stench of annoyance or the too-vivid memory of a kiss.

One must, at the close of day, separate oneself from the woman one loves, from those one visits, from the group one belongs with, in order to regain one's own personality, which was diminished by caresses just as much as by the examples and the doings of those whose interests you share.

To fall asleep in the grip of a too-sweet memory; or in the desire to do like someone else, with no other reason than to imitate him; or convinced without proofs of some opinion dictated by the company you keep—these are circumstances that diminish you, and exert influence on the day to come as well as the succession of tomorrows, forever after.

In your social or emotional life, never permit a woman to influence your thought; listen to her confidences, her dreams, her grooming, do not allow her to speak a metaphysical word, unless it is an "amen." Do not allow a woman you honor with your caress to think otherwise than you do about abstraction; a woman must share the same faith as the one who shares her bed, and nothing else. As my book addresses itself only to Catholic minds, I don't have to tell you that Protestantism renders a woman odious, and that the woman who explains scripture to you should be whipped or abandoned.

A woman has no cerebrality; never forget it, and you must remind her if she forgets. Everything in her is a passion, in various degrees, even in friendship, even in admiration; her sayings are worthless except aesthetically: for the spectacle of the lips, the eye, the gesture, the poses, and the pretty consonance of voice and tone.

The art of life does not consist of living large, but of living consciously.

Tell me, are there men who make the beast with two backs for twenty years running, with the same pleasure? They would have to be idiots: there are some things one has to do or know, just to get them out of one's mind and imagination.

A window that opens onto a party calls to the imagination: enter and observe, and you will be disappointed. Female skin can be the most beautiful matter in this world; if you look closely at this living bloom you will see acne, blotches of color and nasty little hairs; the flesh so attractive from eight steps' distance is, at close range, neither glossy nor of uniform tone.

What does wisdom counsel you? To view the whole phantasmagoria of the world as you would view the skin of blondes, from a bit of a distance.

At the least, if your frailty pushes you beyond the distance that's required to maintain your pleasure as much as your virtue, then after the intoxication wears off, step back and come back to yourself.

Returning to yourself, such is the strength of the individual, to put one's being back into order; the seated cat rolling its tail over its paws provides you the image of a truly solitary being; that is to say that neither man, his master, nor his fellow felines, nor other animals, can change him. Within the bounds of charity, walk apart from society like a cat, never allow yourself to be treated like a dog. Abuse no one, believe in no one.

Devote yourself, for to devote yourself to something worthy is beautiful. Suffer and die for an idea; but do not take your country for an idea, and if, as a lion, you are made to jump through the hoops of the law, let loose your personality and make the earth tremble where they dare to mess with lions.

Against solitude two legions join forces: comrades and women.

The comrade, quite different from the friend, is one that similarity of circumstance rather than choice brings to you; it's the one you meet out of habit. Flee him, he steals your time.

The woman, as I have revealed to you, is ruled by a faculty that is destructive when not kept passive: Wagner incarnated femininity in his Kundry, who did good and bad in turn, according to the influence of the Grail or of Klingsor, and who really only loved the one who resisted her.

No woman can dominate you if you have the strength never to pass twelve hours with her, never to sleep beside her.

The more you covet the celestial goods of reason, the more you will be assailed. Resist without anger, as it is the mission of her sex to bring down the beings feeble enough to yield to her. Be the master then, in order to be beloved, because no woman loves one who yields to her; her pleasure is to be ruled, all the while her instinct pushes her to rule—remember that!

Even if you are in love, do not change yourself in order to seduce. To please, act dynamically, not from cleverness. You will never be loved for your merits: you will captivate to the degree that your soul wills without desiring.

After these defensive considerations, learn that nothing is deadlier than to believe you are thinking, when you are dreaming. Spend a few years steadily holding to one of the great traditional ideals. Live among the masters of understanding, nourish yourself exclusively with masterworks, and above all, do not concern yourself to be current with the literature. That will come later, after initiation, an affair of a few months. Do not think of the present; be first and foremost a student of the past and a disciple of the divine.

Beware of the theories that first inspired your readings in the search for truth. There are spells of giddiness more dangerous than splendid.

Beware above all the works of Éliphas Lévi,[114] an admirable mage, who would give you the illusion of knowledge and comprehension and the boldness to dare—an illusion even more deceptive than magic, if it becomes firmly seated and unspeakably multiplied by resonances and corollaries. You may

---

114. [TN] **Éliphas Lévi**, see note 97, p. 97.

learn Fabre d'Olivet[115] by heart, along with Éliphas, Paracelsus and Lully,[116] Agrippa[117] and Khunrath,[118] Saint Thomas[119] and Boehme[120]—and you will become nothing more than erudite.

You must create your own magic: not as an expression of vanity, but as you would create an original work of art. Let your own vision of truth grow slowly within you; let a prism form that will refract, according to your personality, the eternal ray. The men who have astounded the world were men of

---

115. [TN] **Fabre d'Olivet**, see note 9, p. XXXII.

116. [TN] **Ramon Lully** (1232–1316) was a Catalan philosopher and writer known for his contribution to the Art of Memory, in his *The Abbreviated Art of Finding Truth* (1290). The *Art* embraces religious and occult ideas that came out of the mixing of Muslim, Jewish, and Christian cultures in Andalusia, as well as Franciscan mysticism and troubadour poetry.

117. [TN] **Heinrich Cornelius Agrippa von Nettesheim** (1486–1535) was a German astrologer, physician, theologian, alchemist, and occult writer best known for his work *De occulta philosophia libri tres (Three Books of Occult Philosophy)*, printed in 1531–1533. This encyclopedic compendium of occult and magical knowledge covers the topics of classical Neoplatonic and Hermetic philosophy, Jewish Kabbalah and Christianity, astrology, divination, occult correspondences, spells, talismans, and demonology, upon which much medieval and Renaissance magic was based.

118. [TN] **Heinrich Khunrath** (c. 1560–1605) was a German physician, hermetic philosopher, alchemist, and the author of *Amphitheater of Eternal Wisdom*. Khunrath's work is a link between that of John Dee and the Rosicrucians, drawing upon alchemy and Kabbalah to formulate a religious philosophy compatible with Lutheran theology.

119. [TN] **Saint Thomas Aquinas** (1225–1274) was a Doctor of the Church and an immensely influential philosopher, theologian, and jurist who was canonized a saint. In his *Summa Theologiae* (1265–1274), he provided the Church a rationale whereby orthodox Christian doctrine can be reconciled with the kind of knowledge produced by reason and scientific investigation. A formidable intellectual, Thomas also received direct experience of the Divine, powerful enough that he left his *Summa* incomplete, saying, "Such secrets have been revealed to me that all I have written now seems like straw to me." (Brian Davies, *The Thought of Thomas Aquinas*, Oxford University Press, 1993, 9.) The prayer on page XXXV of this book was composed by Aquinas.

120. [TN] **Jacob Boehme**, also spelled **Jakob Böhme** (1575–1624), was a German philosopher, mystic, and Lutheran theologian. In his youth he underwent a series of mystical experiences, among them a vision triggered by the beauty of a ray of sunshine reflected in a pewter dish. From the content of his visions, Boehme wrote twenty-eight published books; his ideas were discussed in intellectual circles of Protestant Europe, were taken up in anti-authoritarian and mystical Christian movements, and influenced English poets such as John Milton, Coleridge, and William Blake.

concentration; from the very first, all the theocrats have been hermits, at least figuratively: only solitude gave proof of moral grandeur and strength of mind.

Works written far from the public have a grander character than those conceived in the turmoil of life.

It requires frequent solitude for the ideal to manifest to you: retain nothing of the evocative morass of the occult but the spirit of silence; it alone will explain the mystery to you, only it will make you perceive God.

The spirit of silence brings with itself the spirit of peace; avoid all competition; know this: if you want nothing but wisdom, you will get it by renunciation of all human approval; and if you want glory, follow the example of Wagner who, instead of intriguing to get exposure, forged in his solitude a formidable tetralogy, and created a destiny to fit his genius, a destiny that founded Bayreuth.[121]

For wisdom, renounce; for glory, persevere. These two verbs suffice to conquer time and colossal human stupidity: wisdom is the only egoism permitted; glory the sole acceptable reality when one has conquered it atop the heights; lesser benefits such as wealth are of a low nature and not the objects of sacred magic.

---

121. [TN] Péladan refers to **Richard Wagner** (1813–1883) as a well-known and recent example of his own ideal of the inspired artist as mage. (See note 4, p. XXXI.) Unlike most composers and artists of his time, Wagner did not affiliate himself with any academy, school, or style. He concentrated his energy on creating works that lived up to his own vision of what opera could be and did not expend energy on political maneuvering in any institution except the one he created for himself.

CATHOLIC CONCORDANCE

NINTH ARCANUM

The Church, through the voice of its preachers, counsels us to retire from the world and set ourselves apart from our times, similar to radical measures taken to obtain salvation. Attaining salvation and becoming a mage are two parallel routes that can converge in many places.

While mental prayer is the great instrument of mystical practice, meditation appears to be the great artifice of occult practice.

The two disciplines differ in the plan of evolution: piety purifies the soul and culture elevates the mind/spirit.[122] Beings in whom spirituality dominates are qualified to guide those dominated by emotion; but where my teaching differs from that of recent writers who rally around the Catholic Church, is where I require the recipient to undergo moral training as well as intellectual instruction. I am persuaded that the spirit does not take its wings except from an already beautiful soul perfectly similar to those that are the sign of spiritual masters.

---

122. [TN] The French word *esprit* has no precise equivalent in English but includes spirit, mind, and wit. Any time the French speak of *mind*, they are also speaking to some degree about *spirit*, and when they speak of *spirit*, they are also speaking of *mind*. This is true in this English translation as well, even when it is not explicit.

III
RAPPORT or DESTINY

Divine Name: צבאות אלהים (Sabaoth, Elohim)
Sephira: Binah
Spiritual Rank: Thrones
Sign: Gemini
Arcanum: The Ten

Magic can make of any intellectual, or even enthusiast, an extraordinary man—but only within the vocational plan of his destiny.

Not all wood is good for making a Mercurius,[123] no individual is omniapt.

What is commonly called misfortune is usually a complex movement of life that works itself out in the individual, as in the collective.

Fabre d'Olivet, the immortal restorator of Pythagorism, has painted a transcendently beautiful idea-picture of the threefold law of collective destiny

---

123. [TN] One of the most constant themes of alchemical work is generating a **Mercurius**, a spiritual embryo, and then developing and deploying it in a series of transformations. As in astrology, the Mercury in alchemy is associated with the mind and consciousness and is called the universal solvent. It is no coincidence that the patron god of alchemy, sometimes represented as a Jehovah-like hierophant, is called the *Mercurius Philosophorum*, while the alchemist must conceive and develop his own Mercurius, often pictured as a boy.

through universal history, with a panoramic philosophy incomparably greater than that of Bossuet.[124]

The three factors of humanity correspond to the threefold human and the divine Trinity; God the Father gave us the body, God the Son gave us the soul, and God the Holy Spirit gave us spirit-mind. The law of the body, or the secondary cause of the Father, is called Necessity; the law of the soul, or secondary cause of the Son, is called Destiny; the law of Spirit, or secondary cause of the Holy Spirit, is called Providence.

Necessity corresponds to instinct, destiny to emotion, Providence to understanding.

Confronted by these three essential points of orientation, man's will submits to Necessity, combats Destiny, and can conquer it in the name of Providence.

The will that constitutes the entire freedom of man is the instrument of his salvation or his perdition. To steer the course of one's own destiny or that of a continent—the steering wheel being the will—steer according to the compass of the abstract. True north is always in the direction of Providence; that is the direction one must take—except for temporary diversions in the midst of a storm of necessity or destiny—and the destination you must reach.

If you have understood my exposition of the seven planetary methods, you may already judge the combination of the Chaldean septenary with the Pythagorean quaternary.

The will of Samas, the Sun, must hold to Providence alone.
The will of Sin, the Moon, combines with destiny.
The will of Mérodack, Jupiter, consists of both Providence and destiny.

---

124. [TN] **Jacques-Bénigne Lignel Bossuet** (1627–1704) was a French bishop and theologian who was considered by many to be one of the most brilliant orators of all time and was court preacher to Louis XIV of France. Bossuet argued that government was divine, and that kings received their power from God. His 1681 work *Discours sur l'histoire universelle* (*Discourse on Universal History*) purported to show that the whole of human history is an actual war between God and the Devil, in which God moves those governments, political/ideological movements, and military forces most closely aligned with the Catholic Church in order to oppose by all means those forces most closely aligned with the Devil. The *Universal History* was extremely influential into the nineteenth century.

The will of Nébo, Mercury, takes up all three orientations without holding to any.
The will of Ishtar, Venus, is always subject to necessity.
The will of Nergal, Mars, is reduced to itself, rejecting Providence and destiny.
The will of Adar, Saturn, is composed of destiny and Providence.

You see then, my disciple, you must set your goal according to your planet, and take the wind that suits your temperament. Look carefully and study, and you will find very few lives that are truly unfortunate. They are mostly just incompatible with personalities.

You may be sure that among all the ways of making a living, there is one that comes naturally to you; among all the paths, one that will be comfortable to you; among the labors of mankind, one that will become your own.

Chance is the name given to the phenomenon of destiny coming before one wills it, without opposition from necessity.

But do not imagine that all your intentions are conceived according to your own true interests; your wishes sometimes blaspheme your destiny, and their realization would be your ruin.

Always and through all vicissitudes, the initiate wills his chosen ideal, but he must allow life to furnish the mode of realization.

The most powerful help will come to you with the collaboration of time. Knowing how to wait removes most of the force of assaults and outrages. But to wait is not to give up: I imagine you desire glory, and that necessity confines you to a small corner in the middle of nowhere. Wait for destiny to come to you, to your little corner; but so that he will not forget you, continue to will it, that is to say, continue to perfect yourself in your art and in your work, as if your every effort was eagerly awaited by the world.

Cleverness is the way of mediocrities. While some people—that is, the whole world—intrigue, beg and strive, the initiate and the genius intend without fidgeting, they accumulate works or force of will, confident that on some day that is indeterminate but inexorable, they will be hailed as conquerors.

This path, the only one worthy of the superior man, seeks no other power than the accumulation of his own power. This path of Wagner and Balzac leads even to posthumous omnipotence.

But if you want immediate satisfaction, then become a girl; leave off the magic and go prostitute yourself in all the houses of ill repute in the media world.

There is always some advantage that can be taken from even the worst of circumstances, and the art of life takes good advantage of necessity more often than it claims to be hindered by it. The initiate stalks his opportunities; life is so changeable that, provided he pays attention, it always provides him with a favorable wind at some point.

It is as difficult as it is necessary to halt your efforts when circumstances turn unfavorable; and I insist upon this capital point: The initiate, unshakeable in his intent, never predetermines either the means or the moment. After desiring, one must know how to will; without this, it will be called obsession. In exaggerating the theory of will, one risks violating Providence and failing to recognize Destiny.

Absolute within oneself, will must acknowledge its dependence upon the triple relationship of necessity, fate, and Providence.

The initiate examines himself then, before formulating his word. Before any undertaking, go through this questionnaire:

Relative to the Law of the Divine, or Providence, do I have the right?

Relative to the Law of Man, or Destiny, do I have the duty?

Relative to the Law of Nature, or Necessity, do I have the power?

One must have permission, equity, and the capacity to begin to will.

Continually, in the course of willing one must rectify one's will according to the triple compass of three secondary causes.

Your destiny is not blindly opposed to another destiny; first, examine the horoscope of a rival or competitor according to my three questions; and exaggerate in yourself the principle in which he is most lacking; this is enough to give you the victory.

A destiny only rarely evolves by itself; others always modify it. Do not leave it to chance, then—govern your relationships. As a rule, favor intelligence and goodness above all; after those, prefer beauty over pedigree.

As for the rich—that ever-changing class that swarms with every idiocy—view it with perpetual disdain, from the noble-born to the bourgeois; but make it your business sometimes to visit them, because the spectacle of luxury is infinitely useful for embellishing the mind and refining sensibility.

I defy you, after having studied any individual, to wish to switch personalities with him. Certainly, you would like to be Czar, but not to be the criminal who usurps the Papacy, who has the impudence to wear a miter along with his sword. You might desire the power of the one, the sanctity of the other, but not to be one or the other.

Reflection will teach you that each individual, under compulsion from the same laws, differs very much in what causes him suffering and weariness—and not only quantitatively. The best apportioned are those who suffer only in the sense of their nature.

From a simply physical point of view, imagine Lucullus[125] with heartburn, and there you see how easily his happiness might be destroyed.

Being prepared is the biggest component of good luck, and the first requirement is health. The body, the most inferior and the only entirely perishable of your three elements, has this world as its kingdom, while the soul and the mind depend not upon their instincts, but on their Being.

Body obeys mind insofar as it is healthy, and disease renders it unresponsive to the bridle or the whip; it is a horse that is dead or broken down.

Therefore, maintain the physical frame in perfect condition, but do not uselessly overdevelop your musculature. You cannot be a Leonardo who can both bend a steel beam with his bare hands and also paint *The Last Supper*; consciously allow the nervous faculties to predominate.

Physical strength—let it not be confused with health—does not even serve anymore for self-defense. The body must neither be a hindrance nor require your attention; a docile and decorative neuter.

What destroys the most destinies, after women, is habit; and one must consider habituation as a danger—except for aesthetic habituation that, on the contrary, creates a barrier of nobility between us and vulgarity.

To succeed immediately requires wrongdoing; wrongdoing compromises your future, and even more so, your evolution. For those who would be thaumaturges, pressing too hard on circumstances corrupts them; impatience for results marks one as mediocre, and then one abandons magic.

Money saves effort and time—do not despise it. But you must do nothing to acquire it. It must come to you, and it will come on the day you have your

---

125. [TN] **Lucullus** was a famous gourmet in ancient Rome.

destiny, in other words, a word made according to the dimensions of your soul and thought. It will come to you in limited amounts, that will leave you always looking for more; but remember to be the James II[126] of fortune, do not ever seek it.

Do what you must in order to live; you do not have the right to do servile labor for its own sake. Only mediocrities and criminals work for the sake of money. Except for that which comes by inheritance, all money is stolen, it is all dirty, a convenient filth that is acceptable in the finest social circles.

That is why, apart from the case where you have a personal acquaintance, you must be haughty toward the wealthy, who are almost all complete idiots. Withhold your courtesy for those who show moral or spiritual merit, and never allow genius to be insulted in your presence—genius is the true divine right and the dazzling miracle among all.

Bad luck comes from the disparity between temperament and circumstances; it is always easier to modify yourself than the situation.

If you have profited from my indications on the influence of the stars, you know that one may rather easily attract the regard of a planet, that is, modify its influence.

Sun, Moon, and Saturn are genial influences.

Mercury, Mars and Venus are conquering influences.

Jupiter is the star of command, supremacy, of the Papacy and empire.

To bear poverty, borrow the insouciance of the Moon or the renunciation of Saturn.

In the sorrow of love, take refuge in Sol, the Sun, who gives without expectation of return.

Put all transitions under the rubric of Mercury.

Invoke Mars when audacity is called for.

Call upon Venus to tame, soften and sweeten your nature.

---

126. [TN] **James II of England** (1633–1701) inherited his throne upon the death of his elder brother Charles II. He lost it by attempting to reinstate Catholicism as the state religion in opposition to the Protestant convictions of the vast majority of his English subjects. Before and after his reign, he took refuge in France.

Your astrality, always composed of two or three planets, may be corrected by developing the influx most apt to strengthen you for the challenges of life you face in the moment:

Through the contemplation of masterworks, the color yellow, an atmosphere impregnated with incense, and the pardon of grievances, you conjure Sol.
By poetry, by looking upon the ocean, through nightlife, and by travel, you conjure the Moon.
Through attending religious services, oratory, a roomy red robe worn around the house, through the habit of noble gestures and the absence of worry or fear, you conjure Jupiter.
By grooming your body, feminization, perfumes, cushions and low chairs, physical lassitude, and pantheistic reveries, you conjure Venus.
By changing locations, name, accent, and ways of doing things; by the color gray, by associating with the clever rather than with the willful, you conjure Mercury.
By the color red, a fire always near you, by brusque speech, abrupt movements, overbearing and military manners, you conjure Mars.
By the color black, meditation and solitude, obsession and fanaticism, you conjure Saturn.

To change the malefics of the Septenary into benefics, recall that the moral key of the heavens is harmonized like this:

Samas (Sol),	the throne of light.
Sin (Luna),	the throne of shadow.
Mérodack (Jupiter),	the throne of divine right.
Ishtar (Venus),	the throne of voluptuousness.
Nebo (Mercury),	the throne of changes.
Nergal (Mars),	the throne of aggression.
Adar (Saturn),	the throne of concentration.

Samas (Sol) creates,
Sin (Luna) intuits,
Mérodack (Jupiter) reigns,
Ishtar (Venus) seduces,
Nebo (Mercury) schemes,
Nergal (Mars) attacks,
Adar (Saturn) ponders.

There are also seven personalities:

The artist, the poet, the statesman, the voluptuary, the practical, the murderer, the thinker.

CATHOLIC CONCORDANCE

TENTH ARCANUM

In mysticism, conformity to God's will is regarded as an *a priori* condition for any event: according to piety—that is, according to the ideal of passivity that considers life only as a thing to be submitted to—good or bad fortune is of no significance. As a preparation for eternity, earthly existence is valuable only as voluntary suffering.

The mage, on the other hand, blasphemes by viewing events as manifestation of Providence, which is God's will; he holds to an ideal that can be realized in this world. This essentially active ideal presents existence as an ocean he must cross on a course toward doing justice, bringing light, and performing the role of a militant angel. The mage fashions from his illuminated will the sword of life; whereas the pious man, after having set his cap on paradise, joins his hands in prayer and does no more.

IV
MATERIALITY or EFFORT

Divine Name: אגלא (Agla)
Sephira: Chesed
Rank: Dominations
Sign: Cancer
Arcanum: Eleven

You yourself are the material of your great work. Become the intellectual emperor obeyed by your soul and body, and then you will be a mage: but do not imagine that the path is wide or easy that leads to such a summit. Utilize pain as modern science utilizes energy—that's what I can teach you. As soon as he suffers, the ordinary man swears, the devout man gives up, while the initiate sees an advance toward perfection in each pain.

First one suffers physically, which is most bothersome, as it does not contribute to cultivation. Emotional suffering is very productive because it heals the soul even as it chastens vain desires. Finally, mental suffering is the only suffering you cannot extinguish without diminishing yourself, and that does not affect your own person, but rather the material outcome of ideas, and attacks against the ideal.

One obtains from a practice all it promises, if the will is full and constant: this explains how the hair shirt and other such tricks yield results. But such barbarities are suitable only for superstitious women; a woman is such a completely material being, that she must use her body for everything, to her salvation or to her perdition. For you, beware of spurring the flesh with stimulants, drink, or particular foods: never mortify your flesh, but be hard on your soul.

Of the emotions, some come out of ourselves; they are named weariness, despair, loneliness, impotence; they are combated by art, piety and spiritual effort. Other emotions come to us from our company and our surroundings, and often from our researches.

Never forget that a woman is accustomed to tortures for the sake of becoming attractive, and that love is nothing but the sweetest form of suffering.

As an initiate who can suffer in spirit, you have no need to abandon yourself to the sexual inquisition that is so necessary to more material beings, laborers or bankers. For the masses, a woman is the only art, all the poetry, and every dream; the exceptional man partakes of art, poetry and dream aside from women. Limit love to your eyes, if you can—to your lips, at least; to intermittences, at worst.

This very sorrow, which is the only emotion in Balzac's Nucingen,[127] and his finest sentiment, becomes in d'Artez[128] a distraction that diminishes him.

Pay great attention to the resemblance that develops between an intellectual and a guy, as soon as either falls in love. And do not become the foolish dead weight that a woman shakes off in order to raise herself.

For her, love is everything; for you it should be just one thing among the others, at first hesitant and inevitably curious, analyzing later, serene afterward. Do not accept any drama or trouble from a woman; let her be relaxation for your nerves, recreation for your eyes, balm for your soul.

Summon her to give you calm tenderness, and leave her if she refuses. Never yield to jealousy or caprice; you will dwindle imperceptibly. Reduce, reduce the woman to a friend, reduce love to a brief conjugal routine.

---

127. [TN] **Baron Nucingen** is a predatory financier whose schemes ruin his investors, as recounted in Honoré de Balzac's *The House of Nucingen* (1838). In *A Harlot High and Low*, Nucingen falls helplessly in love with a woman who exploits him; he becomes melancholy and lovesick while dissipating his fortune on her.

128. [TN] **D'Artez** is a self-made man, with his heart in the right place, who makes an honorable career for himself while living a solitary and frugal existence, in Honoré de Balzac's *The Secrets of a Princess* (1839). After he inherits a fortune from a rich uncle, he is persuaded to live it up in society, and falls in love with a woman with the titles of duchess and princess. Inexperienced in love, he is inept in his courtship. She plays hard to get, while d'Artez learns about her scandalous past.

You are astounded; everything you have heard about love comes back to mind and protests.

My boy, a woman has no other personality than that of her love; without orientation, her heart beats sometimes for good, sometimes for bad. It is for you to make her calm or foolish.

Now it is certainly not mistreating her to steer her toward serene affections, but it does reduce her theatrical value. I am here to tell you that art has no correlation with strict reality, and Sophocles' Oedipus, so pure and so unfortunate, never existed.

A man must suffer in order to perfect himself; the ordinary man suffers from sexual love; you, an extraordinary man, suffer otherwise.

Suffer by renouncing the contentious but prestigious joys of passion; forbid your senses such impetuosity, forbid disquiet from your heart.

Be serene in your ardency, and master in yourself what is called intoxication. For that, you must impose rules upon yourself that hem in the instincts and chasten sexuality.

I know what you are thinking: You calculate that it would be simpler and more logical to follow the precepts of the Church, which is to flee sexuality altogether, or to make a sacrament of it.

That is too simple. To flee women and to flee love is to risk becoming dry, and to renounce a world of fertile impressions; and part of the problem with women is in the institution of marriage.

No, flight is never called victory. The question is not about one fornication or many; but about a balance of giving and taking on the sexual level.

As pride is the supreme virtue, the dynamic of all perfection, it is that upon which you must work.

Start by admitting your failings; let them serve to measure out for you how far you must rise in your ascent to the holy ideal, and in the privacy of your own soul, suffer from them.

The Church teaches that a life of voluntary suffering elevates and purifies, that perfect contrition consists of feeling pain at having offended God, rather than in incurring penalties. This perfect contrition that the Church does not require, magic imposes.

Whoever abstains from wrongdoing for fear of reaping more trouble than joy is a miserable Christian of narrow salvation. An adept must regret his deviations from beauty and righteousness, and let it be his pride that weeps.

I do not know of anything so great or so small as man; and reasons for self-infatuation are equal to reasons for self-blame.

The man who made the *Divine Comedy*, the *Last Supper*, the *Ninth Symphony* or *Parsifal* is well-nigh a god, and Mr. Carnot,[129] to cite a well-known example, is well-nigh an animal. I do not know that the archangels themselves are not envious of Dante, Leonardo, Beethoven and Wagner; and I am strongly persuaded that the tiger and even the least of felines, the housecat, would despise the President of the Republic, if feline instinct could go so far as to conceive of such abject mediocrity.

By everything you have in common with the President, you hold to a level lower than an animal; by every rapport you have with Dante, Leonardo and Wagner, you rise almost to the level of God.

The divinity of my Lord Jesus was shown by his voluntary death for the sake of taking away the sins of the world.

The Phrase "Imitation of Jesus Christ" contains the pinnacle of all magic; the goal of high culture is always charity.

Our duties increase along with our elevation, and this also extends into the moral as well as the social sphere.

The first duty of the initiate is to seek beauty; then to recognize what is good; from beauty and goodness the idea is born.

To defend ideals is the true chivalry of all times: to defend theocracy against social forms, hierarchy against all law, aesthetics against all customs.

In speech or writing, be a perpetual crusader against the threefold abomination: nationalism, equality, bourgeoisie.

There are patrician forms of suffering infinitely nobler than others, those undergone for the sake of principle.

Those without heretical tendencies who suffer from the current policies of the Holy See; those who, disdaining to fear power, express their indignation at the criminality of the national government; those enraged at seeing César

---

129. [TN] **Sadi Carnot** was President of France in the Third Republic. See note 43, p. 20.

Franck[130] slandered while another two-bit painter has his statue erected at public expense—all these suffer nobly.

For you must understand, my disciple, I have not urged you to become an individual so that you may become self-satisfied, but so that, rescued from the collective, you give all your heroism to ideals.

To suffer for an idea or principle, this is the apogee of human dignity, but beware of employing the principle to serve your own interests, rather than giving your service to it. That would be a great crime.

In undertaking any bold enterprise, weigh the suffering that necessity will impose on you and decide if the benefit is worth the price.

I will tell you a secret: to strengthen yourself, on the eve of your perfection, a secret that religion employs but does not formulate: the metamorphosis of suffering by exaltation.

The enthusiast turns pain into pleasure by the strength of his energy and soul, and the martyrs did not suffer unless their faith was feeble. Customarily, modern life shows ongoing examples. Are there not soldiers, that is to say, draftees, who reenlist? The Newfoundland fisherman,[131] did he not refuse work as an urban laborer, a position almost paradisiacal compared to his own, in order to continue to earn a thousand francs a year at the price of several months so horrific as to be worthy of a painting of Hell?

The same dulling of sensation that limits sensual pleasure extends to pain; it is unnecessary to feel more pity for a stevedore than for a man who writes forty pages a day.

The initiate does not provoke sufferings, as does the mystic; the initiate prefers to choose his sufferings: and I estimate that the choice, if it cannot be made for each moment, may be made for periods.

---

130. [TN] **César Franck** (1822–1890) was a composer, pianist, organist, and music teacher in Paris who became famous for his fantastic organ improvisations for the Basilica of Saint Clotilde. In his own compositions he strove to make music that was French in character but with the emotional weight and substance of the German tradition, and he made many of his organ students into composers who put the conservatory students to shame. Although he had a glowing reputation with the French public, his simple, unassuming, and trusting nature made it difficult for him to contend with the petty politics of the Conservatory, and he suffered at the hands of partisan critics.

131. [TN] From the sixteenth to the twentieth centuries, European fishermen, mostly from the coasts of France, left their home shores to fish for cod on the Grand Banks of Newfoundland.

Pride preserves vanity, and the initiate so despises general opinion that public disapproval means nothing to him; when it exceeds all measure, it becomes his badge of honor.

It is unnecessary to maintain one's good or bad reputation: there is no more advantage in offending one's society than in obeying it.

For you, the dictates of public opinion should come from the Testament of all the Wise. Consult Confucius or Pythagoras about a matter, but regard the authorities of your country, your city, and your class as grotesque caricatures masking paltry souls.

A single point upon which your life should avoid raising scandal is that of Catholicism; be officially one of the faithful, and always consider that you are only a good son of the Church to the degree that you live as an execrable citizen.

Sweet and good within yourself, be a prudent tiger to preserve your personality.

Don't let yourself be controlled or caged. Defend yourself against society, and make trouble if oppressed.

You understand, finally, that I would not have written such things under Louis XIV, and that I would have you renounce the city because the city has renounced God.

There are sinners for whom one must never pray, there are prevaricators for whom charity runs out; and your country is one of those.

These sentiments will close you out of all ordinary paths and opportunities for success.

You are like the mythical character who knew all trades, but who, fallen into a world ruled by the Devil, did not wish to serve in any capacity, and preferred to live by digging up roots.

In sum, as a Catholic (I will not allow you not to be) you are destined to injustice [132] in every courtroom, subject to all the robberies of the law, and to all the tender mercies of the bourgeois rabble.

Suffer this, because it is to suffer for the sake of justice. Suffer this in order to continue the work of Jesus Christ. Suffer this because God sees you, applauds you, and will crown you with the palms of an eternal personality.

---

132. [TN] The French government of that time did, in fact, have a policy of trying to keep Catholics out of positions where they might exercise power or public influence.

CATHOLIC CONCORDANCE

ELEVENTH ARCANUM

On the matter of suffering, the Church gives the same orders as initiation does, without a hierarchy of sufferings; and here it appears that magic can contribute, not only to the religion that is the community of ideas, but to the individual who is the exception to the rule. In honoring St. Labre,[133] among those saints who are more familiar than radiant, above Fra Angelico,[134] and instead of Joan of Arc, the Church has wounded the soundest instincts of human intelligence, and forced the laity to build altars to those overlooked by Rome; and

---

133. [TN] **Saint Benedict Joseph Labre** (1748–1783) was a French mendicant, member of a Franciscan lay order, and Catholic saint. His piety consisted of living as a beggar, visiting most of the religious shrines of Europe, and bearing the difficulties of that life in a Christian manner. He was canonized in 1881, largely because great numbers of people who had begun praying to him as a saint were being cured of illness. He is now known as a patron saint of the homeless.

134. [TN] **Fra Angelico** (c. 1395–1455) was a Dominican friar and painter in the Early Italian Renaissance. While displaying the exquisite decorative detail, delicacy of execution, and jewel-like colors of late gothic miniatures, Fra Angelico's painting was also at the forefront of artistic innovation in Florence, with its use of spatial perspective and the volumetric modeling of figures. He was commissioned by Cosimo de' Medici to decorate the convent of San Marco in Florence, and he also received papal commissions to fresco a number of chapels in the Vatican Palace. His compositions have a luminous atmosphere, purity of color and line, and serene spiritual vibrancy that suggests mystical vision. Although he has not been canonized as a saint, Pope John Paul II beatified Fra Angelico in 1982, and in 1984 declared him patron of Catholic artists, noting the beauty of his work and the integrity of his life.

alongside the exoteric work for the masses, to do another work for the few, in order that ideals may be incarnated, revealed and always present in forms eternally new and beautiful.

The mage does not offer personal salvation except as the first part of self-perfection, preparatory to the true hermetic work, which is that of expanding the light.

V
RITUAL or SACRIFICE

Divine Name: מקום (Makom)
Sephira: Gebura
Spiritual Rank: Power
Sign: Leo
Arcanum: Twelfth

Anyone acquires merit, reward, and self-mastery at the price of perpetual renunciation, analogous to his aim. If you want to prepare a great feat of will, throw your ballast overboard, in other words, abandon other possible satisfactions.

Pythagoras, when he acknowledged previous incarnations on this earth, explained sufferings at the hand of fate as the result of misdeeds in former lifetimes. I must raise my serious objections to such a theory, in spite of my almost unbounded admiration for this philosopher: I believe that this life is the first life for our soul and spirit.

The problem of original sin is not worth all the embarrassment it has caused for theologians: Adamah [135] had a fevered life, a dullness of being, a foul personality; he was a drunkard like Noah, and his inebriation was the first dissonance that disturbed the primordial harmony.

That was for the double reason that free will can only be born from an abuse, and life from an excess. Original sin must be understood as original imperfection, that is to say that Adamah was not a sinner, but imperfect. Given the novelty, the suddenness of conscious existence—no being could awaken into such a life in a state of equilibrium. The creator had foreseen the partial displacement of his work, as a master architect takes account of the deflection of his vault, according to the size of its arches and their buttresses.

The fault of Adam was fated and not his own; divine logic created him perfect but not established in that perfection. Furthermore, it is a great mistake to want to criticize the creation of man according to the standards of the angels. It was God's plan that man immediately lost his happy equilibrium, for the sake of greater glory to come.

So remember, my disciple, that the very first man was imperfect, but not blameworthy in the ordinary sense of the word. See in the drunkenness of Noah the oblivion of Adam.

In another work I have advanced a theory of human aristocracy that I will not repeat here, although it applies.[136] It would be misunderstood without a lot of commentary. It will be enough for you to know that it is your nature to be out of balance, and that balance is not a weighty negative, but the condition in which mind/spirit commands the soul and the body.

Now, a succession of phenomena started with the exuberance of physical life, leading to a development of the sensibility, finally culminating in the faculty of thought or abstraction. Since you are an Adamah, you must start by fighting the instinct that is the most immediate danger for you; afterward

---

135. [TN] **Adamah** is a Hebrew word literally translated as *ground* or *earth*. It is used in the account of the Creation in Genesis 2:7: "God [Adonai Elohim] formed man [Adam] out of dust of the ground [Adamah]," signifying that man and the earth are interdependent. In Eden, Adam's close relationship with the adamah associates him with the serpent that crawls upon the ground, thus emphasizing his animal nature. (See note 92, p. 90.) After the fall of man, the adamah falls along with him, and Adam is condemned to lifelong agricultural toil. Later, God punishes Cain for murdering Abel by making the ground barren to Cain, alienating him from the adamah.

136. *Istar* is the fifth novel of Péladan's ethopoem *La Décadence latine*.

against emotion; Cain and Abel symbolize a pair of emotions, equally excessive. Cain represents active dominance, rebellion, male brutality, impatient and ferocious rivalry; Abel, passivity, vulnerability and resignation, tameness without strength, effeminacy without resources.

Only spirit can give to Cain the notion of generosity and manliness, and to Abel the firmness, skill or stubbornness to defend and protect himself.

Whether Cain or Abel, those obedient to spirit have to sacrifice their dominant tendencies; the one will seek to tame himself and the other to become firm.

In this way, whether you count among the strong or the weak, the active or the passive, you must, my disciple, pursue with ardent desire the ability contrary to your own that will complement it.

Are you Cain? Cultivate the spirit of justice and of peace, lighten your force with generosity, be sweet and you will be complete.

Are you Abel? Cultivate the spirit of defense and steadfastness; firm up your accommodating nature with courage, be valiant and you also will be complete.

But if Cain, you remain Cain, if Abel you remain Abel; you will continue to suffer in the state of original sin.

Redemption has erased it, claims the Church, but not for all, as all men are not accomplices to the executioners of Jesus; there are beings I have referred to elsewhere as *elohites*, who certainly benefitted from the sublime sacrifice that was consummated at Calvary, but who are not culpable for the death of the Savior. The murderers of Jesus have gone by all the names born by the wicked imbeciles, from Luther to Carnot; they all prostituted their intelligence to the service of lies, all were partisans who profited from disorder.

If I have given you the task of liberating yourself from all duty to society, it is in order that you will belong entirely to sacred ideals, certainly not so that you can take your ease in what is commonly referred to as happiness.

Happiness is to know God and to raise oneself toward him; the rest is vanity. Now, this requires that you sacrifice social advantages and the increase of personal power in order to consecrate yourself to a sort of priesthood that is secret but nonetheless all-powerful.

Even if you were the acme of perfection, you would still have a revelation to seek; and you get an inkling of what can put a man beyond perfection: the gift of self, conscious, complete and serene.

To be conscious requires favorable circumstances; in the completeness of your being, stake your eternity upon a word; in calmness, contemplate only the beauty of your sacrifice.

If in one inspired phrase I could tell you the supreme work of all religion and all gnosis, this divine act that heaven itself has come to teach us, it is this: that sacrifice of the sentient self that accomplishes love, becomes charity, charity that is no longer of the soul, but the precise point where thought takes heart, or the heart becomes brain. This ideal was brought to us by Our Lord Jesus Christ, who infuses our souls; his precursors were never more than half of Christ. Some, like Oannes,[137] Orpheus, Prometheus, were spiritual torches; others such as Shakyamuni,[138] brought a charity without metaphysics.

The mystic sacrifices intellect to morals. One sees that the Church is not interested in beauty: she consecrates frightful churches and defaces them with a million pious fripperies.

Similarly, Catholic ritual has no use for art, as if it were satanic. With all its many virtues, Christianity is becoming backward with respect to its civilization; forgetting its sublime traditions that unite form to thought, paraphrasing dogma in frescos.

Magic does not sacrifice the body; magic obliges her disciple to render himself as decorative as possible. She does not despise the form that Jesus wore, or the forms of Mary and of so many saints and geniuses.

She appreciates how effectively allure, noble gesture and eloquence of tongue serve to spread the kingdom of God. She sacrifices nothing of the soul, either, but she strips it of what is contingent and temporary, and turns sentimentality into abstraction.

To imagine that one may be worldly and a mage, bohemian and an initiate, lazy and an adept, a Gnostic and vulgar—what aberrations!

---

137. [TN] **Oannes** was an amphibious being who instructed mankind in writing, the arts, the principles of geometry, building cities, and creating laws. The name is the Greek form of the Babylonian *Uanna* (or *Uan*) in Mesopotamian mythology.

138. [TN] **Shakyamuni Buddha, Gautama Buddha, Buddha Siddhartha Gautama,** or simply **the Buddha**, was an ascetic and sage on whose teachings the Buddhist religion was founded. He is believed to have lived and taught mostly in India sometime between the sixth and fourth centuries BCE.

Taking up occult life is like taking up a religious vocation with its distinctive garb: just as roomy as priestly robes, yet shorter and more easily adaptable to the changes of life, a bit undefined in its ways. One relies neither upon a director, nor a confessor, but only upon the theosophical word of tradition and—to tell the whole truth—one must invent one's own salvation and create one's own ritual.

Certainly, one runs risks, grave, numerous, ineradicable; the occult path, always bold, threatens as much as it tempts; but only boldness gives birth to great deeds. I speak to you of becoming a hero; if you know you are only a soldier, only a believer, go back to your pastor; his word is full of security.

When we bring up the matter of longevity or ease of life, the question of Achilles's destiny comes up. No one is forced into martyrdom or adventure; examine yourself before boarding the *Argo*; are you a sailor who wants to make landfall in Colchis?[139] If you are hesitant, give it up. Upon that shore there is no place for anything but enthusiasm and audacity; one howls along with the storm winds; one knows that to die on this path is never to die again.

Do not count on magic to be your trump card in the game of life; do not count on using secondary causes as helpful genies in the service of your passions.

Far from it, you must sacrifice yourself on the altar of mystery—not your heart, but the biggest part of what you imagine to be the joys of the heart; all the routine and moral naiveté that make up the baggage of bourgeois respectability—all must be thrown overboard.

The morals of your country and your century no longer serve; you will not enter the temple except with your ideal, your banner and the sword of your will.

Are you a Knight Templar? Do you aspire to deliver the Holy Sepulcher and defeat the infidel? For mediocrity has no part in the kingdom, and you will not find there any compromises between heaven and your century.

Antiquity bristled with material and moral ordeals; such a price was exacted for admittance into the mysteries not so much to put off traitors as to preserve the bold.

---

139. [TN] In other words, "Are you looking for a life-or-death struggle?"

Magic, like the priesthood, leaves an indelible mark on one's character; one who has taken even a simple minor grade retains a visible mark of his temporary and partial consecration; in this way a dilettante who approaches the sphinx retains the incoherence of his imperfect initiation.

I am not going to sacrifice the method and style of my book to recite the dangers you run if you are thinking you can just touch your lips to the cup of mystery. If you are not enlivened, you risk being poisoned.

Do not take magic for a study like numismatics or heraldry; you can penetrate the mystery only if your soul makes a magic vow. A vow changes a life.

To love your art more than you love yourself, and masterworks as much as your own art, that is the aesthetic precept.

To love the truth above everything and to declare it at whatever cost, that is the author's precept.

To prepare oneself for a mission that is undefined, long-delayed, and may never come at all; that is the word of the mage.

To forge and temper one's personality is only half of initiation; the other half consists of a mystic marriage to the ideas that, in the course of your labors, strike you as the most beautiful.

Chivalry, having come from the East, became grossly sexualized in France; one must read Boethius [140] and go as far as Dante's *Convito* [141] to see that the lady of primitive gallantry and the faithful lovers of Florence were an abstract ideal.

One who weds himself to the abstract must, like the chevalier Lohengrin, continuously sacrifice happiness to his vow; submit everything to the divine, and constantly wear the colors of his eternal lady, chosen from among Justice, Beauty, Truth and Subtlety.

---

140. [TN] **Boethius** (c. 477–524 CE) was born into the Christianized Roman aristocracy, after Rome had fallen under barbarian rule. While serving as a senator and holding senior posts under Ostrogothic King Theodoric the Great, Boethius made enemies at court leading to his imprisonment and execution in 524. While jailed, Boethius wrote his *The Consolation of Philosophy*, an imaginary dialogue between himself and Philosophy, personified as a woman.

141. [TN] **Dante's Convito** (Italian: *Il Convivio,* English: *The Banquet)* is an unfinished work written by Dante Alighieri between 1304 and 1307. The *Convito* is a kind of encyclopedia of the knowledge of Dante's time, focusing on Dante's love for Lady Philosophy, "the most beautiful and dignified daughter of the Emperor of the universe."

The modern man tries in vain to reconcile an imperious ideal to his own material interests, but one cannot dupe Heaven; schemes have no effect in the serene regions; the Templar is not free to stop and take off his white mantle; one who does not renounce the swooning of instinct and emotion will never wear the helmet of mystery. Adhesion to the divine will, if it is not absolute, becomes a blasphemy, and blasphemy, the deadliest poison of the spirit, erects an impassable barrier between man and eternity.

CATHOLIC CONCORDANCE

TWELFTH ARCANUM

That which anyone has done, it was all done from strength; the first man has wavered as all men will waver; serial imperfection remains inherent in every individual.

As for hard necessity that presses upon us every second, it is not punishment for our inherent ignorance, only the consequence of that imperfection.

It fulfills the conditions required by justice for entry into eternity.

The Angel never goes beyond the level at which God created him, and his place is eternally the same. Man, on the other hand, in the next life as in this one, will continue to improve and to rise toward the intangible and inevitable cause. Without attaining it, he approaches ever nearer, by the consequences of original imperfection that force him to perfect himself, aided as well by the merit and example of Jesus who has come to teach the same love to mortal hearts that illuminates the nine choirs of angels.

VI
DEATH or REBIRTH

Divine Name: אדני (Adonai)
Sephira: Tiphereth
Spiritual Rank: Dominations
Sign: Virgo [142]
Arcanum: Thirteenth

Of all the shadows that weigh upon us, that of death appears by its permanence and its inevitability to be the best argument against skepticism. The founders of religions, unanimous in this sentiment, would put off beyond death all the difficult solutions to the problem of justice, and on this point, humanity has never disagreed.

The future, eternal life must be for each the fitting recompense or the rigorous punishment; but on this point every Demiurge has called forth its own vision of joys and sufferings inspired by local and ethnic anthropomorphisms.

Valhalla is a consolation for brutes, and the Paradise of Mohammed a glorified brothel. The Buddhist heaven evokes an immobile dream without object, and the Christian version, full of sociability, music and joyful dance, although thoroughly policed, does not quite rise to the level of this incomparable theme.

---

142. [TN] In the original French edition, this chapter heading is given the same astrological sign and Arcanum number as for the previous chapter. We judge that the author's intention was to follow zodiacal and numerical sequence, and therefore we have listed Virgo rather than Cancer, and Thirteenth rather than Twelfth, here.

Someday I will present, in a theological work, the process of becoming mortal; here I must keep to practical lessons.

There are three deaths.

Voluntary artificial death is the entry to initiation and mysticism; it consists of killing instinct and spiritualizing the soul. It has been called, in occultism, the creation of a man by himself: the ancients, even the aged, spoke of being seven years old, or eleven, because that was the length of time elapsed since their reception into the mysteries.

Physical death, the only one well-known, foreseen and thus prepared for.

Finally, astral death, that ends purgatory as physical death terminates earthly life.

I am always reminding myself that Catholicism has pronounced on every subject the words most generally true, and I would not take issue here with any part of it. This incomparable and only true religion cannot, any more than its predecessors, obtain from the masses anything but the negative virtues.

Strict observance of the rules of the Church gives, without the shadow of a doubt, salvation and eternal repose; but not glory.

There are distinctions of class in eternity, a rigorous hierarchy, and the bourgeois who are saved do not mix with the choirs of geniuses and poets. Joan of Arc will be out of sight above the general run of pious devotees, and the admirable Fra Angelico to whom the Church has preferred a Saint Labre, will be closer than any respectable woman to the Virgin Mary, however respectable she may be.

Furthermore, without losing my train of thought, I do not consider either Joan of Arc or Fra Angelico as human, any more than Leonardo or Wagner. Those who bring the heavens down into this world come from heaven; earth does not produce beings who create as God creates.

I do not think theology has said of purgatory, as it does of hell, that those who suffer there have no hope of a better condition, and can only expiate.

In any case, it is as prudent as it is sincere to teach that a personal judgment marks our life to come.

Pay great attention, my disciple, that in leaving this life you will be judged less upon your faults than upon your soul and the spirit of your life. Many assume that if you have failed in a big way with a great Word, you have much more to expiate than if your Word were lesser and you had lived more perfectly according to it. But this point of view, a completely miserable point of view, rules only in little minds.

For the initiate, the primary consideration is not risk of suffering, but the limitation he puts upon his eternal elevation.

Raphael committed fornication; Raphael painted pornography. Imagine that for fear of sinning this sublime master had renounced the study of forms, he would have been able thus to spend less time in purgatory. But by the same token, his splendid eternity would have been reduced to simple calm.

Spiritual guidance has played a rather too disingenuous role, here, and I have no doubt that the least rosary-sayer to pass by the chapel of Saint-Anges is confident that he is in better standing before God than the great painter Delacroix. Interrogate a pious devotee, and tell him that Wagner and Balzac, who have created great theater and literature, receive heavenly awards of an altogether different nature than his own, he would be outraged.

Having fallen behind contemporary culture, lacking aesthetics, the clergy perpetually conspires against the poet and the artist, and rouses the pious against art and its priesthood. This is not to be borne: even in religious instruction, we desire that the geniuses be counted among the saints, in the name of the third person of the trinity, and this Word has presided over the foundation of the Rose+Cross of the Temple.

Expect then, to be judged upon your Word, on the general sense of your life, and expect that your eternity will be according to your own ideal. What you have not created, you will never possess; you will experience God according to what you have evoked of God, and your heaven will be what you yourself have created. You can see, then, the importance of clinging to the divine.

The first death, that I have called artificial and voluntary, removes you from the heaviest material limitation.

Pride being a strength rather than a vice, as you have seen, I take it off the list. The six other deadly sins can be seen everywhere, in perennial and unconscious forms. For the sin of lust, my view is that this sin is not so grave as opinion would have it: there are some disorders it produces that have been exaggerated in the theological mind, while it often excuses greed and envy. As for gluttony, wrath and sloth, even envy, these are four deadly sins both acknowledged and official. Who has not dined with a bishop who styles himself as a gourmet? Who has not known cantankerous characters who attend mass like clockwork, rich people who are lazy, and the envious, who are actually everyone?

Now if there is a truly absurd sin, it is gluttony, which I would call a misdirected lust. Those who seek a woman's kisses are, in my estimation, infinitely less blameworthy than the prelate who indulges himself with an old wine. We should damn gluttony, and not go soft on it just because it is practiced by the high clergy and financiers.

If I insist upon this, it is because it is the most degrading of all the sins. Sloth sometimes dreams; envy will sometimes emulate; but gluttony stupefies. I ask you, what kind of theologian routinely puts away a twelve-course meal and plays cards all evening? Lust, on the other hand, stirs the being, cultivates sensibility, and in the case of overindulgence, makes him suffer—a suffering more educational than a poor digestion.

I consider lust as a useful fermentation in the ordinary being, an antidote against stagnation, a motive for making efforts—whereas sloth and wrath, not bringing with them their own immediate punishments, are the deadliest. Must I defend myself against an imbecilic interpretation? I say that lust contains a ferment that uplifts many natures that, without it, would only stagnate; I consider every work of the flesh to be vain, inferior, diminishing; perfection is to renounce them, wisdom is to sublimate them.

I wish only to denounce gluttony because it has no constructive effect; whereas sexual instinct may be transmuted into works of art; I wish only to protest against the Protestantism that has invaded the Vatican, and to proclaim that the body has a right to be beautiful, that one must dominate the flesh, but not despise it.

French civilization has never been very advanced, and for a century the people who have Paris as their capital have returned to barbarity. As examples I need only cite the three ignorances, the worst, the three family arts: the art of engendering, the art of educating, and the art of dying.

Among the French barbarians, one is conceived by accident, educated idiotically, and dies like a dog.

I view death according to the science of the orient, not as a Catholic, and I discover the simple circumstance that one who falls into the water dressed only in a simple robe will float and will swim much more easily than another dressed in numerous heavy garments that cling to the body.

Now, to die is to fall into an oceanic fluid; the soul that is detached from its body in advance suffers infinitely less, and acclimates quickly to its new existence. But the soul that clings to the body tears itself away only with atrocious suffering and wounds, and tosses about in the unknown of the second life in deplorable conditions.

What is more, corporeal obsessions, craving for food or lust, persist even though the being no longer possesses physical organs. Evidently, the sensualists suffer the most in dying, and have the most difficulty in adjusting to the second life.

This second life has for its object the purification of the soul to the point of complete spiritualization—that is to say, to the point where emotion resolves into charity, and the mind into subtlety.

So the soul dies as the body dies on earth, with this difference, that all that has been sublimed in the soul becomes Spirit; one loses only the part corrupted by animal desires.

Entry into the life of the spirit constitutes what is called the happiness of eternal life; the being confirmed in grace can no longer descend, and at that point begins his peace, if he is simple; his glory if he is a saint or a genius. I said begins, because eternal life is a perpetual progression, an always active ascent, a gravitation without end into the light, toward the Cause.

The state of mortal sin is an aggravation of that original imbalance called original sin, further augmented by free will. What they call falling straight into Hell is to exit the body so violently that the soul disintegrates, and the spirit immediately solidifies, abandoning a fluidity too corrupted to contain it. What happens to this disintegrated soul, abandoned by spirit, I do not wish to speak of here.

The state of purgatory is made up of two operations: the work against what remains of sensual attachments, the result of which may be for a long time undecided; afterward a slow purification ending in the metamorphosis of the entire personality. We enter eternal life only after the complete erasure of all earthly impressions.

Understand now, my disciple, why I would take you away from the temporal and local, why I steer you toward things that are eternal, and into the development of your capacity to abstract.

CATHOLIC CONCORDANCE

THIRTEENTH ARCANUM

Purgatory is the state or period named by the Church as the one in which the discarnate man raises up his soul-spirit to make it pure spirit.

Relying on two texts by Saint Augustine (*The City of God*), Bellarmine's Catechism [143] declares that the resurrected body will be of the same sex as one had in life. This strange decision has no other purpose than to compel the individual to the virtues proper to his or her sex.

Until a pope declares in favor of the Bishop of Hippo,[144] I judge that theory as deplorable and contrary to all traditions.

Adam was created as an androgyne, and I cannot accept an afterlife in either a male or a female form; but in the name of all art, the ternary form resulting from the two mixed at puberty.

---

143. [TN] **Robert Bellarmine** (1542–1621) was an Italian Jesuit, Cardinal of the Catholic Church, professor of theology, and later rector of the Roman College. Bellarmine supported the reforms of the Council of Trent, and his catechism was a Catholic version of the small manuals in question-and-answer format, which had proved so effective in educating Protestant children and adult converts on basic elements of religious doctrine. As a Cardinal Inquisitor, Bellarmine took part in the condemnation of Giordano Bruno, and persuaded Galileo to abandon the theory that the earth moves around the sun. Bellarmine was canonized a saint in 1930.

144. [TN] **Saint Augustine** (354–430 CE) was Bishop of Hippo Regius, a city in the Roman province of Numidia (on the coast of the present Algeria). He is one of the most important Church Fathers of Western Christianity, a preacher, theologian, and author of *The City of God, On Christian Doctrine*, and his *Confessions*.

Furthermore, if one wishes to assert that only one sex possesses spirit and soul, one must consider that the elect, upon the example of the geniuses, believe they are androgynous by virtue of their receptivity of soul united to penetration of mind.

VII
QUANTITY or VARIETY

Divine Name: שׁדי (Shaddai)
Sephira: Netzach
Spiritual Rank: Principalities
Sign: Libra
Arcanum: Fourteenth
Orthodoxy: The Lance

Theologians speak of a sin of sadness, little known among pious laity, and this sin consists of loss of appetite for life, analogous to the sterility of prayer experienced by the mystics. It alone is enough to make the initiate fail at the very threshold of the temple.

There is a measure to observe in one's practice, and a remedy that the Church cannot give because of its danger. The most important consideration is to avoid taking one's own life. One very small pleasure can suffice to dispel an enormous weight of weariness.

Magic requires self-mastery but not self-mortification. Whereas the monastic method eliminates certain elements in order to give to others their true value; the initiatic orders preserve a man's faculties, and balances one by another.

The good itself, in this world of relativity, does not comport with excess; in excess it ceases to be good. We are as strictly limited in the noble sense as we are in view of our lapses.

What is more sublime than faith? And yet even with faith, the fanaticism that it can engender has many times gone beyond the bounds of horror. Torquemada and the Dominicans [145] of Spain will be known for all posterity as abominable monsters; in vain have some fanatics tried to justify these bandits. They will remain the prime example of the dangers run by a civilization when its leaders are not intellectuals.

Violence committed against ourselves counts no more than it does against anyone else, and the method of doing anything must be arrived at by temperaments, in the etymological sense [146] of the word. So, do not shut yourself up as a misanthrope just because men are wicked; do not punish yourself, because the course is a long one.

Moderate all your acts; yield only to enthusiasm and ecstasy, and to those only momentarily. Flexibility doubles your strength by economizing it, and permits better adaptation to circumstances. This is not to simplify your effort, but above all to defend against the law of reaction and backlash.

Depression follows fever and lethargy follows the paroxysm; if you judge the dynamic loss between the two extremes, you will see that less fever means less depression, and that diminishing the paroxysm delays the lethargy; the medium effort, delivering less force, can be sustained longer.

Having worked all through the night, your morning is lost, your afternoon is compromised. Except for the compulsion of a special case, a night of forced labor costs you more time and nervous energy for less result. You will never

---

145. [TN] The **Dominican Order** is a Catholic mendicant order founded by the Spanish priest Dominic of Caleruega in France in 1216. When it became evident that his order's efforts to combat the Cathar heresy were making no headway through persuasion, a group of church institutions known as the Holy Inquisition was created to impose punitive measures, including torture and burning at the stake. The order's leading role in carrying out the Inquisition fostered the pun that the Dominicans were the "Domini canes," or "Hounds of the Lord." **Tomás de Torquemada** (1420–1498) was a Castilian Dominican friar and the first Grand Inquisitor in the Spanish Inquisition.

146. [TN] **Temperaments** is a word derived from the verb *to temper*, as in mixing water into wine for an optimum beverage, or tempering a steel blade to give it an optimum combination of rigidity and flexibility—that is, to obtain an optimum balance of qualities by careful mixing or treatment.

do from midnight to five in the morning what you would have done from five o'clock in the morning until noon.

Physically, the gymnast employs as much skill as muscle; morally, the initiate strains his nerves as little as possible.

Two serious pitfalls are called dread and regret; one weakens you before the event, the other tears you apart afterward.

Consider and make your decision: whether to change or to continue—there you have the preface and follow-up to any matter—and it does not take much time or effort.

See that you do not attempt to do the work of time; recognize what belongs to it, and allow this slow and sure collaborator to relieve you of your worst difficulties.

Allow no room in yourself for impatience. As soon as it appears it stops thought, which should take into account the always-calculable factors that prevent an occurrence.

The life strategy for the one who desires neither the Legion of Honor, nor public office, nor the respect of his neighbor, consists in finding a vantage point from which to view the human comedy without taking part in it except when divine will is in play, in a role unprecedented and grandiose.

A mage is a monk in the world, who conserves in his fashion—a perilous fashion, it must be admitted—dignity, justice and idealism.

To think straight, and feel rightly are much higher functions, and more beneficial to mankind than cultivating the earth.

At the dawn of history, two beings would appear to have been honored as mediators between man and the divine, the astrologer and the virgin, the thoughtful and the pure.

The first function, largely abandoned, takes you to serene joys; yield to the superior attraction, and the immediate reward will be serenity.

You can see such peace on the faces of monks, complete and holy. May the eternal light of thought shine upon your face, not the furrowed brow of mental effort.

You must be comfortable in the hermetic path, and take joy in it, so as to walk radiantly.

Make your climb from whatever side of the mountain best suits your personality, and the effort will not be bitter. You must not be seduced by the immediate splendor of this grand design: to become a mage

Salvation is necessary; initiation is nothing of the sort. Salvation is for everyone, initiation is for the few.

Any village priest must be able to read the prayer book every day, none is required to understand Genesis or the Apocalypse.

Anyone can read and write; nevertheless, one may be a very worthy man and be unable to comprehend, much less to write, this book.

If it is only curiosity that drives you, I think you will fall away quickly, as I can offer you no material advantage.

Instead of ways to accumulate possessions, I ask you to renounce. In place of trump cards for the game of life, I invite you to throw out the cards, to despise the game. The phantasmagoria that could turn this book into a pretty mirage, I have sacrificed, although it goes against my habits as a lyric artist. I tone down my discourse to the level of a friend who gives advice, of an elder brother who guides, of a master who warns.

Although you must either firmly undertake initiation or renounce it, you are free to develop it by various means. I have told you that magic is truth refracted through the prism of an entity, and that you must literally make your own magic, find your own way, and I tell you now that you will establish your own means of ascent.

Imagine a mountain that conceals in its flanks a treasure: each seeker must dig his own tunnel; no one can penetrate by the path that serves another. Use a pick-axe or dynamite, dig a well from the summit or pierce the foundation, do according to your lights and your nature; the treasure will be found in equal weight everywhere; you are assured of reaching the goal of your efforts.

If on one day your fatigue hinders your work, take a rest: the important thing is not to leave the place, that is, not to abandon your intent. Rest in place, figuratively; above all, do nothing contrary to your training, nothing vulgar.

The ennoblement of your personality must reverberate in your words, gestures, your appearance. Even in solitude take care to hold a noble attitude; you are not stupid, and I do not have to point out to you the difference between theatricality and dignity. Mannerisms, whether mimicked or expressive, whatever sort they may be, influence thought and also sensibility. This will reinforce your detestation of vulgarity, and your refusal to suffer boorishness. If you want to gauge your progress, go into a nightclub—you will not be able to stay there without discomfort.

To the degree that you can put up with the music of *William Tell*, the theater of Scribe, the company of girls,[147] the ambiance of a bar, the contents of the news, idle talk—you are still nothing but an animal, that is to say, a Parisian.

After that test, if you do not feel the sublimity of Wagner, Shakespeare, the subtly aromatic sensuality of an honest woman, the vivifying astrality of churches, an ardent interest in metaphysics, a preference for reading over conversation: you are still not an aesthete.

I give you two criteria to use often, for without these two primary responses—horror of mediocrity and perception of the sublime—you will never be able to receive initiation.

By the same token, if you as an artist are pleased with stereotypes, farces, and triteness; as an author, with clownish and meaningless word play; as metaphysician, with unsynthesized paradoxes—you are no more than a dilettante, a frightful modern. Go rot along with the decadence you incarnate, and remove yourself from this study that requires understanding that is like the eye of an eagle that, without looking down, focuses on the highest and most brilliant point.

Superficially, historians attribute the Reformation and its consequences to the exaggerated tastes of the Renaissance popes for the arts and letters. Not at all; when the art is Michelangelo and Raphael, art vivifies and fertilizes; but the

---

147. [TN] The early twenty-first-century equivalent would be commercial pop music, television, loose women, etc. (See the author's special usage of the word *girls* on p. 37.)

Mandragore and the *Célestine*[148] do not merit an audience of cardinals, and the fault of the prelates was to accept the pretty, the witty, in other words, the inferior. They ought not to please themselves with anything less than the sublime, and the pope who will sponsor a production of *Parsifal* will certainly be a very great pope.

On essentials, be immovable, and flexible as to ways and means. You will see for yourself that one cannot do everything that you wish, nor as you wish. You should be indulgent toward your neighbor, so often thoughtless and irresponsible. The occult royalty to which you aspire does not permit hatred or anger any more than competition or intrigue. Your entity as a lover should attract the object of your desire, and if the object resists, blame your entity for insufficiency, or accept that your wish did not serve the purposes of your true vocation.

In this way you will have peace of soul and social peace, both necessary for the perfection of personality.

Temporizing, that is, biding one's time until one's undertaking is favored by the occasion, will give victory to the one who does not hold the false values in which most of humanity wallows. Temperance in asceticism, by regulating it,

---

148. ***La Célestine (The Comedy of Calisto and Melibea)*** is a Spanish novel attributed to Fernando de Rojas, published in 1499. Melibea is the beautiful, innocent young girl who draws the attentions of Calisto, a young aristocrat. Celestina is an old manager of a brothel who plots to deliver the girl into Calisto's hands. Although he speaks the exquisite vocabulary of Castilian chivalry, Calisto is essentially a sexual predator, and the plot is a series of chicaneries and betrayals that result in the deaths of all the principal characters. The dialogue's mix of street wit, obscenity, and cultured rhetoric, along with its realism and the psychological depth, raised the work above the ordinary; it set the pattern for Spanish classical drama and was widely emulated, as in Cervantes's *Don Quixote*. The Spanish church denounced it; nevertheless it was translated into Italian by a favorite of Pope Sixtus II. Although the bulk of the tale was salacious monkey business, it was very popular among French clergy, who believed its tragic ending made it into an admirable moral tale.

La Mandragore (The Mandrake) is a satirical play by Niccolò Machiavelli, effectively a stage presentation of the amoral and cynical political philosophy of his best-known work, *The Prince*. First performed in 1526, the cynical romantic comedy presents characters who are all thoroughly corrupt or easily corrupted; and far from coming to bad ends, they each attain their heart's desire through deceit and pandering to greed and lust. The message can be summed up as "the end justifies the means" or "greed is good."

An underlying assumption of both comedies is that human nature itself is irredeemably corrupt, and therefore we all may as well resign ourselves to wallowing in the filth.

protects it from painful reverses of fortune that waste the best of our accumulated nerve-force.

From a more practical point of view, when our intentions are not feverish, we may take death blows without being wounded. As the wanderer abandons his cloak to the mad dog that tears it to shreds, the initiate knows the wisdom of not fighting a battle he cannot win, whether against an individual or a collective.

The transition in our souls from temporal things to the eternal thing takes place best when we are at peace.

Until one has entered the priesthood of magic, that is, full initiation, the conduct of the novice must be watchful and secret, as initiation is accomplished by methods invented by the individual according to his genius, and the light cannot break unless the adept has behind him six years of silence, labor, and ascent.

CATHOLIC CONCORDANCE

FOURTEENTH ARCANUM

Perfection is achieved by the withdrawal into self and the projection of self toward God. As soon as this orientation takes effect, salvation and gnosis commence: there remains only a question of degree and quantity.

The Christian seeks God by canonical works, the mage by traditional workings. The work surpasses prayer in the way that genius surpasses piety; but as genius is the sign of a superior essence, it is as natural to some as piety is to others, and this does not bear in any way upon salvation. No prayer has uplifted as many souls as the head of Christ painted by Leonardo da Vinci. One must consider the masterworks as the greatest of miracles.

Only with the greatest difficulty can I explain to myself the healing of a paralytic at Lourdes, but the *Christ in the Garden of Olives* by Delacroix plunges me into astonishment, and I say that art is the greatest miracle in this world, since without it we could not imagine heaven.

VIII
QUALITY or PERVERSITY

Divine Name: צבאות אלהים (Sabaoth Elohim)
Sephira: Hod
Spiritual Rank: Archangels
Sign: Scorpio
Arcanum: Fifteenth

Pernicious enough on the conventional level, perversion is deadly in magic: this sin of decadence is particularly notable among the highly cultivated. It infects art with its strong perfume; as it is spiritual, it always projects a peculiar vividness, analogous to those prodigious flowers that secrete a poison. In cerebrality there is a point that combines good and bad, an imperceptible blurring of beauty into ugliness where the chimera and the monster make their appearance. All forms of the sin against the Holy Spirit—malice, willful denial of the known truth—all partake of this depravity. One might say that instinct invades the mind and, clothed in intellectual subtlety, contaminates the understanding with the base tendency of the loins.

The intellectual must take the trouble to defend himself against this patrician debauch, because he must expose himself to a great deal of culture.

Tristan and Iseult is the last word in musical perversity; but it is the entirely catholic work of Balzac that was put on the index of books forbidden to the faithful.

To gauge the competence of the Commission for the Index,[149] one has only to notice the routine ignorance from which they pass their judgments: one would search in vain among their denunciations for a single scrap of music. Is it not comical, that the letters and all the arts are susceptible to wickedness and that only music remains pure, even when it is named Chopin, Balakirev?[150]

It is ridiculous that the archbishop of Lyons, who forbade his flock to attend a performance of *Hérodiade*[151] on account of the blasphemies of the libretto, saw nothing blasphemous in the score. And what of the reverend dunderheads of the contemporary clergy and, for example, Father Cornut, a Jesuit insulter of Catholic talent, who was ranting against the illustrations in *Diabolicals*,[152] at the same time the symphonic intermezzo for *Esclarmonde*,[153] the most cynical filth in the repertoire of musical drama, was being played!

The guardians of bourgeois virtue want to forbid students of art to study the nude, but they are blind to the indecent ugliness of the paintings in the Church of Saint-Sulpice. In literature, I do not believe one must recoil from vivid portraits of concupiscence; but I do believe that we must present them in a clear light, with warnings and protections. As to those who design art or literature to titillate the audience, they are prostitutes, not perverts. I declare very readily that the would-be literary sovereigns who, with tirelessly provocative pens, insult both sexes and seek even to reverse them by sodomy, are filthy and nothing more.

---

149. [TN] The **Commission for the Index** was a committee that compiled the list of books forbidden to Catholic readers.

150. [TN] **Mily Alexeyevich Balakirev** (1837–1910) was a composer, pianist, and conductor of the Russian school, known today primarily for his encouragement of more famous Russian composers such as Tchaikovsky.

151. [TN] *Hérodiade* is an opera by Jules Massenet to a French libretto by Milliet and Grémont, based on Gustave Flaubert's 1877 novella *Hérodias*.

152. [TN] *The Diabolicals (The She-Devils)*, 1874, is a collection of short stories by Barbey d'Aurevilly (see note 84, p. 81), considered his masterwork. Each story features a woman who commits an act of violence, revenge, or some other crime.

153. [TN] *Esclarmonde* is an opera by Jules Massenet to a French libretto by Blau and Gramont, first performed in Paris in 1889. The story is based on a medieval legend and revolves around Esclarmonde, an empress and sorceress of Byzantium, who loves Roland, a French knight. Massenet clearly intended the medieval elements of the story to appeal to the Wagnerian taste, but they lack the mythic force of the Wagnerian librettos, and Massenet's composition follows French musical traditions.

VIII. QUALITY OR PERVERSITY

The perversity that is printable in history books and comprehensible to the general public is not even perverse. So odious and disgusting is this spiritual vice that it is beyond the capability of many, including almost all who pretend to themselves or to others that they practice it. Because a real pervert does not act at all: from the moment his desire is attainable he is a criminal; he ceases to be perverse as soon as the act becomes possible.

Perversion in the occult is called sorcery; it is the biggest fraud in the world, although it is astonishing to discover criminality and simple-minded nonsense mixed up in equal proportions in the same case.

If magic is the crown of religion, sorcery is the basement; the mage is a sublime devotee, the sorcerer a corrupt devotee.

The first sorcerer was a credulous idiot who, unable to obtain satisfaction of his vices through legitimate prayer, imagined for himself a caricature of omnipotence called the Devil, in order to glorify his crimes by a patron God of evil.

Up to this point, the working of the imagination is interesting; there is a curious effort in this human stupidity so obsessed that it created a God to bless its vices.

But the sorcerer, incapable of effectively inventing or gathering a cult, decided upon this infantile idea that since the devil is contrary to God, his rites would be the divine rites in reverse. Right away the brute made the sign of the cross backward, reversed the triangle and said mass backward.

In this way the dim-witted sorcerer, to lend some consistency to his worship of the devil, blasphemes God and pollutes himself. Deranged in paroxysms of madness, without abandoning his game of honoring the devil in everything that offends God, after sodomy and bestiality, in a sort of last burst of drunken rage, he invents—always on the pattern of the rites of the true God in which he believed very firmly—a disgusting parody of the Holy Eucharist in which he slits the throat of a newborn infant.

There we have such a horror that a most holy anger rises in the soul, and dreams of ancient tortures.

After all these crimes, the sorcerer can go even further—into ridicule.

The blasphemer turns quickly into the druggist, the criminal into a lowly dealer, the profaner into the conman. By desecrating materials once consecrated to religious purposes, the sorcerer formulates potions, unguents, and talismans that he distributes among the naïve, and he uses them himself.

The apparent and often illusory result of such atrocities consists of living apart, under general suspicion, frightening people into yielding up morsels of bread; and the crowning glory for the sorcerer is to make a man impotent, to afflict an animal, or to spoil a crop.

It is truly pathetic, and imbecility would be the only word for it, if this naïf were not also dangerous.

Take note of this, my disciple, the sorcerer is indeed formidable—as a bad man, bold and audacious—but not as a magician.

It is his grimaces that are powerful, not his spells. But his grimaces stir up his instincts and take them to a higher level of noxiousness—that is the whole of it.

Now we come to goetic magic, black magic: working a ritual to kill, while looking into a magic mirror; cutting the throat of a black hen at the crossroads at midnight; casting a spell of sexual obsession from a state of trance, or through solitary pollutions embittered with curses; the power lies in the tension of the will and not in the methods employed to project it.

You must see through the fascination of black magic as portrayed in cheap novels, and recognize all the paraphernalia of black magic as occult gimmicks designed to alarm women and yokels.

In our day, there is no longer enough faith to make a sorcerer.

A writer without a conscience [154] has given us a cynical portrayal of a black mass (as it is now called) to inflame the senses of the readers of a vile magazine. Now, a black mass uses for the host a *chevreau*, that is to say, a small infant whose throat is slit; and by his failure to denounce the perpetrators to the police, the author of which I speak has convicted himself of a sick and lying imagination, or complicity in a murder.

What has recently lent an appearance of reality to sorcery is the smoke and mirrors of a skillful charlatan who has undertaken the honor of restoring goetic magic under his own name.

---

154. [TN] **Joris-Karl Huysmans**, in his bestselling novel of 1891, *Là-Bas*.

Over six years ago a friend of mine wrote a letter to me saying there lived in such-and-such a village, a mysterious personage, well versed in magic, and sent me the first issue of a magazine featuring this personage.

The chevalier Péladan, my father, through his office as director of the *Annals of the Supernatural*, was for a long time the best-informed man in France on all phenomena called supernatural, benevolent or malevolent. At the mention of the name of the said personage, he identified him as a defrocked priest, convicted in a court of law on charges of fraud, who had tried to sell to the pretender Naundorff[155] a holy oil made with the blood of white mice that were fed consecrated Eucharistic hosts.

I sent the occultist friend this information; he paid no attention, stayed awhile in the village of the pretended sorcerer, and did not confide his impressions to me. This bad priest revived the nonsense of Vintras[156] and of Rose Tamisier,[157] wrote and sold loads of pious and occult foolishness. He must still be doing it, having been made a celebrity by Mr. Huysmans, to whom I have

---

155. [TN] **Karl Wilhelm Naundorff**, also known as **Charles Naundorff** (c. 1785–1845), was a German clock and watch maker who claimed to be the son of Marie Antoinette and Louis XVI and the rightful heir to the throne of France. He was able to convince former members of Louis XVI's court, but Princess Marie-Therese, his supposed sister, never recognized him.

156. [TN] **Pierre-Michel Eugène Vintras** (1807–1875) was a psychic medium and prophet. In 1839, Vintras founded the "Work of Mercy" (*l'Oeuvre de la Miséricorde*) and claimed to have visions of the Archangel Michael, the Holy Ghost, the Virgin Mary, and St. Joseph. The visions informed him that he was the reincarnation of the prophet Elijah, destined to usher in the Paraclete, the era of the Holy Spirit, and the Second Coming of Christ—and that Charles Naundorff was the true king of France. Vintras used upside-down crosses and performed "miracles" with blood-stained Eucharistic hosts, some of which are described in the works of Éliphas Lévi.

157. [TN] **Rosette Tamisier** (1818–1899), a peasant woman from Provence who received many visions of the Virgin Mary, claimed to experience mystical phenomena such as miraculous Communion, and to have received the stigmata, in the form of a cross, a heart, a chalice, and even a picture of the Virgin and Child imprinted on her body. She became most widely known, however, for one particular "miracle": One day, as she was praying before a painting of the pietà in church, the wounds of Christ began to "bleed." Despite being discredited by the Archbishopric of Avignon, the reports attracted thousands of pilgrims from around the world to the village. Investigators found that the blood coming from the picture was the blood from a leech, and Tamisier was tried in court and sentenced to jail for showing contempt for a cult object. Her case was one of many incidents that polarized secular and anticlerical sentiments in France.

forbidden any instruction in magic from any occultist, in recognition of his remarkable talent for falsification.

The character of Canon Docre from *Là-Bas* is no other than the sorcerer with the white mice who, so prettily spiritual for a sorcerer, recited to Mr. Huysmans his own misdeeds. But he attributed them to a canon of my acquaintance, whom I know to be a cultivated soul, good and only too impatient in his faith. As for Dr. Johannes who cures the poisoning-by-sorcery, it is our sorcerer of Carmel[158] himself, portrayed by the complicit or duped pen of Mr. Huysmans.

So! the plain truth about this so-called black magic is this:

An intelligent, well-instructed priest, but vicious, defrocked, a fraudster, twice convicted, supports himself by occulto-pietistic play-acting, and not only is he given room and board by a good fool who believes him to be holy, but he pushes the astounding farce to the point of getting charge of the good fool's two daughters—for the purpose of helping elementals to incarnate.

Imagine Tartuffe[159] as a prophet against a mystical Orgon, getting not only room and board, but also bedding the daughters of his benefactor who is also his disciple. Then, add to the daughters a few other hysterical-mystical women, and you have a complex imposter, not a sorcerer.

---

158. [TN] **Abbé Joseph-Antoine Boullan** (1824–1893) was a French priest, with a doctorate in theology, who was defrocked in 1875 for heretical beliefs and practices. In 1859, he established a religious community known as *l'Oeuvre de la Réparation* (the Work of Reparation), also known as the **Church of Carmel**. This was later denounced as a cover for his liaison with a mistress; he was accused of doing away with an infant born to her after a mass in December of 1860, although proof was never produced. Boullan served three years in prison (1861–1864) on charges of the fraudulent practice of medicine (using saliva, urine, and feces). In 1875, the Archbishop of Paris expelled Boullan from the Catholic Church. For Boullan's troubles with the Order of the Rose+Cross from 1886 to 1893, see note 31, p. 8.

159. [TN] *Tartuffe, or The Imposter (Tartuffe, ou l'Imposteur)*, first performed in 1664, is one of the most famous theatrical comedies by Molière. The plot turns around Orgon, the father of a family, who is blinded by admiration for Tartuffe, a pious fraud (and a vagrant, prior to Orgon's help). Tartuffe claims to speak with divine authority, and Orgon and his mother no longer take any action without first consulting him. The rest of the family and their friends detest Tartuffe as an imposter, and are alarmed when Orgon announces that he will marry Tartuffe to his daughter Mariane. The family plots to expose him, and Tartuffe responds with blackmail, getting the family evicted from their own house. After many misadventures, things are put right, and Tartuffe is revealed as a criminal with a long history, who has often changed his name to avoid being caught.

It takes a certain force of personality to play such a role and to maintain it, even in the eyes of the clueless; but however lively the comedy, it remains comedy. That this Goetian Tartuffe had fallen for his own tricks, that his impious set-up for serving religion to the satisfaction of his lascivious tastes had clouded his judgment to the point that he started believing in his own powers, this is probable. Although such powers are delusory, M. Huysmans, who asked the personage to bewitch me for the sake of experience, took action thereby against my sweet life, just to get an idea of how Catherine de Medici[160] ruined the house of Valois.

One can only bewitch one's inferiors, neither the just nor the mage. But a spell that fails comes back upon the one who cast it, and I suspect that Vintras II[161] and M. Huysmans may have suffered dreadful migraines in my honor; the one in an effort to impress and to make himself believed, the other obeying a secret law that spurred him on: Huysmans, the popularizer of tales about the horrors of pretended occultism, versus Péladan the novelist, who in 1882 had restored the Pythagorean ideal of the mage of light to literary purity in the person of Mérodack.[162]

Remember then, my disciple, that sorcery is a method of raising the nervous force, used by beings equally credulous and criminal, who can neither stop believing religious doctrine nor renounce wrongdoing, and who, in mixing faith with sin, made a religion of evil. Leave the whole business to the men

---

160. [TN] **Catherine de' Medici** (1519–1589), of the Medici family of Florence, Italy, was queen consort of Henry II of France and subsequently regent of France (1560–1574) during the Catholic-Huguenot wars. Three of her sons reigned as kings of France: Francis II, Charles IX, and Henry III. The first two died natural deaths and Henry III was assassinated, bringing an end to the Valois branch of French royalty. In a large country wracked by religious dissension and violence, Catherine has been faulted for allowing it to get so far out of hand, for instigating massacres, for poisoning political enemies, and for practicing black magic. Whether she ever ordered a massacre or a poisoning is disputed by historians, but there is hard evidence that she hired practitioners of the magical arts, which was far from uncommon among the crowned heads of Europe at that time.

161. [TN] At the death of **Eugène Vintras** in 1875, **Abbé Boullan** assumed the direction of a remnant of his followers in Lyon. They practiced the redemption of humanity from original sin through ritualized acts of love: rapport with spiritual entities and sexual unions between those who had ascended closer to God and the less spiritualized members.

162. [TN] **1882** was the year Péladan began his career as an art critic in Paris. On **Mérodack,** see note 24, p. XLII.

of literary art, this darkness swarming with amusing forms that the poor human brain invented for its crimes in the ages of faith.

Sacrilege presupposes faith, corrupted but strong, and not just the faith of the individual, but a whole social environment of belief. Therefore there are no longer any sorcerers—that is to say criminals—who exalt themselves through religious exercises. There will always be criminals, that is, malevolent wills.

The modern criminal is a skeptic: rifle the pockets of the fellow sentenced to death, and you will find no pact with the Devil. Black magic, the religious form of evil, never existed except as a facade, and even as a facade it is culturally dead and lives on only in scholarly books and the art of telling stories.

CATHOLIC CONCORDANCE

FIFTEENTH ARCANUM

The sin against the Holy Spirit is unforgivable because it includes willfulness, persistence and rationalization: Voltaire, for example, would seem as unsalvageable as Judas, although we cannot know the will of God, whether for justice or mercy.

Any use of occult methods to satisfy one's passions constitutes an unforgivable sin *par excellence*, and he who serves himself using magnetism (they call it suggestion in the Academy) to seduce a woman will be judged not only as a fornicator or adulterer, but also for sacrilege and profanity. Whoever makes a public spectacle of the second atmosphere, called magnetics, must be excommunicated; the working of magic that is not secret becomes criminal; and the Church, in forbidding its faithful to occupy themselves with magic, has great good reason; this subject should not be touched by anyone less than a highly cultured cardinal.

IX
TIME or IMPOTENCE

Divine Name: צבאות יהוה (Sabaoth Jehovah)
Sephira: Yesod
Spiritual Rank: Archangels
Sign: Sagittarius
Arcanum: Sixteenth

When the seas are too rough, the best sailors stay in port; when life is too adverse, the sage bides his time. The struggle against the elements furnishes warnings and parables to the initiate.

Considering existence as a perpetual conflict of forces that must be overcome, you will begin with the simple skill of not offering combat when either the field or the opposition is adverse.

You are alone, against a Providence that more often than not, you fail to recognize as such, and alone against a destiny stronger than your word, and against the necessity of the moment, as well as the wills of others.

Even if you were able to achieve constant harmony with Providence, that would not exempt you from the need for prudence and good management.

The miracle that represents the greatest aid a man can receive appears always in exact proportion to the merit or destiny of the beneficiary. Now, for a rather long time you will be accomplishing little more than acquiring merit in preparation for destiny.

Have I not told you already that the sorcerer takes his power from raising the pitch of his own emotion? That is why you never confront your adversary when he is in dynamic exaltation; otherwise you risk, even if you have just cause, being vanquished.

In all things, there are two parallel currents: knowledge and power. From moment to moment, power will predominate over knowledge, if knowledge is not equally powerful; the same as power will become vain if it cannot be idealized.

Right, and good reasons, by themselves, are never enough in this world; righteousness must be imposed, not by violence, but by the dynamism of conscious inertia, that employs all furors.

Imagine that you have your grievances against human justice and that it has obstructed your defense; what is poor little you going to do? Clapped in prison, you rehearse your speech to the four walls with as much care and force as if you were before the judge and jury: ridiculous, you say? Ah, but it is magic! Do spiritually what you cannot do physically.

Are you dependent upon an unjust man who has not honored his obligations? Refer him in spirit to the tribunal of the archangels, and as if those spirits were in your presence, plead your case. You smile again, and yet I have handed you a great secret and the only way to reconcile firmness of will with necessity.

They do not lie when they tell you that faith can move mountains, and that will can do anything, adding—what should always be presumed—if the faith is as big as the mountain, if the will has accumulated a sufficient quantity of desire, and if there is no overriding resistance from destiny.

Search your memory for the event that saddened you the most, and go back over it in detail. In reliving the conditions of that time, you will conclude by explaining the unhappiness to yourself and by discovering there a personal fault, antecedent or hidden.

I exclude sabotage or a series of accidents, and remain on the realm of ordinary life.

There, injustice prospers, but not irrationality. When Balzac wanted to be an industrialist, this genius-in-obscurity was treated just like anybody else in life: Balzac's will was opposed to Balzac's destiny, a destiny that did not permit him to succeed on that low level. As a creator of art he was invincible, and his enormous output accumulated despite a life full of difficulties; as a speculator, he was a loser.

Pythagoras insists upon our limiting our activities and acquisitions. "Never do something you do not understand." Now, there are some faculties that exclude each other. There has never been a man of action who was also a great artist, or a warrior of great valor in a time of peace. We are born for a certain effort, and our misfortunes come from rigid necessity forcing us to stray from our own path.

I believe then that an intellectual must rely on, and demand everything from, his intelligence, which does not signify that a journalist is an intellectual in obedience to his needs. Nor do I claim that Spinoza, in polishing lenses, or a great mind serving as a minister of state government, degraded himself. One is diminished by the triviality of one's aspiration, not the labor itself.

Established in his specialty, a man presents a smaller target to the blows of life; he can parry them, standing upon home ground; our perils are our recklessness.

After misfortune strikes, our life force reacts, but we usually fail to make use of it, due to distraction and exhaustion. Nothing in life presents itself as complete or continuous, neither a hard destiny nor a happy one. The one who has the fortitude of soul to discern the movement of fate, and use it, preserves himself and rebuilds what was destroyed.

The deadliest of all counselors, despair, makes us act literally like an injured man who enlarges his wounds.

In the face of a cyclone of fate, one must change one's ways and means, but not one's course, if one is following one's aptitude. Should the fatal hazard be intimate and passionate, running away or traveling would be expedient.

The unlucky man is a being with a personality deficit; the more his morale depends upon others, whether the other is affectionate or numerous, the more they will determine his condition.

Womankind, with its perpetual deficit of personality, has not given any solitaries to history; there have been no feminine hermits. The unfortunate man becomes a woman, that is to say, subordinate to a cosmic or social other.

When a life is truly oriented to the absolute, failure does not take on the importance that it has for the adventurer. The man who stakes his life on worldly ambitions, and fails, does indeed lose everything: his design cannot exist without its realization. On the other hand, a thinker unheeded or persecuted, keeps all his valuables: it is enough that he continues to think, for him to not be conquered.

George Cadoudal missed taking his place in history across from Charlotte Corday,[163] but he did not succeed in killing the monstrous Corsican, and his name is forgotten because his word was not realized: for details, read the terrible tale in *Bonaparte and the Bourbons*.

The Corsican escaped physical death; and while it is not only the denunciations of the sublime Chateaubriand[164] that have made his name detestable, those denunciations reverberate nevertheless in human memory, with a growing execration.

Chateaubriand's thinking, even unexpressed, would have influenced the spirit of the West. The act not executed dies; but thought lives on, grows and multiplies exponentially outside of literature, according to laws that cannot be spoken of here.

Bad luck teaches, inspires, and heals, and it should not be cursed; but it wears us down and exhausts us, so it should not be provoked.

A kind of intoxication takes hold of the religious ecstatic, and pushes him to an excess of penitence; he becomes inebriated, and from that point his suffering approaches bliss. The initiate, even if pious and enthusiastic, does not experience the analogy to what is called "the madness of the Cross."

Moral and mental maladies send out a contagion analogous to leprosy, syphilis or diphtheria; I warned you at the beginning of the foul promiscuities of bars and buddies.

The practitioners of alienism may all have nervous tics and delusory perceptions, but then, so do those who live in the diabolical atmospheres of the office and the media, which corrode any moral sense.

Is it not amazing that for twenty years the political brothel that suffices to destroy liberty in France, the Chamber of Deputies, has heard not one memorable speech, not one profound word or wisdom from a thinker or a man of

---

163. [TN] **Charlotte Corday** assassinated Marat, an ideologue of the French Revolution; and Cadoudal tried to assassinate Napoleon Bonaparte (born on the island of Corsica).

164. [TN] **François-René de Chateaubriand** (1768–1848) was a French writer, politician, diplomat, and historian whose novels are considered the first French literature in the Romantic style.

state? Taken individually, the deputies are not all rabble and morons; in a group they put each other under an evil spell with a strange unanimity.

When a country is mad, one must separate oneself from the life of the citizen, for fear of contagion; when an environment is as wicked as that of our young literati, one must flee it.

However, the most pressing danger comes from personalities that impress us intimately.

The criterion that defines good and bad company is the impression it leaves upon us.

If you feel yourself calmer, clearer, or better when you part from your friend, you have proof of a good influence.

If, after seeing a woman, you come to yourself feeling nervous, restless, discontent with yourself and your life, that is proof of a noxious influence that will weaken you.

Every being that approaches us does us harm or good; not in the sense of joy or constriction, but of imparting peace or throwing us into disorder.

Beware of the weak, who can without a doubt exercise a strange dominance, by the simple method of discovering a fault in you and making it into a cause for satisfaction.

Behind our disasters, there is almost always a snickering Mephistopheles, less picturesque than the one in *Faust*, but dreadful nevertheless.

Fear is one thing: useless. It brings disaster in the same way that currents of air bring thunder. I have already said that despair causes us to lose the opportunity of fate that is the response to bad luck. On the other hand, if then one minimizes the effects of anxiety and regret, one has diminished the catastrophe almost to nothing, by firmness before and artificial forgetting afterward.

Prayer, meditation, work, and noble friendships are the shields of the adepts. And finally, the being within which spirit hovers the greatest part of the time, will be always less damaged by life, like sleepwalkers, for whom falls and collisions do not impose the ordinary consequences.

CATHOLIC CONCORDANCE

SIXTEENTH ARCANUM

The theory of compensations put forth by Azaïs[165] is beautiful, profound, and certified by the Church. "We do not know," say the Church fathers, "what is truly good for us; and God sometimes protects us by refusal." Nothing is more probable; but we remember the Pythagorean exclamation, "Captain in peril, do not tear out your hair to conjure Neptune; work according to the art of Neptune."

The perfect Christian does not deny misfortune; he considers it a springboard for a leap toward perfection. The initiate advancing in spirituality, subject to misfortune, extracts the lesson and the moral profit it contains; but he fights it.

The knights of chivalry searched the world for adventure and merit; they rejoiced to encounter a dragon, but they slew it.

Just so, the adept does not despise the moral profit or the merit to be had from misfortune, but he intends to overcome it with real prowess.

---

165. [TN] **Pierre Hyacinthe Azaïs** (1766–1845) was a French philosopher who initially applauded the Revolution but was appalled by its atrocities. By 1809, in his work entitled *Des Compensations dans les destinées humaines (Compensations in Human Destinies)*, he maintained that, on the whole, happiness and misery are equally balanced in life, and that men should therefore submit quietly to a fixed government rather than risk the horrors of revolution. He proposed that the most basic principle of existence is the opposition between forces of expansion and compression, whose cause is God. In the physical world, the forces are manifested in matter vs. action and reaction, while moral and political phenomena are the result of two primitive instincts, progress vs. self-conservation. Perfection, as Azaïs saw it, lies in equilibrium or universal harmony.

X
LIFE or GLORY

Divine Name: אלוה (Eloah)
Sephira: Malkuth
Spiritual Rank: Ischim
Sign: Capricorn
Arcanum: Seventeenth

Glory is one of the highest conceptions there is: like pride—which, from its abuses, has been designated a capital sin—it must be considered according to magic.

The glory of conquerors, military glory, is for the mage a nameless opprobrium, and the Vendôme Column,[166] for example, would be demolished by the initiate, along with the removal of the names of warriors from the streets and plazas. True glory is of beauty and justice. If it could be had from letters of the Academy, it would become ridiculous; if it came from fame, it would be despicable.

Glory is a man's will espoused to the light that gives him a son, that is, a work.

Not the drivel of a smart aleck espousing the opinion of his times, a mirror in which he sees his reflection embellished and deceitful.

Glory is an intent, it involves a very great effort: to wed the light, step out of one's times, and give birth to a form, in other words, to give new life to a passive ideal or eternal symbol, out of your own virility.

---

166. [TN] The **Vendôme Column** is a monument to the French Revolution.

What a confusion there is in the Western spirit on this noble matter, and what clashes among French educators!

For the reader of the *Petit Journal* or the Minister of Public Education, glory gives the same crown to Wagner who composed *Parsifal*, and Bonaparte, who butchered fifteen million souls; there is a Hoche Street near Chateaubriand Street, and in the country where Marat, Voltaire, Gambetta the bad actor, and the journalist Desmoulins all have their monuments, while Balzac and Delacroix must go on waiting for theirs, I ask you what goes on in the mind of an adolescent looking for a clear direction? Petrarch at the Capitol, or Caesar the pederast torturing Vercingetorix, which is glorious?

How many men are there constantly brutal enough to agree to grant the same honor to two opposing generals, and what rare mental disease was going around at the siege of Sebastopol where the French and Russian officers disported themselves together between two vicious battles? Is it not Valhalla minus the Valkyries, which is to say, the worst barbarity of the Goths?

Here we have two armies facing each other: the routine calls for the two armies to be heroic and to fight a raging battle. The savages would have it no other way.

Theosophically, the hero is the one whose cause is just; and the miscreant, be he as valiant as Percy, remains a miscreant.

We must finish by considering the farce of courage from the physical point of view: the more a being is empty, the better bargain he drives for his hide.

For the rest, if you invited no matter which sergeant-major to prove a metaphysical point, I expect it would be a strange vaudeville, while the least of intellectuals is capable of leading a charge and going with a whip against a thousand cannons.

The soldier who goes to war does not believe he will die, and upon the field of battle, becomes a beast of burden, he thinks only the thoughts of his troop or regiment: the glorious 000th is literally unconscious of its glory, as mindless as a bull goaded into a ring where he defends himself against human brutes.

Judas Maccabeus[167] knew why he fought; he incarnated the Jewish ideal, Larochejacquelin[168] incarnates theocracy; only fanatics make sense with sword in hand. But the principals in conqueror tragedies, the poor sots who went to Tonkin as national pirates, strike me as desperate and miserable, or as hooligans.

The word glory must not be applied to society's thieves and murderers, or else we must invent another word for true glory. The dreadful Montauban[169] who burned down the Summer Palace in Peking carries the same golden nimbus in human memory as Leonardo da Vinci. Both are said to be "covered in glory."

The very essence of true glory is to receive universal approval, not to be valued only in one place and time; or to fully incarnate the justice of a time and place.

Charlemagne against the Saxons, and Joan of Arc against the English, fought for the light, still more for the Empire and for France: that is their greatness.

---

167. [TN] **Judas Maccabeus** (or **Judah Maccabee**) was a Jewish priest, warrior hero, and national liberator who led the Maccabean Revolt (167–160 BCE) against the Seleucid Empire. The successful rebellion won religious freedom for the Jews, the permission to live in accordance with their own laws, the official return of the Temple in Jerusalem to their control, and a reduction of Hellenistic influence in religious practice. The Maccabees founded the Hasmonean dynasty, which ruled Judea from 167 BCE to 37 BCE.

168. [TN] **Henri du Vergier, comte de la Rochejaquelein** (1772–1794), was, during the French Revolution, the youngest general of the Royalist insurrection in the Vendée, a coastal region located immediately south of the Loire River in western France. Two hundred thousand people were killed or disappeared at the time in the Vendée, from 1791 to1796. La Rochejaquelein is remembered for issuing his famous order, "Friends, if I advance, follow me! If I retreat, kill me! If I die, avenge me!" After notable victories, he was killed in guerilla fighting against the Republicans.

169. [TN] **Charles Guillaume Marie Appollinaire Antoine Cousin-Montauban** (1796–1878) was a French general who led troops in the Second Opium War. As the expedition approached Peking, they encountered the **Summer Palace**, the main residence of the Qing dynasty Chinese emperor, with its exquisite gardens, architectural wonders, and cultural treasures. French troops took part in the looting and destruction of the complex, but it was the British High Commissioner to China, Lord Elgin, who gave the order to burn it to the ground. Three thousand five hundred British troops were not enough to remove all the priceless treasures from the Summer Palace before it was consumed in a huge conflagration lasting three days.

If the burning of the Palatinate[170] is not a crying shame, I demand that the memory of Cartouche[171] be rehabilitated. Men are so vain that they venerate their foolishness as dogma. They have systematized brigandage and call themselves brave; having replaced the words "homicide" and "robbery" with "war" and "game"; and having renamed assassination "duel," they are said to be civilized.

The English bombarded the coasts of China, because China refused entry to English opium,[172] and there you have the measure of national and corporate depravity.

Outside the defense of civilization and of the oppressed, all glory presents itself as the work of peace and generosity.

If someone confronts himself with this problem—to impose his name upon human memory—he would better be a criminal than a genius. Deutz,[173]

---

170. [TN] The **County Palatine of the Rhine** (later the **Electorate of the Palatinate**) was a wealthy, strategically located, and industrially important German territory in the Holy Roman Empire. When its ruling family died out, Louis XIV laid claim to it. The ensuing **Nine Years' War** (1688–1697) laid waste to the Palatinate, following the French military policy of devastating the enemy's lands rather than engaging in military battle. French atrocities committed in this operation have been blamed for generating the German enmity that erupted in the wars in 1870, 1914, and 1939.

171. [TN] **Cartouche (Louis Dominique Garthausen)** (1693–1721) was a highway thief with a reputation for stealing from the rich and giving to the poor in the area around Paris, until he was executed by means of the Catherine wheel. He became a romantic folk hero, inspiring songs and stories long after his death.

172. [TN] The **Opium Wars**, the First (1839–1842) and the Second (1856–1860), involved disputes over British trade in China and China's sovereignty. The underlying issue was a huge trade imbalance. Wealth was draining out of the British economy to pay for Chinese porcelain, cotton, silks, brocades, and various grades of tea, while the Chinese would accept payment only in silver, as they were not interested in exchanging their products for anything the British had to sell. The British responded by getting the Chinese to pay cash for something they didn't want: opium in huge quantities, grown in the British colony of India. When the Chinese attempted to enforce their laws against bringing the drug into the country, the confrontation erupted into war.

173. [TN] **Simon Deutz** (1802–1852) was a Jewish convert to Catholicism who became an advisor to Marie-Caroline de Bourbon-Sicile, duchesse de Berry, and then the head of a conspiracy against the new King Louis Philippe I. The duchess entrusted Deutz with delicate negotiations to solicit military support for her claim to the throne. Saying he feared civil war, Deutz denounced the duchess to the king. The arrest of the duchess led to a public outcry against Deutz, who was denounced as a Jewish traitor.

Perrinet,[174] Leclerc[175] have immortality along with Iscariot, and nevertheless, who would want such detestable notoriety? Science conducts examinations of monsters, and history records atrocities, both out of a need to study them. What we lack in higher education is a firm ethic to guide young minds toward true glory.

Newton[176] and Murat[177] should not be put on the same level, or glory will be like the Legion of Honor,[178] that is granted equally to the poet and his publisher, which makes for great comedy, and makes a laughingstock of the lovely blue ribbon that France awards to distinguished captains, young diplomats and cuckolds.

---

174. [TN] **Perrinet Leclerc**'s betrayal put the city of Paris into the hands of Burgundian forces in 1418, when France was twenty years into the Hundred Years' War between Burgundian and Armagnac factions. After being insulted by Armagnac occupiers, young Perrinet Leclerc unlocked the city gate of Saint Germain on the night of May 29, 1418, to let in an armed band of Burgundians. Together with Perrinet's anti-Armagnac sympathizers, they killed with unprecedented abandon and violence, spawning reprisals and counter-reprisals that continued into mid-August.

175. [TN] **Charles Victor Emmanuel Leclerc** (1772–1802), a French general, was sent to suppress the Haitian revolt led by the former slave Toussaint Louverture. Leclerc, accompanied by 23,000 French troops, landed in Haiti in 1802, took possession of most of the island, and made peace with the rebel leaders. By treachery, Leclerc captured Toussaint and sent him to France. The rebellion reignited and Leclerc's army was decimated by an epidemic of yellow fever. Leclerc died of fever, the rebels took the offensive, and the French surrendered in November 1803.

176. [TN] **Sir Isaac Newton** (1642–1727) was an English mathematician, astronomer, and theologian, whose *Principia* formulated the laws of motion and universal gravitation upon which rationalist science was developed. Newton studied Rosicrucian literature extensively, and of his unpublished papers, about a third of them deal with alchemy as a spiritual practice.

177. [TN] **Joachim-Napoléon Murat** (1767–1815) was a Marshal of France and Admiral of France under Napoleon. He served alongside Napoleon in Egypt, Spain, Russia, and Germany. For being Napoleon's brother-in-law, as well as for merit, he acquired the titles of First Prince, Grand Duke, and King of Naples, and he was known as the "Dandy King" for his taste in clothing. After the fall of Napoleon, he was captured, imprisoned, tried for treason, and sentenced to death by firing squad. His wife, Caroline, reported that he met death calmly, addressing his executioners, "Soldiers! Do your duty! Straight to the heart but spare the face. Fire!" (Caroline Murat, *My Memoirs*, London: G. Bell, 1910, 23.)

178. [TN] See the **Affair of the Decorations**, note 39, p. 19.

Glory should be awaited rather than pursued: or else it becomes a simple matter of publicity; and an American, using the almighty dollar, can make the world forget even Dante.

What makes the position of the Western intellectual even more impossible than ever is that neither the State nor the wealthy individual possesses the taste for immortality that was so strong in the Italian Renaissance.

Today's social club calls in twenty journalists in order to get their gala covered in the daily papers; but the idea of a literary dedication that would make their name remembered forever has never occurred to them. Likewise, there is not a man in France, enough of an embezzler, enough of a financier, to sponsor great works of art, and thereby attach his name to a name that will be handed down to posterity. The French, and Westerners generally, lag behind the banker Turcaret[179] and the least of Italian currency traders.

The man of intellect and art, between a rock—the lucrative racket of pleasing the public—and the hard place—the abandonment of all dignity to please a Republican government—and the impossible—to please the wealthy, even when pandering to their vices—finds himself quite at a loss.

Never has the epoch been so sterilizing, and those who still labor must seem to have double genius and be colossally obsessed.

Anyone who would win over the voters of these times may count himself literally a non-being; since all ideals are lost and spoiled, one can do no more than curse one's times, which is the worst way to inspire them. Indignation, that sad muse, remains the inevitable replacement for her nine sisters. Instead of taking the material for one's work from the present, it requires a great effort to project oneself into the past and work against the current of the time.

Never have writers and artists been reduced to such hard necessity. Nevertheless, one man[180] has demonstrated what miracles the will can accomplish.

---

179. [TN] **Turcaret** is the main character who gives his name to the comedic masterpiece by Alain-René Lesage, first produced in 1709 at the Comédie-Française in Paris. Turcaret is an unscrupulous, vicious, and lying financier, married to a woman who deserves him and who gives as good as she gets. The Comédie-Française refused to stage the play until the royal government insisted. It was performed only seven times (to enthusiastic audiences) before it was withdrawn, possibly because the actors were bribed by financiers.

180. [TN] Péladan refers again to **Richard Wagner** as a well-known and recent example of his own ideal of the inspired artist as mage. See note 4, p. XXXI.

The theater at Bayreuth is witness that genius can subdue the universe and revolutionize an art from top to bottom.

Imagine that the hero of *Parsifal* is the dove of the Holy Spirit, that this drama endlessly represents the Eucharist and messianism, and that every year skeptical Europe sends fifty thousand pilgrims to the church of art in Bayreuth! Imagine that, and I assure you that behind the beauty of the work and the will of the man, there are angels, that sometimes become impatient, and move to change the course of human stupidity.

Modern glory, even aesthetic, wears a strange shadow that comes from the materiality of its ideal. Compared with Aeschylus and Sophocles, the theater of Victor Hugo is straw drama, but not so the theater of Goethe or Wagner.

The initiate of art sets himself to giving form to the abstract through his imaginings, and to put an underlying mystery into his pathos. There is in art for art's sake a triviality visible to any eye that looks at it, it is true that the last sacred poet, Dante, more honored than understood, more often quoted than read, had no effect on the Western brain.

The artist must be detached, not only from his own time, but from his people, and work as a humanist, that is to say, tainted as little as possible by ethnic color in his work. As beautiful as it is, the Gotho-German trappings of the *Ring* go beyond what one would wish.

Not to portray the life of the present, and to work far from the public, as do the wise, is the only advice I can give.

As the current decadence will be renounced by the new civilization, it would be awkward to be included in that rejection.

The century has no care for art: let art have no care for the century.

CATHOLIC CONCORDANCE

SEVENTEENTH ARCANUM

The Church has for two centuries forgotten its aesthetic mission: it builds the most hideous monuments and decorates them with the most ignoble statuary, the worst decorations. Its canticles, its music, its ornaments, are on a level with its architecture, and soon the anti-Catholics will have nothing for which to envy us.

Therefore, the Order of the Rose+Cross is come at this hour to force the Church to become artistic, and in this way to lend it the prestige that it alone is worthy of.

It will be painful: the priests and laity take genius for deviltry, and insult the glories. Catholicism, confronting the artists, resembles a father who has forgotten his most handsome sons, and recovering them, renounces them because they do not resemble his other children, the humble, plain, and more easily managed ones.

XI
THE METHOD or ENEMIES

Divine Name: גבור אלהים (Gibbor Elohim)
Spiritual Rank: Daimons
Sign: Aquarius [181]
Arcanum: Eighteenth

One must not have enemies, that is, one must not accord to anyone enough importance to oppose himself to one's own personality.

Hostilities are inevitable, but not always deadly.

The initiate works upon himself, in himself, by himself, all that the agnostic depends upon from others.

According to doctrine, what is necessary will come into the life of the adept, if he holds steadfast to his destiny. But only meditation makes us aware of the limits on the degree to which we can express our will without overreaching the power of our destiny.

We are born with predispositions, as much as to say, with the beginnings of failure, and the ancient astrology was a calculation of the strength of will against the weight of necessity.

---

181. [TN] In the original French edition, this chapter heading is given the same astrological sign that was listed for the previous chapter. We judge that the author's intention was to follow zodiacal order, and therefore we have listed Aquarius rather than Capricorn here.

The mercenary Boulanger[182] is said to be Venusian, and that is enough to put his ultimate success in doubt: he seduced the crowd; instead of being faithful to them, he gave them a rival in the person of a countess who lost her destiny. This inferior man did not have enough character to substantiate his ambitions. Without personal worth, given prominence by a destiny that put into his hands all the power of the popular discontent, he has cooed like a dove without abandoning his desire to reign; but the destiny that had done so much for him has abandoned him. Reduced to himself, he represents nothing, and does not possess enough personality to bear his exile with any dignity.

Our lack of success always comes out of a contradiction between our desires and our will. We lack moral unity, integrity—that is the most common weakness. It is not the target that moves and shifts, it is we who lose sight of it. The ambitious man faithful to his design will not fail to achieve it if he avoids wasting his strength on other passions. The scholar may ascend to the highest pinnacle of knowledge if he lives as a scholar; that is to say that in his behavior, as in his research, he does not have to keep repeating and dwelling on a fact once explored, such as sexuality, for example. The artist will not finally achieve his masterpiece except by the employment of all his passion in the making of art. There is no true impotence; we waste our energies, and that is the reason for our failures.

It is less a matter of repenting and renouncing our passions than of accommodating them to our commitment; a painter who is incontinent, for example, nevertheless restricts his pleasures to women fit to pose for a beautiful picture.

Besides solitude and living apart, one must mix socially with the highest class possible, in order to profit from special privileges and the conveniences of corruption.

The good and the beautiful, by their nature, benefit from many evils. By analogy, metaphysical rot, like material rot, engenders under a skillful hand

---

182. [TN] **Georges Ernest Jean-Marie Boulanger** (1837–1891) was a French general and politician and an enormously popular public figure during the Third Republic. He won a series of elections and was powerful enough at the height of his popularity in 1889 that many feared he would become a dictator. He promoted an aggressive nationalism, known as *revanchism*, which opposed Germany in the name of avenging the Franco-Prussian War, which appealed to the working class, traditionalist Catholics, and royalists who were his base of support. The Boulangists were defeated decisively in the elections of 1889. See also note 57, p. 39.

things that are perfectly noble. One does not sufficiently appreciate how divine alchemy constantly sublimes the worst elements, and how evil becomes a stimulant to virtue, and the misdeed an occasion for doing good. The mage collaborates attentively with this great work of providential reactions that preside over the beneficial use of sin.

Massillon,[183] in his immortal homily on Mary Magdalene, expounds a theory similar to that of Fourier:[184] instead of recommending to the sinner a prototype of the Christian, he shows how the most diverse tendencies may lead to salvation, there is no potential we need to eliminate from ourselves—it is only a matter of using it to serve salvation.

Of itself, no temperament is incompatible with goodness; the least spiritual quality, physical courage itself, may be employed luminously, and any tendency may be turned to noble purpose. Today, the enmity of individual toward another has lost its force, and the pitfalls are called laws. The enemy of all is the State: the difficulties of life are called horrid education, military recruitment, judiciary without justice, police who threaten honest men.

The principal dangers for the intellectual are: the university, the army, the government and the police.

There is no trap that can compare to the stultification of French public schooling, to being reduced to abject passive obedience; to the insecurity of a country without protections of *habeas corpus,* to the depredations of police that for twenty years have operated as much against honest men as against the wretched.

I have commanded you to forget everything that France teaches; as for you, if your parents did not have you born in Jersey, reproach them for failing in their strict duty, and let the genius of necessity inspire you. In matters of human

---

183. [TN] **Massillon**, see note 96, p. 94.

184. [TN] **François Marie Charles Fourier** (1772–1837) was a French philosopher and one of the founders of utopian socialism, who envisioned a new world order based on unity of action and harmonious collaboration. The transformation of labor into pleasure is one of his central ideas, and he was a proponent of a basic income for those unable to work, championed education for every man, woman, and child, and is said to have coined the term *feminism* in 1837.

justice, just remember what Montesquieu said about stealing the towers of Notre-Dame,[185] and stay out of clashes down on the streets.

Anyone whose job is to obey strict orders is a special hazard: he is a boundary-stone, don't cross him; stay out of the way of the military, avoid the police or bribe them. I do not do the country of France the honor of believing honesty stands a chance in it, or that innocence has any value in court or in public opinion.

Moreover, the ever-powerful mage can only be opposed in his works; his word defies the conjurations of society and hatred.

In the lions' jaws, the Christians persecuted were more Christian than when Constantine raised them to triumph. Was Joan of Arc any less the Maid at the stake? The Chouan counter-revolutionaries,[186] massacred but not defeated by the grandfathers of those who now govern us—are they not also martyrs of the faith, dead or alive?

Defeat and victory designate the contingencies by which the word abides without end. Jacques de Molay,[187] from the stake, pronounced death-curses upon the Pope and the King, showing himself to be more the grand master of

---

185. [TN] "If I were accused of stealing the towers of Notre Dame, I would start running!" This warning about the French system of justice is an anonymous proverb that Péladan attributes to **Montesquieu** (1689–1755), a French judge, diplomat, writer, and political philosopher.

186. [TN] **Chouans** were royalist resistors against the French Revolution, who staged a major revolt in Bas-Maine from the spring of 1794 until 1800. Members of this revolt (and French royalists in general) came to be known as *Chouans*; the revolt itself came to be known as the *Chouannerie*.

187. [TN] **Jacques de Molay** (c. 1243–1314), was the last Grand Master of the Knights Templar, from 1292 until it was dissolved by order of Pope Clement V in 1307. King Philip IV of France, who owed huge monetary debts to the Templars, had Molay and many other French Templars arrested and tortured into making false confessions. Brought to the stake to be burned, de Molay reportedly asked to be tied in such a way that he could face the Notre-Dame Cathedral and hold his hands together in prayer. According to legend, he called out from the flames, "God knows who is wrong and has sinned. Soon a calamity will occur to those who have condemned us to death." Pope Clement V died only a month later, and King Philip IV died in a hunting accident before the end of the year.

the Temple than his happy predecessors; whereas, if Louis XVI[188] had not been sent to the scaffold, he would have died as an idiot, not as a victim.

No matter how a man leaves this world, his earthly glory, like his eternal glory, depends only on his enthusiasm: Archimedes,[189] killed as he traced out geometrical figures, was not defeated: his contemplation of science was taken up again on the other side of life.

So you see, my disciple, the grandeur of the ideal, how it defies all adversity and all accident.

But recognize also that what applies to the idea does not apply to the individual, there is no Law dedicated to your happiness, and that the worlds are indifferent to your desires and vain pleasures.

For you to participate in the power of the ideal requires you to become a knight of a Grail; search history for a great man who was no more than himself, and you will not find one.

"Only God is great," said Massillon before the council of Louis XIV,[190] and he could have added: man is worthy only insofar as he loves the divine.

In the communion of saints and the communion of geniuses, there is no room for anyone but those who aspire to holiness and genius; the one who does not desire perfection, be it only in the form of art, is only a mammal, unworthy of a discourse or even a word.

Man reduced to himself is only the most perverse of the animals: in order to approach God, he needs help from his elders in the effort.

---

188. [TN] **Louis XVI** (1754–1793) was the last king of France before the monarchy fell to the French Revolution. Food scarcity prompted the masses to revolt; this, followed by crippling debt, financial crisis, and Louis's indecisiveness, contributed to a general loss of confidence in the monarchy. In the midst of civil and international war, Louis XVI was arrested, the absolute monarchy was abolished, and the First French Republic was proclaimed. Louis XVI was tried for high treason, found guilty, and executed by guillotine in 1793.

189. [TN] **Archimedes of Syracuse** (c. 287–c. 212 BCE), the famed Greek mathematician and inventor who is said to have shouted "Eureka!" when he discovered his principle about water displacement, was killed at the end the Siege of Syracuse when he rebuffed a Roman soldier who had been sent to retrieve him because he was so engrossed in his mathematical calculations.

190. [TN] **Louis XIV** (1638–1715) of France was known as the **Sun King**. His reign brought France to a pinnacle of international prestige, at the price of growing fiscal and social problems.

Do not seek intellectual support from your peers, unless they are connected to rare mystics and enthusiasts. Evoke the illustrious dead, not by rituals and séances, but by meditating upon their works.

Do not, like the idiot spiritualist,[191] ask Shakespeare or Plato to appear for the entertainment of a roomful of credulous fools, but reread the great William, and sound the depths of Plato: you may not see the phantom, but your own spirit will be illuminated.

Illumination from the genius of the sages is the lamp that must light your path through this rotten century. At this point I can tell you that progress is a blasphemous word invented by journalists to make nations forget both their duty and the holy truth. Baudelaire has properly removed that word from several of his pages, and Dutens[192] has demonstrated that the ancients were not ignorant of our supposed discoveries.

Despise above all the history of Rome in the cornelian form given by that idiot Duruy,[193] and look with disdain upon the infamous people of Rome that had no art of its own, no goodness, who pushed collective or national criminality beyond the bounds of obscenity.

Detest all force without justice; detest in the State what you blame in an individual, detest the State unless it is theocratic.

But detest in spirit; do not go explaining to the glorious French officers who starved the monks of Frigolet that they are wretches. If you bump into Ferry,

---

191. [TN] **Spiritualism** is an occult movement that developed and reached its peak from the 1840s to the 1920s, predominantly in English-speaking countries. Spiritualists believe that the spirits of the dead have both the ability and the inclination to communicate with the living, and often rely on spirit mediums to carry on such communication, but believe that anyone may become a medium through study and practice.

192. [TN] **Louis Dutens** (1730–1812) was a French philologist, diplomat, and historian who wrote *Recherches sur l'origine des découvertes attribuées aux modernes (Research on the Origin of Discoveries Attributed to Moderns)*, first published in 1766. He cites evidence that the natural philosophers of antiquity understood the movement of the earth around the sun, the force of gravity, the makeup of the Milky Way, and the lunar influence on ocean tides, and used steam engines, telescopes, and microscopes, along with many other achievements claimed by the moderns.

193. [TN] **Jean Victor Duruy** (1811–1894) was a French historian whose *Histoire des Romains et des peuples soumis à leur domination (History of the Romans and Their Subject Peoples)* led Napoleon III to choose him as an assistant in writing his own biography of Julius Caesar and then to appoint him minister of education in 1863.

don't kill the monster, because his officers will react like the mindless stooges they are, and Ferry has his role to play as the prime traitor in the Latin demise.

Arm your spirit, forge yourself a sword of eloquence, a lapidary style, and wait for your mission to be offered to you. If it comes late, or never, so what? You have honored the truth in your soul; you have prepared your eternal reward.

In this life, consider the next, and while you suffer, never depart from the conception, or the design of the eternity to which you fly.

If you hear me, your salvation in the catholic sense is sure, and your unhappiness in this world is immediately reduced.

The portion lost from your earthly life is regained in heaven, if you follow the divine law. Is that not invincibility? The world may paralyze your strength, but your will projects itself to where the angels rejoice.

What have you to fear? Peace of mind heals the body; disdain for men and their laws armors you against their injustices and oppression.

Friendship betrays you and love deceives you, but behold—do you not see this new star that shines in the sky? It is a world vaster than ours: does not the sight of it lift you to where you no longer suffer, if for a few more hours you must submit to the tyranny and the foul promiscuity of the terrestrials?

CATHOLIC CONCORDANCE

EIGHTEENTH ARCANUM

The Church, in putting the goal of life beyond death, preserves the faithful from becoming too sensitive to the setbacks of life.

In obliging us to charity, the Church makes charity to our neighbor possible and sometimes sweet; but in counseling the faithful to renunciation, the Church falls short of cultivating the whole individual. The one who is faithful to perfection, that is, saved in eternity and good in the present, does not yet have in himself any power of illumination.

Obsessed with its saints, the Church has forgotten genius; busy with prayer, it abandons action; into this breach magic comes to render both aesthetic weapons and a willingness to fight.

I believe that three iron stakes in the chest of certain monsters would be of great service to the reign of God: it is true that these three iron stakes are secular and profane, and in *Istar*, I have said how the Holy Father disposes of anyone's life when he says mass.

I cannot profitably go any further in the expectation that this ardent fire of God's wrath, from the hands of the Holy See, will fall like bolts of lightning.

XII
ACCOMPANIMENT or PROVIDENCE

Divine Name: אל (El)
Mixed Rank: Androgynes
Sign: Pisces
Arcanum: Nineteenth

Theocracy has been the political form of the great empires of Babylon and Memphis, of India and Mongolia, next to which our modern histories look like the chronicles of primitive tribes. What is true of humanity is also true of man.

The greatest commandment is this: that divinity be both the foundation and the crown of all our undertakings. As various as it can be conceived, divinity is not reducible to a single observance for all.

It is present in the studio of Delacroix,[194] of Sigalon,[195] in the garret of Balzac,[196] as it is in the cloister. The courtesan who induces an officer to lighten the sentence of an intellectual condemned to the galleys makes sublime use of her charms; and if Marie Antoinette hadn't been the sublime torture victim of the monarchy, she would still be the patron of Gluck,[197] the only genius and the only majesty of the eighteenth century.

---

194. [TN] **Delacroix**, see note 91, p. 89.

195. [TN] **Xavier Sigalon** (1787–1837) was a French painter of historical scene, and portraits. In 1833 he was commissioned to copy the Sistine fresco of *The Last Judgment* for a hall in the Palace of Fine Arts in Paris.

196. [TN] **Balzac**, see note 77, p. 74.

197. [TN] **Christoph Willibald Gluck**, see note 105, p. 101.

The number of Providence is also that of generation and radiance, and all culture of self remains imperfect that does not aim at expansion.

It is permissible to raise oneself above the law and human solidarity, on the explicit condition that this pride bows before the infinite pride that is God's.

"Look to your salvation" says religion; and magic: "You will not be saved unless you become a savior."

The choir of angels sings in *Parsifal*: "Redemption to the Redeemer," explaining thereby that the man who raises himself above the others assumes a new dignity with special duties.

The Sepher Elkana [198] explains it:

"Judge, if you have justice living within you."

"Command, if you have the power within you."

"Sacrifice, if you have within you a chief priest."

"Reign, if an invisible crown weighs upon your head."

"But remember, you who pass judgment, you will be seven times judged."

"Remember well, you who rise to command, you must bow seven times in obedience to Bel."

"Remember, you who recite the all-powerful names, you will be seven times called to obedience."

"Remember, you who lay a heavy scepter upon the people, you will be humbled seven times by Ilou the Supreme."

"Judge, chief priest, mage, Sar, remember!"

That is how Sâr Elkana acknowledged in all men the right to wield the scale, the rod, the censer and the scepter, but he warned that divinity exacts a toll for such high ambitions. This price is designated in the text as "seven times," signifying in occult terms "expansion" or "creation," the world having evolved according to the number seven.[199]

---

198. The *Book of Marvels*, Elkana the Chaldean, manuscript of the thirteenth century, with the seal of Hugh de Payens, First Grand Master of the Temple. (Unique copy belonging to Sâr Péladan.)

199. [TN] Among the Hebrews, the **number seven** always carried connotations of holiness, perfection, and completion: hence, Genesis tells of the Creation being completed in seven days.

Thus, anyone who arrogates to himself such dignities is obliged to consecrate to the abstract a septenate of his power. Now, three is the number of the complete man, while seven signifies that the mage retains for himself nothing of his power.

We are far, far above those miserable essays of egoism in the form of ethics that are so often attempted.

The modern hero who suffers if his cigars are too fresh, from the dreariness of life, from indigestion, is not worth a word in passing. One must aspire beyond oneself to be worthy; we are not freely allowed, like animals, to blindly pursue our appetites; dilettantism is nothing but a decorative form of impotence; aesthetic emasculation.

Anyone not in need of certitude is a false thinker; and metaphysically, Renan[200] defined himself as a eunuch.

The notions of charity and work have been wrongly separated from each other.

The painter of the Chapel of Saint-Anges has worked a miracle of another power than those of Lourdes, and should the church-goers of the universe be offended, certain phrases of Bossuet, certain verses of Lamartine, certain pages of Wagner astound me just as much as an instantaneous healing of a whole hospital would.

I do not differentiate between the merits of charity and those of art. The Sistine Chapel and the *Last Supper* are for intellectuals the equivalent of all charities and all the blessings.

I know one must do terrible violence to the pious if they are to make room for genius, but no hesitation is permitted in the Order of the Rose+Cross; through genius, Beauty will return to Catholicism, and if its portals are presently too narrow for it to enter, we will break through the portals.

For much too long an ignorant and narrow-minded clergy cast the artist out with the profaners. We want our pews in the Church, or if denied, we will build our own cathedral to Our Lady of All Beauty, in the certainty that soon she will be blessed by the Virgin and blooming with angels on joyous wings.

Never sacrifice form: beauty is God made visible, as truth is God made conceivable.

---

200. [TN] **Ernest Renan**, see note 101, p. 98.

Do not imagine, my disciple, that it is a matter of preferring the ideal to oneself, or of existing only as the sword-bearer of an abstraction. With the victory, the archetype will bring you indescribable and continual joy in rhyming your life with the harmony of the pure spirits; then you will hardly hear the human noise.

The sufferings that Hamlet enumerated, saying that death would put an end to them, the slings and arrows of outrageous fate, these injustices can all conjure together, the wrongdoers and the Law, and the whole horror will be dissolved by the clarity that will descend upon you.

Art, with its images, gives tangible form to every wisdom; you will find in *Parsifal* the sublimity of the century, the holy work seven times august, the very notion of my teaching on the figure of Montsalvat.[201]

Lohengrin, conqueror of Frederic de Telramund, is the initiate-conqueror of evil. His power was not his own; God delegated to him a supernatural power. Now, be apprised that Wagner is even more extraordinary than his heroes, and that having conceived them, he has been them.

Go down on your knees with your very life, before a Grail, a precious relic of the past; be your own champion, pious and valiant.

The process described in this book prepares you for the light, but the light comes from above. One receives it, it is not a matter of creating it. One receives it, warmth and joy, and one radiates it, color and power.

No mind gives birth to itself, no being nurtures itself; one emulates some prowess, some saint, some genius; one nourishes oneself with a certain example, certain words, certain masterworks.

This commerce, or rather, this worship of greatness and beauty, perfects the heart in submitting it to the breath of spirit. Egotists try in vain to elevate themselves without devoting themselves; dilettantes refine themselves without love; the highest degree of any path is not attained except through sacrifice; neither the book nor the fresco allow themselves to be penetrated without enthusiasm.

Give honor to form, my disciple, firstly in yourself; be noble in manner, noble in speech, and do not be satisfied with anything less than nobility in anything.

---

201. [TN] **Montsalvat**, see note 12, p. XXXIII.

Your presence must never be complicit in common vulgarities, and anywhere you cannot impose beauty, you must leave. Require of yourself an impeccable dignity that will be your defense against the attacks everyone launches against everyone else. These detachments I demand, these necessary renunciations serve to unify your strength, and increase it in the uniquely beautiful path of love for ideas.

I promise you so many joys of spirit that you will decline excitements, so much inspiration that you will retract your instincts, so much beauty of heart that you will reduce your passions. See for yourself to what limits your sanctified ambitions will carry you.

If you want to get rich and be your own man, to be something rather than someone, to wear a ribbon in your buttonhole instead of the Rose+Cross in your soul; forget this book. It will leave a troublesome restlessness in your mind; one cannot reconcile one's material interests with the ideal.

Return to the crowd, you who desire the illusory goods of this world. Here is the university that offers to make you a poisoner in your own turn, here is your country that will give you a colorful costume if you give it that passive obedience that Pascal[202] could not comprehend, that is customary in the imbecile Occident; here's the priest of mob rule: in the French constitution it is written: *to the most unworthy*. Go, live like the pigs.

And here is the fruitful prostitution of the press; do like the girls, be an atheist professor, judge, journalist and deputy, be all of that, but be accursed like the country in which you are a respectable citizen.

For you who remain, already dazzled by the splendors of the Grail, a beginner today, Parsifal tomorrow, my disciple for a while yet, soon to be my peer and my brother: O you who will be a mage, I salute you! Welcome, welcome, dear soul who has resonated with the ringing of blessed bells, soul of sweetness and strength, soul of a saint and artist, future tabernacle of divine charity, you whom the passions will soon abandon forever, I salute you, and salute you again! Noble spirit, who has perceived through my pale language the lovely white light of the ideal, spirit of subtlety and peace, spirit of glory and overwhelming mystery—

---

202. [TN] **Blaise Pascal** (1623–1662) was a French mathematician, physicist, inventor, writer, and Catholic theologian. Following a religious experience in late 1654, he began writing influential works, including the *Lettres provinciales* and the *Pensées*, which have been regarded as some of the finest prose in the French language.

future reverberator to the absolute, you who soon will be crowned with the golden wreath of pure truth, hail to thee!

Mage, I salute you! To ordeals, to works, to present gnosis. I have opened the temple to you as Gurnemanz opened it to Parsifal: I can do no more.

Someday after suffering, after weeping, after creating, you will wear the black and white cross, starred with the holy Rose. Then, knight of the Temple, remember him who loves without knowing you, who writes this sincere and good discourse to illumine you, and pray for your initiator, O Rose-Cross, that God may, judging only the beauty of his plan, pardon the imperfection of his word for the sake of your own vocation. May it be so.

CATHOLIC CONCORDANCE

NINETEENTH ARCANUM

Religion and magic differ only in the predominance of soul in the one, of the spirit in the other.

I repeat, the mage assesses a work by its merits, the masterpieces as miracles, the geniuses as saints, the artists as priests, the enthusiasts as the faithful, and the arts as sacred rites.

On this point, on this point alone, magic concedes nothing; because it defends a part of the truth that the customs of the Church, and not the Church itself, opposed.

The year two thousand is the date prophesied for the inauguration of the reign of the Holy Spirit; the works of intellect become thus most fully realized when grace is with us; and the office of the mage has always been to recognize in advance of the priest the manifestations of the divine.

As Balthasar, Caspar and Melchior welcomed the Son of God; Péladan-Sâr here adores the Holy Spirit that is to come.

BOOK THREE

THE TRINITY
of the
HOLY SPIRIT

Holy Spirit, O most offended
by this century; O least prayed to
of the Three Persons of God.
(*Istar*, fifth book of the ethopoem
La Décadence latine; Dentu.)

I
THE WORK OF THE FATHER

The divine unity creates a being in his own image, but the Scripture and the Kabbala qualify the body as the gift of the Father; and human history from the primordial revelation up to the Messiah might also be called the cycle of the Father.

I have defined original sin as vertigo at the newness of existence.

In the newly started sculpture there is a work of sorting out the actions and reactions of force between the active and passive parts; just so, at his birth, a man created perfect in spirit and soul would have been able to keep his balance, if his will, amplified by intoxication of the instincts, had not made a destiny outside of Providence.

Man, born an androgyne, had the human (species) form, and a body that was fluidic, not organic.

That is why his dizziness of will rendered him incapable of remaining on the plane of forms: God the Father, out of mercy, lowered man from the formal to the organic plane.

Adamah,[203] darkened in soul and spirit, soon began a life similar to our own.

The sin of the primitive world, also seen among the Israelites, Ninevites, Phoenicians, and the Goths, is cruelty, militarism and torture.

Mohammed also belonged, despite his times, to the period of blood, while Shakyamuni,[204] despite his anteriority, initiated the Messianic principle.

---

203. **Adamah**, see note 135, p. 136.
204. **Shakyamuni**, see note 138, p. 138.

The Celts, so brutal that their Valhalla prolongs their drunkenness and butchery into eternity, these Gothic sons of the suicidal Odin, like the Nimrods and the Mongol Khans, incarnated this same giddiness of instinct that tainted Adamah, the giddiness that would come to an end in the Christians thrown to the lions.

The ancient world evolved largely as strength and thought; the State always abused power and bloodied itself without dying: the ancient mages continued, through the dynasties and their overthrows, to celebrate in the inner sanctuaries of the temples a cult of divine truth that was unified but sterile.

In this respect, the first phase of initiation corresponds to the first phase of history.

Thus, in order to remove the original imperfection, we must willfully transpose ourselves from the organic plane to the species level, that is to say, to live no longer according to entirely organic sensations.

To be capable of taking part in an orgy, whether sexual or military, is so degrading that greatness is no longer possible.

The beginning of perfection is in the struggle against the instinctive Nahash, known as both sensuality and brutality.

One must be able to make the negative confession of the Egyptian:[205] to be just or well balanced and, in consequence, able to respond to the call of the ideal, able to prefer principle to contingencies.

The cultivation of sensibility is said to be the work of the Son, and cultivation of understanding that of the Holy Spirit; as for the work of the Father, it is the work of the will in conformity to divinity, as Moses accomplished. That Chaldean seems to have set up the pillars of Hercules of the will; his physique surpassed in complete sublimity that of Orpheus Kasd, his emulator honored in Ionia,[206] that daughter of the Hindu Yavanas.

---

205. [TN] In order to be judged fit to enter the afterlife, the dead were required to recite a **negative confession**, containing a long list of attestations that one has not harmed anyone, neglected duty, offended the gods, and so on.

206. [TN] **Ionia** (7th–6th centuries BCE), named after the Ionian tribe of Greeks in the Archaic Period, was the northernmost territory of the Ionian League of Greek settlements, located on the central part of the western coast of Anatolia in present-day Turkey.

I. THE WORK OF THE FATHER   213

The invention of Israel accomplished the ideal of providential will: and the impression of greatness hinders one's perception of the defects of the enterprise.

The word of Moses set him with astounding wrath against that of other theurges: only Jesus can make us see and feel the barbarity of Jewish customs. I believe it was the masterwork of its period and that it was the best that could be done at the time. But if it is necessary to infatuate a people, to crown them the people of God and to vomit injustice upon all their rivals—from the higher point of view of the mage, the wisdom of Shlomo [207] does not suffice to raise his wicked people above the Egyptians, nor to dupe us into believing that Jerusalem was anything more than a pale reflection of the greatness of Babylon.

Israel is nothing but a Chaldean work; the latest in date and whose vibration has been transmitted to us. Its providential role was to serve as the transition between the two hegemonies of Orient and Occident; Moses prefigured the work of Saint Paul.

But most of the notions the Hebrews lived by yielded to the word of Jesus and the course of the centuries.

Saint Louis, and even Louis XIV submitted to the notion of a chosen nation; the *Gesta dei per Francos* [*The Deeds of God Through the Franks*] was a Mosaic motto that was shown to be a fiction when the collective Nahash caused France to fall below the level of the least tribe of Oceania.

At the same time, archaeology has revealed to us the wisdom of the East, and today's intellectual recognizes that Paris is a barbarian village and the State is an abomination lower than the hordes of the past. What is called progress is nothing but a regularization of wickedness, developing in extent and not in elevation.

Robbery concentrated in the hands of anonymous power goes on continually; slavery that engulfs the whole population takes the name of the law, of recruitment: up to one's forty-fifth year, every able-bodied Frenchman is whipped out of bed like a black field slave. That dishonor to the cardinalate

---

207. **Shlomo**, meaning "peaceable" in Hebrew, is a common Jewish given name. It is often used in Jewish discourse to refer to King Solomon of ancient Israel, renowned for his wisdom.

named Lavigerie [208] rails against the black slave trade to the accents of this *Marseillaise* that serves as the hymn to the white slave trade.

What worse tyranny than that which forbids the individual to consume anything other than what comes out of the filthy national monopolies? What despot commands every one of his subjects who has been away traveling for two months to submit, on pain of imprisonment, to questioning and inspection at the point of departure and the point of arrival?

I defy you to name an oriental empire where the poor pilgrim would be imprisoned just for being poor. The workman, the artist or the dervish who arrives in Paris and falls to sleep on a bench will be condemned to a month in prison on charges of vagrancy, and this in the name of the State, and this under the accursed pretext of the fatherland.

Put it in your mind, my disciple, that the crown of the mage obliges you more than it frees you. You will change duties by initiation; and let your only remaining right be to disobey national laws.

Make of yourself what Moses made of a horde, make yourself an Israel, in other words, be a providential will.

In two points, will and theological conception, you will accomplish the work of the father and the first phase of magnification.

My instruction mixes the three paths because it is both elementary and synthetic: the most imperious urgency is for you to change—by conscious choice, following arcanum twenty that embraces the right and left hands of free will.

Base your life on a theocratic principle so that, being prepared by firmness of intent and serenity of mind, you will receive without fail the divine touch of the sacred heart of Jesus.

If you are a knight who prays, that is to say, a sword with a cruciform hilt, soon the rose of charity and art will bloom and blunt the point of its blade, because strength is a form as well as a movement.

Hold in memory this vision of God, that bears the name *Elohim of Yahweh*, and invoke the Cause, by Geburah.

---

208. [TN] **Charles Martial Allemand Lavigerie** (1825–1892) was a French cardinal. (See note 59, p. 46.) In his first pastoral letter as Archbishop of Algiers in 1867, he deplored the abuses of slavery; and after Pope Leo XIII issued an encyclical appealing for an end to slavery in 1888, Cardinal Lavigerie toured the capitals of Europe, telling of the horrors of African slavery and urging the formation of anti-slavery societies.

Make an effort, without lying, to classify your adversaries with the unjust. Whoever obstructs you on the path of the Good will be struck down, because in this path one is protected as long as one follows it.

But each time that you mistake your selfish interests and your passions for holy anger, you will be struck down yourself as a blasphemer.

God is on no one's side but God's, and avenges only himself; that is, you exist in the manner of a cleric, unremarkable in himself, but august when he carries the Eucharist.

Man is nothing in himself and cannot do anything by himself; but man as the faithful knight of Providence is like God and can do like God, because the divine is always omnipotent, and radiates everywhere. Call, receive, and keep this beam of light; you will have accomplished upon yourself the work of the Father.

II
THE WORK OF THE SON

The three divine persons in the creation were called the One God; even the character of Israel, known as the people of God, was clearly believed to be a divine unity. This high prestige was given them by the Chaldean Moses.

The *Discourse on Universal History* gives the strange impression that, before Jesus, only the Israelites were not idolaters. Today that historical fantasia by Bossuet[209] has only aesthetic and decorative value.

During the reign of the Father, the Holy Spirit was always given honor in the secrecy of the sanctuaries; the Atlanto-Egyptian red race, the Semitic or Chaldeo-Etruscan race, the Aryan Indo-Europeans and even the Sumero-Turanians were theocrats, hierarchic, and ruled by priesthoods of magic that possessed the whole knowledge of metaphysics.

Whether it was because the idea was not strong enough to restrain the collective passions, or because the priesthoods, like that of Misraim [the Egyptians] in the era of Moses, never sowed abstract ideas among the people, the truth became sterile. Goodness became totally separate from ideas, and when the ignoble legions of Rome took over from the abominable military brutes of Assyria, there was no more goodness in the land: heartless humanity could only die. Then the second divine person was embodied, and we saw God immolate himself on the cross so that his suffering and death would give birth to that compassion, sweetness and peace of mind that we call charity.

---

209. [TN] Bossuet's *Discourse on Universal History*, see note 124, p. 118.

II. THE WORK OF THE SON

The work of the Son was a work of soul, it came not to reform the understanding, but to bring it the expansion of love; it imposed goodness on the mind.

From that time, the reign of the brute and the murderer was done, from that time on, a soldier was called a bandit when he was not the arm of justice. Golgotha gave proof that the victory belonged to innocence, that royalty is nothing but the right to devote oneself, that from then on only voluntary and conscious victims would make conquests and receive the homage of the centuries.

The second phase of initiation corresponds to the second cycle of history.[210]

Love succeeded to Strength in history; let it succeed likewise in you. One does not conquer Nahash except through altruistic and disinterested emotions.

In the reign of the Son, it is not enough to resist Temptation, one must annul and repel it.

To be capable of egotism, of an interest that is completely selfish, prevents the approach of the second degree.

Justice is no longer sufficient before God the Son, one must have mercy. To take pity is higher than rationality; and he who pardons surpasses the one who is simply equitable.

Cultivation of the will requires hardness upon oneself that one must not extend to one's neighbor.

Perceiving the deplorable motives of the worst deeds and faults, the initiate does not vent the wrath of the prophets against anyone but the State, that is to say, the institutionalization of evil.

Never has a word been so much obeyed as that of Jesus; the passivity of the martyr was a fitting emulation of Calvary, and the eternity of the Church was provided for by innocent blood, the blood of the lambs of God who, bejeweled with radiant rubies, served as the foundation for the Gospel and its law.

---

210. [TN] Péladan's exposition of three epochs of history corresponding to the three persons of the divine Trinity is a faithful rendering of ideas originally developed by **Joachim of Fiore** (c. 1135–1202), an Italian theologian who was respected and encouraged by Pope Lucius III. Joachim's idea of an apocalyptic arrival of the epoch of the Holy Spirit became widely influential and was taken up by the spiritual wing of the Franciscan Order, as well as by a number of heretical groups. Thomas Aquinas refuted Joachim's ideas, and they were declared heretical in 1263.

Christianity, in becoming Catholic, went from passivity to vigorous activity. The Pope was sovereign because it was the essence of the Papacy not to submit to any oppression and to possess an inviolable holy city.

Here again it is the detestable idea of the Fatherland, or collective banditry, that has stained the honor of the Church. Some, like Simon de Montfort,[211] pursued their own secular ambitions in the program of exterminating heresy; others like the deplorable Spaniards, ungrateful, unprincipled and murderous, took the pretext of Catholicism to plunder and massacre the Moors, without whom they would still be entirely lacking in culture.

As much as Lavigerie betrayed the Church by using the crucifix to conquer the Arab by way of converting him, it was equally stupid to believe that prayer should be the sole arm of the Catholics.

The propagation of the Faith should be undertaken first of all in Paris, rather than among the nomads who have never in any way influenced the progress of humanity. If one intends, despite the climate and the differences of race, to catholicize the East, the only worthy way would be for the missionary to convert the marabouts, the holy men. Truly, there is no honor in converting the vulgar from Manitou; and there is an unconscious evil whenever the soldier and the tax collector march in behind the missionary; by this deed making sweet Jesus the symbol of conquest and spoliation.[212]

Until the Roman clergy will have converted the highest Brahmins, the propagation of the Faith, in spite of its martyrs, will still be a work of Western plunder.

The missionary carrying his French routines into Algeria and China must espouse the Algerian or Chinese collective, become a patriot in the land he evangelizes and oppose the West; it would be less abominable, whatever else might result of it.

Meanwhile, the priestly role would appear to be neutral and in fact, devoted only to justice, or openly supportive of the weak and the oppressed, following

---

211. [TN] **Simon de Montfort, 5th Earl of Leicester** (c. 1175–1218), was a French nobleman, soldier, and prominent leader of the Albigensian Crusade, feared for his ruthlessness. In 1208, Pope Innocent III declared the crusade against dissident Christians in Occitania, and offered the lands of the Cathar heretics to any French nobleman willing to take up arms. Simon's military efforts were rewarded with confiscated lands that made him the most important landowner in this rich and commercially strategic region of southern France.

212. [TN] The French colonial wars in Indochina and Algeria were often justified as military protection for Catholic missionaries and their activities.

the order given by the Holy Father which, spoken from such height, would become a veritable ruling of Providence!

The conduct of a Catholic, like that of an initiate, is composed of tolerance toward anything that does not hinder genius or culture. But one should not take laxity for gentleness; the bishops who have allowed their seminarians to dress in the uniform of homicide, and then to practice it, deserve to be hooted down. When these seminarian-soldiers are ordained priests, I predict not a single Catholic will attend their mass or accept the Holy Eucharist from the sacrilegious hand of a national assassin.

To reconcile the strength of the Father with the goodness of the Son; to be gentle and firm, strong-willed and compassionate, not to weaken and not to become rigid, to abide unshakeable in one's intent and benign in one's actions, this is the formula of the second degree.

Jesus Christ, from the height of his cross, inaugurated a new heroism and a new love.

He has given the victory to the deserving; he has given his example.

This example, that is the whole of religion, teaches the sublimity of voluntary self-sacrifice; for the last word of one's will is to accept pain and death, and accept them even for the sake of the unworthy. There is nothing higher than self-sacrifice for the impersonal "all."

Until Golgotha, one had seen proud posturing, furious rivalries, great acts of intoxicated brutality; but not innocence marching to immolation, so that grace could come from the triumph of crime.

Born in the course of the Passion, this novelty of soul, charity, had cast its truly celestial reflection into the human heart.

Through charity the saving work of the Son is accomplished, by charity the will of the Father becomes solar, life-giving, and saving, irradiated by the subtlety of the Son.

III
THE WORK OF THE HOLY SPIRIT

Human unworthiness has exhausted the grace of God the Father who reigned resplendent over the Orient; it seems that the merits of the Passion of Our Savior have been overtaken by the growing iniquity of mankind.

Our hope still awaits a new outpouring of grace, as a third work of salvation. To anticipate the manifestation of the Holy Spirit would be impious, to announce its imminent triumph is to reiterate a hope common to all great spirits through the centuries, for a conclusion to the present spectacle of Western sacrilege.

The specific character of the actual sin is nationalism.

The French do not murder and rob a great deal: France robs and massacres all the French in the form of taxes and tariffs, and military vexations. As individuals, deputies and ministers are just doing lawful business, but as functionaries they are criminal. When interrogated, they are not found to be mad or vile, yet nevertheless, France is mad, and vile to the greatest possible degree. Nowadays evil has only one name, and that name is "nation." In his private heart no man believes in equality, but the State fouls all of its monuments with this eight-letter filth.

I know no other atheist than the State, no other thief than the State, no other bandit than the State.

Confronting this horrific phenomenon of error cultivated into evildoing that is honored above all other acts of patriotism. I foresee a catastrophe without name that will crush the useless nationalities; and upon the ruins of the

Latin world, the Law will manifest the Holy Spirit, just as Jesus appeared over the ruins of the Roman world.

Abuses of power and fraudulent science fall under the jurisdiction of the Holy Spirit, just as the sins of the will cry out to the Father for justice, and hardness of heart demands vengeance of the Son. Individual malevolence is restrained of itself, to the extent that the pursuit of happiness makes any spectacle of suffering egoistically painful to witness. We lack the ferocity of the Dominicans, but the anonymous French nation equals both Torquemada[213] and Tiberius, without the pomp of the one and the enormous fantasy of the other.

Thus, the third phase of initiation corresponds to the cycle of the Holy Spirit; so to achieve in oneself the miracle of sublimation, one must violently reject any nation that sets itself against celestial subtlety.

Whoever deals with democracy, whoever votes, whoever does not execrate the State today, these men and their works will never be magical, and I flatter myself that if any one of them should try to reconcile one of their modern aberrations with my teaching, a sudden dementia will strike that profaner of ancient wisdom.

One does not need to consult astrology to know which star will rule the future, and the signs are enough to show that the revelation is from the Holy Spirit, because Western prevarication forces it to a terrible intervention.

Depart then, by inner renunciation, from the Five Latin Cities; shake the ashes from your feet upon the people who evicted God; and since the idolatry of nationalism has replaced Jesus, let the Fatherland collapse. France has renounced God and his Church; renounce France, my disciple, in the name of the Church, your Motherland.

When you close this book, take one over-arching and sincere counsel from it. I advise you never to stray from the Church, for any reason.

The Papacy is the only institution still standing; rally to its standard. There is no truth to enunciate that will challenge hierarchical authority, and Catholic solidarity remains the only possible salvation.

Save all your indulgence for Rome, all your patience in her favor.

You may boldly name names of sworn bishops and diplomatic cardinals, but the motto of the order is "Save the Pope." That is because the Holy Spirit

---

213. [TN] **Tomás de Torquemada** of the Spanish Inquisition, see note 145, p. 154.

manifests only from the balcony of Saint Peter, and magic, this corona, has no foundation without the religious edifice.

Speak, cultivate, write exclusively in the divine French language, as tomorrow after the yellow invasion, it will be the third classic language, and the predominant. Present in all the mysteries of faith, the Holy Spirit looks with approval upon the intellectual, as the just will soon be called the mage. The defense of the faith is no longer in the folded hands of piety, but in hands that work.

The saints to come will be the geniuses and theosophers; the rule of the simple is at an end, the future belongs to the subtle and the wise.

The clergy, no longer producing the great effects of sainthood, will see loss of faith in their prestige, at least if they do not bring into their ministry that steadfastness that causes people to say of a man: "That one, he is a character."

Without a doubt, the just must be incomparably cultivated. In an era when everyone reads the papers and fancies himself literate, the leaders must become mandarins. I chose that word so as to express a concern for esoterism in thought and in aesthetic. From now on the work of art must be of such a high order that the people feel it without comprehending it; we must raise literature, sciences, and arts above the grasp of the crowd, so that a new aristocracy arises, uniquely literate, uniquely knowledgeable, uniquely hard-working, in the face of the old human rabble.

The mark of the Holy Spirit is subtlety; as charity is the mark of the Son, and will is the mark of the Father. No one of them can exist without the other two, but the one most appropriate to the exigencies of the present time is the holy subtlety.

Now, my disciple, to pursue this direction any further would be to begin intellectual instructions, and I will wait for the results that come from this primary lecture. If it finds a real echo I promise to present the whole subject of occultism in an appropriate way. If it meets only indifference I will, like a mage, keep silent, and return to writing about the arts that give me so much pleasure.

Whether you give me praise or blame, it matters only that you profit. Having come to this last page, do you feel yourself a better man, nobly inspired? Have I communicated to you a taste for the mystery? Have you felt within yourself the birth of sublime ambitions?

If I have done you any good, I have been granted my wish, and my goal is attained.

This book is more an act than a work of art; I wanted to be clear on each idea, but I had to let go of making it stylistically perfect.

As a stranger, a Catholic and a Sâr, I find malevolence lurking even in the libraries, and I work in an environment of such insecurity that I do not produce what I am capable of.

It took ten years to produce this book: and I would consider it a victory, except that I would much prefer to be raising a cry of impatience from the Holy Spirit, whose work will be accomplished, and for whom I hope to serve as the herald who runs through the villages, crying, "The Holy Spirit is being born, the Holy Spirit is born!"

Amen!

AFTERWORD

*By Jean-Louis de Biasi,
Illustrious Grand Patriarch–Grand Master of the
Kabbalistic Order of the Rose-Cross*

Like any drug, a book can be precious medicine but can also endanger the life of a sincere seeker! A writing, especially from someone professing to be a magus or a prince, can advocate practices and values that are not appropriate for a beginner or for society.

This book, like others from the same author, was not written to be balanced or restrained or to please adepts. It is provocative, uncompromising, contemptuous of people, and misogynous, to say the least. Péladan talks about the way to become a mage, but his own culture, as well as his frustrations, get in the way. As this book is supposed to help the reader progress on a spiritual path, we should rise above the historical context and evaluate what could be helpful today, leaving the author's personal anger as only contextual.

I have been honored to receive the spiritual authority of the Kabbalistic Order of the Rose-Cross,[214] an initiatic lineage that was entrusted by Péladan to Stanislas de Guaita, who formally organized this association in 1888. I have learned from inside the history, philosophy, and rituals of the original Rose-Cross school, but also how and why it was progressively recreated later by Péladan. In this afterword, I want to highlight some elements of this heritage that will help you understand how the character of the mage depicted by the author is a reflection of his own life. I will also highlight some of the essential

---

214. See https://www.rose-cross.net/.

principles that can still be useful today. Then you will understand why most of the occultists of his time strongly rejected his initiatives as anathema.

While reading this book, you surely noted the intertwining of politics, religion, spirituality, and art. This is something we must keep in mind as we seek to understand Péladan's intent. In the first chapters, he uses the famous symbol of the statue coming from Plato and Plotinus. Imagine a statue of God that fell into the sea. Over time, it became covered by shells and other sea creatures. Upon finding it, you would have to remove the layers of impurities to progressively unveil the wonders beneath. In the same way, we should distinguish the author's human passions from the timeless wisdom he presents.

Joséphin Péladan came from a politically engaged family. Their fight was to reject and oppose the modern values of the Enlightenment that were claimed by the French Revolution. At the time this book was published, the monarchy had already been abolished for a hundred years. The French restoration of a fifteen-year monarchy had ended sixty years prior, and France was officially a secular republic. However, nostalgia for a Christian monarchy was still strong and would remain so in this country for a long time. Science and philosophy, praised during the French Revolution, were still seen as superior to religion. Following his family, Péladan strongly advocated for the conservative values that had belonged to the former political system. Consequently, he supported the return of the monarchy and the Catholic Church.

Rooted in Péladan's deep faith, the Catholic dogmas became the absolute standard for his personal ideas. As he repeats throughout the book, the teachings of the Church proclaimed by the Pope are infallible. The "Credo" (declaration of faith) is absolute, and everything in life must be in accordance with it. As a strong believer, he explicitly submits his ideas and teachings to this standard. You found this concordance after each chapter.

You can ask yourself if such behavior was common at the time. The answer is no. For hundreds of years, initiates, esotericists, and sometimes even priests were exploring other venues. They were reading pagan philosophers and practicing rituals that mixed pre-Christian knowledge with an esoteric gnostic heritage. Others were using rituals containing fragments from the Egyptian civilization. This was true, for example, of Egyptian Freemasonry, which was created by Cagliostro, and the Sacred Order of the Sophisians,[215] created in 1801.

In the opening statement of the book, Péladan claims to belong to four different lineages: the Templar Order through his father, the Rose+Cross through his brother and Simon Brugal, the Chaldean tradition through his name and writing, and finally the Catholic Church. These spiritual traditions are his main inspirations.

It is undeniable today that the small group Rose-Cross from Toulouse (South of France) really existed. Knowing what kind of practices and rituals this group used is very difficult; nevertheless, we can find some interesting clues.

As defined by Péladan, the mage is above the crowd by nature. The vision he developed can be associated with fragment 153 from the Chaldean Oracles, which says, "The theurgists are not counted in the herd of men who are subject to Fate." The philosopher Nietzsche, a contemporary of Péladan, speaks also of a "superior man" who has risen above the common people. Even if this vision is traditional, there are several ways to interpret it. Of course, it can be a disdain of others, but also the surpassing of ourselves by overcoming the illusions of the material self.

At this phase in his life, Péladan reacted more than he acted. Everything that did not follow his will was opposite to what he perceived as a mage. While he linked art, beauty, and spirituality, as a Platonist would normally do, he rejected everything and everyone who doubted his own ability to recognize what art is. Consequently, journalists criticizing his work or work he favored were rejected as enemies. No nuance here: just a large and complete rejection of all journalists. The same applied to the army, to women, and to politicians. As a matter of fact, everyone who opposed and criticized him was banned as a whole. This uncompromising character might be tolerated in a writer who lives with panache and disdain. However, it cannot be the attitude of an initiate eager to rise to the divine.

The occult tradition that was enacted in the nineteenth century, following a common Western philosophy, emphasizes humility. This spiritual attitude is different from publicly claiming to be humble. It is a realistic vision of our own

---

215. See https://www.sophisians.org/.

self in comparison with what has been achieved by others and what we must achieve in our life. This is not a virtue that should be directly cultivated by an adept. He should only be aware of the work that remains to be achieved. He should remove the veils of illusion that surround him and that have been thickened by his pride.

Humility is also linked with tolerance. An initiate is aware of the world and the people in it. As such, he must know that it is not possible to place everyone in the same box. Journalists do not become enemies of the people just because a few of them criticized someone. There is no reason to ask the people to insult them and throw them out in the mud. Some are bad and some are good, just as in the army and politics and other areas of life. We can understand such behavior coming from uninformed people, but this is less understandable from someone who is presenting himself as a model of what a magus should be. I must admit that in some parts of his book, Péladan was right in saying that we have to fight for our ideas and place them above all. This, however, does not excuse the dangerous behavior of encouraging his students to follow his example. This tendency can also be found in his Catholic militancy. It seems that neither humility nor tolerance were mastered by Péladan.

It is also essential to take his words about women very carefully. Obviously, he is closely following the teaching of Paul and the Catholic Church. The latter has always been very clear about women. As we can read in the Bible, more precisely 1 Timothy 2:11–14: "Let the woman learn in silence with all subjection. But I suffer not a woman to teach, nor to usurp authority over the man, but to be in silence." In 1 Corinthians 11:7 we read: "A man indeed ought not to cover his head, forasmuch as he is the image and glory of God: but the woman is the glory of the man." Then, as Colossians 3:18 states: "Wives, submit yourselves unto your own husbands, as it is fit in the Lord." As a proud son of the Church, Péladan follows these teachings and provides a similar model in which women must be kept dependent on and subjected to men. He writes: "The woman, as I have revealed to you, is ruled by a faculty that is destructive when not kept passive; [...] Be the master then, in order to be beloved, because no woman loves one who yields to her; her pleasure is to be ruled."

Of course, men have needs, and they can have wives, Péladan allows, but men should never forget the real essence of women: "In your social or emotional life, never permit a woman to influence your thought; [...] Do not allow them to speak a metaphysical word, unless it is an *amen*. [...] A woman has no cerebrality; never forget it, and you must remind her if she forgets." The Bible has taught misogyny for thousands of years, so we should not be surprised by Péladan's claims.

Is this a good model to follow if you want to become a mage? Absolutely not! It may be useful if you want to become an adept of Péladan and follow the Catholic teachings, but initiates and those who attain the rank of magus are different. Since the beginning of the Western tradition, women have been part of the initiatic chain. They have played an important role in the continuation of this tradition. Hypatia is a good example. She was a Hellenistic Neoplatonist philosopher who lived in Alexandria during the fourth century CE and was savagely killed by a mob encouraged by violent priests. Another woman called Asklepigeneia, a contemporary of Hypatia and daughter of Plutarch, initiated Proclus into theurgy, according to the rituals and teachings she received from her father.

During the Dark Ages, women were often persecuted as witches. Christianity offered them few spiritual roles, none of them on equal footing with men. However, since the beginning of the nineteenth century, women have been initiated into all the important esoteric organizations. This was the case in the Egyptian Freemasonry of Cagliostro, which even created a feminine Egyptian Freemasonry. We also see a lot of women among the Sophisians. The initiatic orders managed by Stanislas de Guaita and Papus, the Kabbalistic of the Rose-Cross and the Martinist Order, were largely open to women. The Hermetic Order of the Golden Dawn, founded in 1888 in London, welcomed women as equals. Their names are countless. On the other hand, and as expected, every organization rooted in the Catholic Church was either male only or placed women in a secondary position. The historic Rose-Cross movement seems to have been this way at the beginning. When Stanislas de Guaita took the direction of the Kabbalistic Order of the Rose-Cross, this tendency was abolished, and so it remains today.

Anyone who is eager to undertake a real spiritual or initiatic path should recognize the real origin of these misogynistic ideas. They have no justification except for a fear of women. If you believe in the existence of a soul of some sort, how can you differentiate between the soul of a man and the soul of a woman? You cannot. If you believe in reincarnation, for example, this question is absurd. Of course, bodies are different and can interact with the expression of our emotions. Trying to maintain a difference between genders and justifying it spiritually is usually detrimental to women. This is the opposite of any initiatic path.

The main justifications come from male-dominated religions. Prophets conveniently received messages from God justifying this inferior status of women. Greco-Roman civilization was not exempt from this attitude, which was integrated into the theology of the Catholic Church. This is a manifestation of the fourth heritage claimed by Péladan: subjection to the authority of the Church.

In the context of his time, Péladan's fight was to reject and oppose the modern values of the Enlightenment claimed by the French Revolution. Following his family, Péladan strongly advocated for conservative values belonging to the former political system.

The members of the original Rose-Cross group from Toulouse practiced alchemy and wrote about the preservation of health and life and about treating sickness. They were also concerned with the preservation of local cultures dating back to the Middle Ages by way of the troubadours. Péladan's brother Adrien, who was part of this organization, expressed this heritage in his life in a consistent way with the Rose-Cross teachings. He was a doctor and precursor of homeopathy, who manifested humility all his life. He was the one who initiated his brother Joséphin.

Following his example, Péladan initiated Stanislas de Guaita and Papus. With the support of other well-known occultists, these two created and organized the Kabbalistic Order of the Rose-Cross. It was the first Rose-Cross order open to outside candidates, and it became a real organization, with inner rituals and outer Kabbalistic diplomas.

As a matter of fact, the values claimed by this organization were neither conservative nor Catholic. Its members were occultists. The teachings focused on reincarnation, magnetism, divination, etc., and were not so concerned with art.

Their vision of a mage was very different from the one claimed by Péladan. The same year Péladan's book appeared, Papus published a work called *The Science of Mages*, which presents a clear contrast to Péladan's. Papus was the spokesperson of the Kabbalistic Order of the Rose-Cross and most of the leaders of the occultist movement.

In his introduction, Papus wrote: "Occultism does not pretend to possess the only truth. [...] We consider that the use of titles [Magus] from another age as satisfaction of fool vanity, excusable for a beginner, but ridiculous for a serious writer and very detrimental for anyone who pursues an honest research." In another chapter of the same book, Papus continues, saying: "If religious education [Catholic] would not lead your mind to sectarianism, by wanting to impose this basic mistake that a religion alone is capable of saving humanity, if this teaching would not encourage war for questions of faith [...] I would be the first one to say to you: use this ideal. But, in all conscience, I cannot, because you would be deceived. [...] The first criterion of the truth is to be global and not sectarian."

You can understand that this vision of the spiritual path is very different. In one case, truth is delivered by the power of the Church and no research is necessary. All that needs to be done is to read the message and follow it. For occultism, on the other hand, truth and the spiritual world are the subjects of research and experimentation. This is the only way to avoid being intolerant and keep from fooling ourselves while lost in the illusions of egocentricity.

Surrendering one's own will to dogmas and living as a martyr or messiah is undoubtedly the major pitfall facing a would-be mage or magician.

This tendency is well known on the spiritual path, and this is what Papus had in mind when he wrote: "When, today, you will see individuals calling themselves 'Magi' or 'Hierophants' or 'sons of God,' as there is no occult assembly able to deliver such titles, you can be sure that you are dealing with the ignorant or conceited, if not worse."

A few months after the publication of these two books, Péladan created the Rose+Croix Catholique, which soon transformed into the Ordre of Rose+Croix of the Temple and Graal. His convictions led to the formation of a separate Rose-Cross organization with very few members. As initiates in charge of the Rose-Cross tradition, the Kabbalistic Order of the Rose-Cross published a strong denial of this clerical interpretation, which had moved away from the original mission and doctrine of the Rose-Cross. This interesting document restated the essence of this heritage and pronounced that Péladan could no more be seen as part of this inheritance.

However, this deep divergence didn't diminish the recognition of Péladan's talent and personal experience.

Undoubtedly, his vision gave birth to an artistic movement that lasted for decades, although it is more in accord with the Wagnerian mythology than the Rose-Cross movement itself. This elevation to the divine using art is truly traditional. It can be found in the troubadours of the Middle Ages and the Italian movement of the Fedeli d'Amore. This ascent, based on an aesthetic ecstasy, is a deep and real esoteric path. But, as for any prophet, the personal experience cannot always be shared properly. Unfortunately, what works for one person cannot be easily given to someone else.

It is difficult not to be touched by Péladan's sincerity and honesty. Even if victimized by illusions and blindness, he spoke with a strong voice. He was not trying to lie, and we can learn from his example, although maybe not in the sense he was expecting.

We wish we could believe that a Babylonian prince came back to life, showing us the marvelous original tradition of the Rose-Cross blessed in Rome by the Catholic Church. We could imagine Péladan bringing back the Grail to the Pope and having his books blessed by the heir of Saint Peter.

It could have been so, but as the original title of the book indicated, only an "amphitheater of dead sciences" remained as a precious stone half-buried in the mud. Knowing this book is important as a testimony to a human, artistic, and esoteric experience. It is essential in life to follow the call and understand our vocation, but every experience is unique and personal. Let us follow, as Péladan did, the motto written by his contemporary Nietzsche: "Become who you are."

APPENDIX

The Golden Verses of Pythagoras
According to the Commentary of Hierocles

PART I—PREPARATION
1. First, render consecrated worship to the immortal gods.
2. Make your holy vow, and keep the faith. Revere the memory of the beneficent geniuses of the divinely inspired heroes.
3. Give due respect to the divinities of the earth, by rendering them the worship lawfully due to them.

PART II—PURIFICATION
4. Be a good son or daughter, treat your brothers and sisters fairly, treat your spouse tenderly, and be a good parent to your children.
5. Choose for your friend the one who is a friend of excellence and good values.
6. Pay attention to friendly advice and criticism, and learn from the virtuous and useful actions of others.
7. Do your best to avoid breaking with a friend over a trivial fault.
8. Be aware that power is a near neighbor to necessity; develop your own abilities, for what is possible is very near to what is necessary.
9. It is in your power to overcome the odds against you; start by working to eliminate the habits by which you defeat yourself:
10. Overindulgence, laziness, sexuality, and anger.
11. Do nothing evil, neither in the presence of others, nor privately;

12. First and foremost, respect yourself.
13. Next, always aim for justice in your acts and words.
14. Do not get into any kind of habit that involves acting without rule or reason.
15. Remember that death comes to everyone, and let that thought inform your judgments in life.
16. Remember that material good fortune and the approval of your fellow man are very easily lost.
17. Some misfortunes are fated; do your best to gain insight into the reasons for them;
18. Bear your circumstances with patience, whatever they are, and do not complain,
19. But do whatever is in your power to improve them.
20. And consider that fate does not send most of these misfortunes to the blameless. The gods give help to the wise in escaping the worst of them.
21. There are people who love error as well as those who love truth; there are many ways of thinking, good and bad;
22. Do not be too quick either to adopt them or to reject them outright, but consider and judge prudently.
23. Where you see that lies prevail over truth, put on the armor of patience, get out of the way, and wait.
24. Engrave on your heart what I am going to say next—
25. Do not allow anyone whatsoever—not by words or deeds—to fool you, rush you, or tempt you into doing anything not good for you.
26. Beware of what everybody knows—THINK FOR YOURSELF.
27. Before taking action: think, seek the best advice you can get, and then do what seems best to you.
28. Speaking and acting mindlessly is the way to a life of misery. In the present, you should think of the future.
29. Take care not to do things that bring evil consequences upon you later, or cause regret. Do only those things that will not harm you, and consider before you act.
30. Never do something you do not understand; but get a thorough knowledge of the realities at work in your own life.

31. Do not despair over your mistakes and your ignorance, but instruct yourself. Time and patience will favor you, and you will be able to live well and pleasantly.
32. Do not neglect the health of your body;
33. Give it food, drink, and exercise in due measure.
34. Due measure is the amount that strengthens without dulling you.
35. Follow clean habits of life, but do not grow accustomed to luxury.
36. Avoid all things that will attract envy.
37. And do not be wasteful out of season, as if you did not know what is decent and honorable.
38. Greed and stinginess are as bad as improvidence and waste;
39. A happy medium is your ideal in these matters as well.

PART III—PERFECTION

40. As soon as you wake up in the morning, consider calmly what you need to accomplish in the coming day.
41. Never allow yourself to fall asleep in bed until you have made a mental review of all your actions of the past day:
42. Where did I make mistakes? What did I accomplish? What did I leave undone that I ought to have done?
43. Whatever was wrong, mistaken or inadequate, do not repeat it;
44. And if you have done any good, be glad in it, and persevere.
45. Make it your most serious business to practice all these things continually; meditate on them well; you will grow to love them with all your heart.
46. They will put you on the path to becoming the strongest, best and wisest you can be.
47. I swear it by the Power that has planted in our souls the basis for Divine Realization, by the eternal Source of all existence.

PART IV—THE CONTEMPLATIVE VIRTUES

48. Never begin any work until you have prayed to the gods to bless your undertaking.
49. You must begin the work, but only the gods can bring it to successful completion.

50. When this way of acting becomes your habit, you will fathom the ways of gods and men, you will learn how everything passes and returns.
51. You will learn how far the different Beings extend, you will know the bond uniting the Immortal Gods to mortal men, and you will also know about the One who contains them all in Himself, being their Foundation.
52. You will know that the entire universe is a Single Whole, and all things alike contain the same nature.
53. Having come to know your own nature, you will no longer place your hopes where there is no hope; and nothing in this world shall be hidden from you.
54. You will also see clearly that men bring down misfortunes upon themselves voluntarily, and of their own free choice.
55. In their trouble and distress they seek their salvation everywhere but where it is to be found—from within.
56. Few know how to rescue themselves from their misfortunes, for most are blind to the law of the formation of their destinies.
57. They are the playthings of the passions that keep them running around in circles until death comes.
58. Like a magnet, they draw troubles that follow them everywhere, tossing them up and down; and they cannot see it.
59. An endless inner conflict upsets them wherever they go.
60. Instead of seeking conflict, people should avoid it, conceding to each other without arguing.
61. Oh! Father Jupiter! If You want to free men from all the evils that oppress them,
62. Show them each the genius that is their guide!
63. But you need not fear, for every human has a Divine root that recognizes error and sees the Truth.
64. Sacred Nature reveals to them the most hidden mysteries.
65. If she shows you her secrets, you will easily accomplish all the things I have prescribed here.
66. And by the healing of your soul, you will free it from all evils, from all sorrows.
67. But avoid anything that would contaminate your body and darken your soul.

68. Investigate things to find essentials and principles, in order to see clearly and act surely.
69. Always request the understanding that comes from above, and allow it to guide and direct you.
70. And after having divested yourself of your mortal body, you will enter into the purest Æther,
71. You will be immortal, incorruptible, a God, and Death shall have no more dominion over you.

TRANSLATOR'S NOTE
K. K. Albert

This version of *The Golden Verses of Pythagoras* in the appendix of this book is an adaptation drawn from a number of earlier translations.

The most widely used English translation is that of Florence M. Firth, from 1904, taken largely from Antoine Fabre d'Olivet's French. I consulted Fabre d'Olivet's 1813 version, both in the original French verse and in Redfield's English translation from 1916. In addition, I studied the valuable commentaries provided by Fabre d'Olivet and Firth, which are drawn from antique sources.

Kenneth Sylvan Guthrie wrote his English translation of 1921 directly from the Greek, making it a valuable check against the other translations, but, unfortunately, Guthrie's faithfulness to the Greek wording and figures of speech renders much of the text rather obscure to a general reader.

The eighteen-century poetic treatment of Nicholas Rowe gives the verses a decorative style that does not reflect the potent pragmatism of the advice, or the spiritual potency of the conclusion. The biblical tone of Firth's translation is not optimum, either. A number of versions in clean, modern English fail to convey some of the important meanings carried in the earlier, more old-fashioned translations. The version given here is an attempt to present the best elements from all of them.

Here are the principle sources used:

Firth, Florence M. *The Golden Verses of Pythagoras and Other Pythagorean Fragments.* Hollywood, CA: Theosophical Publishing House, 1904. http://www.sacred-texts.com/cla/gvp/index.htm.

Fabre d'Olivet, Antoine. *The Golden Verses of Pythagoras*. Translated by Nayán Louise Redfield. New York: G. P. Putnam's Sons, 1917. http://www.sacred-texts.com/cla/ogv/ogv00.htm.

Guthrie, Kenneth Sylvan. *The Complete Pythagoras*. Disseminated in mimeograph form, 1921. Edited by Patrick Roussel. https://archive.org/details/CompletePythagoras/page/n1.